The Complete Idiot's Guide Reference Card

Top Ten Secrets to ~~...~~ and Future

1. *Understand what is really* ~~...~~ ce should begin with a look at what's at ~~...~~ buying too little or too much coverage. Thi~~...~~ you about risk.

2. *Stick to the safest insurance companies.* You have too much at stake with most insurance needs to take any chances with companies that are not financially sound. You want to know that the protection will be there when you need it most.

3. *Find an insurance agent you can rely on.* There will be times when you don't need an agent to help you determine what you need and how best to buy it. But there are some needs and solutions too complex to tackle on your own. Learn the difference in this book.

4. *Be more concerned with the big loss than the little one.* You can absorb the small dollar loss more easily than the major, catastrophic loss.

5. *Reduce your premium expense and expand your coverage at the same time.* Use deductibles, coinsurance, and elimination periods to reduce your premiums while protecting against the major threats to your financial well-being. Again, be concerned about the loss that devastates your wallet, not the first $100 of a claim.

6. *Remember to consider yourself a valuable asset.* Consider the impact of a loss of your earnings on your financial condition. While you won't be able to find insurance that protects against layoffs, you can protect against a loss of income due to sickness or accident.

7. *Don't buy insurance solely as an investment.* Insurance is protection against the risk of financial loss. Some life insurance policies have investment features that can make them more attractive. However, unless you need the coverage, invest elsewhere for a better return. If you need the coverage, weigh the potential return as just another factor in your decision-making process.

8. *Help protect yourself by avoiding risks.* Don't just rely on insurance to protect yourself against loss. Wherever possible, avoid or minimize the conditions that give rise to losses. Recovering under insurance policies is still less preferable than not suffering a loss in the first place.

9. *Look at annuities for tax-deferred growth of assets and income.* The contemporary annuity can be an excellent vehicle for accumulating wealth for retirement. It can also be a valuable tool for ensuring an income you cannot outlive. Learn about the various types of annuities in this book.

10. *Price is secondary to protection.* The goal of any effort to shop for insurance is more than finding the lowest premium. The right coverage should be a higher priority. If you can accomplish both objectives at the same time, you've done a great job.

alpha books

tear here

Locating Your Insurance Policies

This guide to locating policies describes types of insurance coverage and where interested parties can find the policies and other documents important to their financial well-being.

HEALTH INSURANCE

Insurance Company _____

Policy number _____

Type of plan _____

Deductible _____

Coinsurance _____

Location of policy _____

LONG-TERM CARE INSURANCE

Insurance Company _____

Policy number _____

Elimination period/Daily benefit _____

_____

Location of policy _____

DISABILITY INCOME INSURANCE

Insurance Company _____

Policy number _____

Elimination period/Monthly benefit _____

_____

Location of policy _____

LIFE INSURANCE

Insurance Company _____

Policy number _____

Death benefit _____

Type of policy _____

Location of policy _____

AUTOMOBILE INSURANCE

Insurance Company _____

Policy number/Auto insured _____

_____

Policy limits _____

Location of policy _____

_____

HOMEOWNERS/RENTERS INSURANCE

Insurance Company _____

Policy number/Date of last review _____

_____

Policy limits _____

Location of policy _____

UMBRELLA LIABILITY INSURANCE

Insurance Company _____

Policy number _____

Policy limits _____

Location of policy _____

_____

Insurance Company _____

Policy number _____

Death benefit _____

Type of policy _____

Location of policy _____

The
COMPLETE
IDIOT'S
GUIDE TO
Buying Insurance
and Annuities

by Brian Breuel

alpha
books

A Division of Macmillan General Reference
A Simon & Schuster Macmillan Company
1633 Broadway, New York, NY 10019

International Standard Book Number: 0-02-861113-6
Library of Congress Catalog Card Number: 96-084571

98 97 96   8 7 6 5 4 3 2 1

Interpretation of the printing code: the rightmost number of the first series of numbers is the year of the book's printing; the rightmost number of the second series of numbers is the number of the book's printing. For example, a printing code of 96-1 shows that the first printing occurred in 1996.

Printed in the United States of America

Note: Reasonable care has been taken in the preparation of the text to ensure its clarity and accuracy. This book is sold with the understanding that the author and the publisher are not engaged in rendering legal, accounting, or other professional service. Laws vary from state to state, and readers with specific financial questions should seek the services of a professional advisor.

Publisher
Theresa Murtha

Editor
Debra Wishik Englander

Development Editor
Faithe Wempen

Production Editor
Michael Thomas

Copy Editors
Theresa Mathias
Brian Robinson
Whitney Ward

Cover Designer
Mike Freeland

Illustrator
Judd Winick

Designer
Barbara Kordesh

Indexer
Chris Wilcox

Production Team
Heather Butler, Angela Calvert, Kim Cofer,
Beth Rago, Pamela Volk

Contents at a Glance

Contents

Foreword

Unless you like giving away money, you need to understand insurance. Every year you're throwing away thousands of dollars on the wrong policy. That has to stop before the insurance industry names you customer of the year.

You've picked up a book that will protect you from that dubious honor. The key is understanding the product you're buying.

It is amazing how many otherwise savvy consumers will throw up their hands when it comes to insurance. They'll do tons of research before buying a cappuccino maker, yet can't be bothered when it comes to insurance. They don't understand insurance and don't want to understand it.

Without any advice other than the salesperson's, they'll spend big bucks on a policy that someone tells them is good. And many times, they end up buying a bad policy from a bad insurance company and an agent who gave them bad advice.

When I was the Regional Manager in Consumer Services & Enforcement for the Pennsylvania Insurance Department, I encountered thousands of bright people who knew absolutely nothing about insurance. Usually, these people came to our department after something bad happened and that bad insurance company wasn't paying them. Unfortunately, in too many instances, it was too late to help those consumers who only then developed an interest in insurance.

Hopefully, you're reading this book before running into your own insurance snafu. Almost every insurance pitfall is avoidable, if you're a well-informed consumer.

There are many fine insurance companies who will be more than happy to take your money. Maybe you'll get lucky and find one. On the other hand, you might wind up with a policy that will only pay when pigs can fly.

The Complete Idiot's Guide to Buying Insurance and Annuities can help you separate the good policy from the bad one and the good company from the kind you read about in John Grisham's *The Rainmaker*. With Brian Breuel's guidance, you'll even be able to distinguish the good insurers from the excellent ones.

You'll also get advice on saving money. You shouldn't have to spend an arm and a leg for the best policy, and the author makes sure you don't. By reading this book, you'll have a leg up on the insurance company and the agent whose livelihood depends on your buying a policy. At last, you'll be on an even footing with the folks who live to sell you insurance.

Buying insurance is like purchasing most products. You need directions on how it works. In this book, you'll find charts and graphs that are a lot easier to follow than most instruction books I've ever read.

The Complete Idiot's Guide to Buying Insurance and Annuities is written in plain English, not insurance jargon. You'll learn how to interpret your life, health, auto, and homeowners policies. The book also provides inside information on shopping for an annuity, long-term care insurance, and disability policies. Insurance doesn't have to be a foreign language, if you're willing to read this book.

The alternative is buying the first policy that catches your eye without knowing what you're doing. If you're going to fritter away money on impulse buying, spend it on a cappuccino maker. Insurance isn't an impulse purchase. With Breuel's guidance, you'll finally know what you're buying after years of throwing money away.

Unlike most insurance books, you won't need caffeine to keep you awake. You'll be entertained as you learn. The author sprinkles humorous quips throughout the book.

Wake up and smell the coffee. You can't go through life without understanding insurance. Get started before it's too late.

Les Abromovitz

Introduction

Insurance protects individuals and businesses against financial losses from risks they may not be able to avoid. This concept is relatively simple. Yet the process you have to go through to buy the right insurance is often complex and confusing. As a result, most people view insurance as something of a necessary evil. That is, until they have to file a claim. Then it becomes a life preserver.

Well, what is the truth about insurance? The answer is that insurance is a sound and efficient way of protecting your assets. And as such, it is like a savings account and a will—a part of your overall financial planning. And if it is approached in an informed, responsible way, you'll find that the protection will add to your sense of financial well-being, just like a savings account.

You can achieve this level of comfort by becoming better educated about insurance. That is the goal of this book—to make you more knowledgeable about all types of insurance. It will also make you a better shopper by teaching you what to ask for and what to avoid.

How This Book Is Organized

The book presents insurance by category, and is divided into six parts.

Part 1: Risk and Needs. Insurance is an alternative to dealing with risks—to your health, home, car, income, even your life. There are also other ways of meeting life's risks head-on, and you'll read about them in this part of the book. You'll also learn some of the basic guidelines for buying any insurance plan or annuity.

Part 2: Life Insurance. Life insurance *needs* are often confused with *wants*, and you need to understand the difference before you buy your next life insurance policy. There are many new and innovative life insurance plans available today, but they are designed to meet different needs and client profiles. This topic explains the various types of life insurance available today.

Part 3: Disability Insurance. Most people fail to consider the impact of being out of work on the family's finances. The current corporate downsizing trend has put you on notice if you are a candidate for a layoff or early retirement. But what if you are unable to work because of sickness or accident? Part 3 explores the various types of coverage and how to shop for what you need.

Part 4: Health Insurance. There is possibly no topic more explosive in today's rapidly changing environment for health care. There is a trend toward managed care, which can reduce your premium but sometimes at the expense of quality and extent of coverage. In this part, you'll learn about health care alternatives, including the all-important long-term care insurance.

Part 5: Annuities. The growth of annuities in this country has been nothing short of phenomenal. Tax-conscious savers and investors buy annuities to help create the assets necessary to fund retirement. But there is the often overlooked use of annuities to provide an income you cannot outlive.

Part 6: Property and Casualty Insurance. Part 6 explores homeowners and renters insurance, automobile insurance, and liability protection. You will learn what those coverages are and how to read those confusing policies.

Conventions Used in This Book

There are several special items that are presented apart from the text. You will see them as boxed notes among the text. They are set apart for several different reasons.

Insider Tip
"Insider Tip" boxes are where you will get helpful hints and ideas to save you money, from someone with an insider's view of the insurance industry.

Jargon Alert
The insurance industry has a language of its own, much of it created to meet legal requirements of the policies. You will find the more common terms defined in these "Jargon Alert" boxes.

Bet You Didn't Know
"Bet You Didn't Know" boxes will give you background information or little-known facts about the insurance industry and the business of insuring you and your assets.

Watch It!
"Watch It!" boxes contain information about problems and pitfalls you will want to avoid.

Acknowledgments

This book would not have been written by me if my publisher at Macmillan had not had the confidence that I was the person to write it. My sincerest thanks to that publisher, Theresa Murtha.

To the extent that you find this book readable, I must share considerable credit with the editors on this project. My initial editor was Debby Englander, who shared the labors with Faithe Wempen, a wise critic. She in turn enlisted the able eyes and pens of Theresa Mathias, Whitney Ward, and Brian Robinson. Special thanks to the production editor, Mike Thomas, and the insightful Les Abromovitz. You've taught me that good editing is about more than clear writing. It is about clear thinking. Thank you.

During the writing of this book, there were two "professional life underwriters" who shared their expertise in the area of life insurance. My appreciation to Fred Abrams of ITT Hartford and Gene Kweeder of The New England.

Some careers meander like country roads. Others roll on like expressways. In my wanderings, there have been several people who helped with directions. My thanks to Tyler Potterfield and Sam Holloway for beginnings. And to Robert Shoemaker for a return to the road.

Finally, I sincerely want to thank my partner and closest friend, who just happens to be my wife, Shirley Cribb Breuel. A special person with immense talent, she has been the one who enabled me to exit the expressway and roam the countryside. I will forever be grateful, because my greatest experiences have been off the highway.

Part 1
Risk and Needs

Insurance itself isn't a problem. Suffering a loss without adequate protection is a problem. Insurance is part of the solution. But most people are more afraid of the solution than they are of the problem. This part of the book examines insurance as a solution to the problem of a loss.

Once you understand the nature of the risks that are threats to your security, you are on your way to being in control. You can determine the best road to take to financial security. And insurance is about security. It is about peace of mind.

So sit back and read about risk, insurance, and security. Take a major step toward gaining control over your financial affairs.

Chapter 1

What You Don't Know Can Hurt You

In This Chapter

➤ The reasons most people avoid facing insurance matters

➤ What you should understand about risk

➤ Alternative ways to deal with risk

➤ How to decide when to insure against risk

This chapter will introduce the comprehensive and often complex world of insurance. It starts at the point where most of you are now—in need of insurance coverage, but with an unclear understanding of your needs, the types of coverage available, and how to decide what to insure. Risk, an important concept for you to understand when considering insurance, will be introduced in this chapter.

Avoiding Insurance

If you're like most people, the word "insurance" makes you anxious. While you know you need some insurance, choosing the right kind and amount seems so complicated and threatening that you'd rather do almost anything than think about whether you have enough or the right coverage. But deep down you know that you'll be far more anxious if you ever suffer a loss without it.

Jargon Alert

Insurance is an agreement or arrangement that shifts the risk of loss from the insured to another party, usually an insurance company. An *annuity* is a contract between the insurer and the insured whereby the insurer promises to accumulate and/or pay out income to the annuitant for a long period of time, often life.

Nobody wants to think about the unpleasant and painful events that usually trigger an insurance claim: death, serious illness, an automobile accident, earthquakes, hurricanes, tornadoes, and so on. These are not pleasant subjects, especially when you're discussing them in the context of yourself and your family.

A second reason you may avoid dealing with insurance is that you don't understand what it is or how it works. It's natural to avoid what you don't understand. Unfortunately, the insurance industry usually doesn't help. The literature, the proposals, and the policies themselves are difficult to read and comprehend.

Another reason is that you might want to avoid the sales call. To many buyers, an insurance agent is almost as offensive as a used car salesman. Even though the need for the coverage is obvious and the insurance company is a pillar of strength and security, you put off the coverage because you're afraid the salesperson will be untrained, inexperienced, pushy, or worse. You avoid the purchase just to avoid the hassle.

A final reason for avoiding insurance is your fear, generated by all of the negative press. The financial pages regularly report policyholder lawsuits for unscrupulous insurance sales practices, not to mention company bankruptcies or seizures by regulators because of the insurers' deteriorated financial condition. You may be afraid to trust insurance companies and their salespeople.

WOW! Bet You Didn't Know

The insurance industry is separated into two categories: life and health insurance, and property and casualty insurance. This book will address the life and health insurance categories first.

While these are all valid reasons for wanting to avoid dealing with your insurance needs, the fact remains that, like death and taxes, there's almost no way to escape this lifetime without having some kind of insurance coverage. The best advice, then, is *caveat emptor*—let the buyer beware.

This book will help you understand what insurance and annuities are and how they can benefit you. If you understand the principles, practices, pricing, and products of the insurance industry, you stand a better chance of getting the right coverage at the best price.

The Risks You Run Every Day

Have I not walked without an upward look
Of caution under stars that very well
Might not have missed me when they shot and fell?
It was a risk I had to take—and took.

Robert Frost, *Bravado*

Understanding insurance is about understanding the concept of risk. *Risk* is an uncertainty of loss. For the purposes of this book, it is an uncertainty of a financial loss. A *loss* is a decrease or total elimination of economic value. Homeowners run the risk of a fire in the home. A fire could result in a partial or total loss of the value of the home itself, depending on the extent of the damage.

Here a Risk, There a Risk

On a typical morning you clutch at an alarm clock that jars you awake, prompting a yawn and a stretch that could throw out your back before your feet hit the floor. You hustle to roust the children, encouraging, threatening, cajoling them to get to school before third period. In the process, you light a combustible gas stove or sleepily dial up the microwave, exposing yourself to unimaginable calamities.

The drive to school, complete with bickering teens, presents the most severe threat of the day. Most auto accidents occur within a few miles of our own homes. The children, their friends, and your associates at work repeatedly cough, sneeze, and otherwise propel their germs into your face. You eat lunch at the new restaurant where raw foods are the specialty. After work, you go to a reception for visitors from another part of the country and expose yourself to who-knows-what-sort of germs from the streets, playgrounds, and homes.

The point is, you're continuously exposed to risks that could result in a financial loss. If you thought about them all the time, you'd be paralyzed into complete inaction. Your own home wouldn't be safe enough.

How, then, do you decide which risks are worth your attention? And, if worth your attention, how to deal with them? There must be some risks like Robert Frost's (and Chicken Little's), that are just worth taking.

Jargon Alert
Risk is the uncer-tainty of any kind of loss, although this book concentrates on economic losses that can be insured against. Therefore, *loss* is measurable and definable in dollars and cents.

The Triple Threat of Risks

There are three types of risk that you need to consider:

➤ *Personal risk* is the uncertainty that you will suffer an illness or injury to your body. It includes the financial loss that results from death, disability, illness, or accident.

➤ *Property risk* encompasses assets you own or possess. It may be a *direct risk*, such as the risk of loss caused by a fire in a home you own. Or it could involve *indirect risk*. For example, the risk of loss of rental income from a fire in a rental property you own is an indirect risk.

➤ *Liability risk* is the risk that results from the law of liability, whether by state statute or case law. You could, for example, be liable for damages caused by the negligent operation of your car.

Insurance is the most common approach to managing each of these risks. However, it is not the only response, as you learn in the next section.

How You Deal with Risk

In some cases, you can simply avoid risk altogether. This option is available whenever you have a choice to make. If you're worried about your safety on a flight across the country, one alternative is to not take the flight. This choice eliminates the possibility of a loss to you on that flight.

A second method of dealing with risk is to assume it. This was the approach taken by the narrator in Robert Frost's poem. While the risk of stars dropping on his head wasn't great, it was still a risk, albeit not a risk likely to be insured against.

A third approach is to reduce the *hazard*, the condition that increases the likelihood that a loss will be severe. If you store highly flammable cans of paint thinner in your garage, you are increasing the chances that a fire that strikes your home will be more damaging. You can reduce the hazard by disposing of the flammable materials, properly and with regard for the environment.

Physical hazards relate to specific tangible conditions, such as oily rags in a corner near a furnace, or worn-out brakes on your automobile. Each of these conditions increases the likelihood of a severe loss.

Moral hazards relate to the mental attitudes of individuals. The moral hazard of greatest concern to the insurance industry and society is dishonesty. Moral hazards can sometimes include *morale hazards*. A morale hazard is a condition caused by indifference or laziness, such as a lack of concern with the condition of one's automobile brakes.

Needless to say, reductions in both moral and morale hazards can significantly impact risk. The use of antitheft devices in autos can reduce the losses from stolen vehicles. They protect against laziness in leaving cars unlocked and vulnerable to theft, and they also reduce the opportunity for dishonesty. Medical advances and safety improvements are also examples of hazard reduction.

The fourth approach to risk reduction is to reduce the loss, which is often referred to as *loss protection*. The aim here is to minimize the extent of the loss. Loss reduction and hazard reduction usually go hand in hand. A fire alarm and fire extinguisher will not prevent a fire, but their presence certainly can reduce the damage or loss caused by the fire. Removing combustibles and cleaning out chimneys can likewise reduce the hazards that can lead to a fire in the first place.

A fifth strategy is to shift the risk. In this case, the burden of the risk is actually handed off to another party. A *surety bond* is an example. A surety bond is a promise by one party, called the *surety*, to be liable to a third party, the *obligee*, for the debt or obligation of a second party, called the *principal*. The risk is not usually impacted at all. It just becomes someone else's responsibility.

The final approach is insurance, which is in itself a form of risk shifting. It is the primary focus of this book, but, as is probably obvious, it usually works best in tandem with the other risk-shifting strategies. Just because your car is insured is no reason to leave the doors unlocked and the keys in the ignition. Not only is it a hassle to deal with the entire claims and replacement process, but anything you can do to reduce auto theft generally will reduce premiums and save everyone money.

Bet You Didn't Know

WOW!

The insurance industry, composed of approximately 6,000 companies, represents well over $2.5 trillion in assets and employs over two million people. This represents a significant commitment to help you protect yourself against loss, and illustrates why you should assume responsibility for minimizing loss on your own.

When Is a Risk Acceptable?

The key question then, becomes *which risks should you assume, and which ones should you insure against?* There is no scientific test or slide rule that will give you the answer. The test is more of a gut reaction to the alternatives.

Suppose you're a 35-year-old with significant family responsibilities, including young children, a mortgage, and debts, and that you can reasonably expect to earn an average of $40,000 a year for the rest of your working life. Should you insure your life against premature death? (Realizing, of course, that when you contemplate your own death, it's always premature.) Assuming a retirement age of 65, you'll earn $1,200,000. You probably wouldn't want to replace the entire amount, but let's assume you would want to provide $250,000 for your family. Would you do it with insurance?

The next question is obvious: How much will $250,000 of life insurance cost? Would you buy the insurance if it cost $3,000 a year? What if it cost $300? The $300 would probably be affordable, but are you easily convinced that this is a fair cost? Probably not.

The Big Mistake/Small Mistake Test

The next question to ask yourself is the big mistake/small mistake question: "If I die without this coverage, is it a big mistake or a small mistake? If I write a check for $300, and I don't die this year, is that a big mistake or a small mistake?" If you answer "big mistake" on the coverage and "small mistake" on the cost, you probably should insure against the risk. Basically, you're asking yourself if you're willing to assume all of the risk all by yourself.

With this new perspective in mind, consider the number of people who spend $1,000 or more each year to insure an automobile worth $12,000, and yet do nothing about insuring their future income, worth in excess of $1,000,000, because it costs $2,000 a year. By asking the "big mistake/small mistake" question, you will be able to recognize and prioritize your needs for insurance protection.

To summarize, you have read why many people are reluctant to address their insurance needs. You don't need to fall into that category. You now know what risk is and various ways to deal with it. And you have a powerful tool in prioritizing your protection alternatives, the "big mistake/small mistake" test. In the next chapter you'll learn more about the insurance industry as a source of protection.

The Least You Need to Know

> ➤ By assessing your needs ahead of time, you can usually afford some form of protection against loss.

> ➤ You can aid your own cause dramatically by employing more than one means of dealing with risks, such as reducing hazards and insuring against loss.

> ➤ You should weigh the potential loss against the cost of the coverage.

> ➤ Apply the "big mistake/small mistake" test to determine whether to insure against the risk, be it your car, your home, or your life.

Chapter 2

What Is Insurance and How Do You Get It?

In This Chapter

➤ How to recognize when a risk is insurable

➤ Who the players are: insurance companies, agents, and brokers

➤ Keys to selecting the right insurance advisor

This chapter looks more closely at the risk requirements of insurance companies. Not all risks will be insurable. Once you have a risk that can be covered, you will need to know who is in the business of providing insurance. There are many different companies and people, all playing different roles. Finally, this chapter will give you the guidelines for selecting an insurance adviser.

Uninsurable Speculative Risks

In Chapter 1, you learned that insurance is a means of shifting risk to another party. In effect, you're saying that the loss you could incur is more than you're willing to assume on your own. But that doesn't mean that an insurance company will automatically insure the risk. The risk must satisfy an insurer's requirements.

Insurance companies will not insure *speculative risks*, but only *pure risks*. Speculative risk exists when the outcome could result in either a gain or a loss. For example, if you wanted to go to Las Vegas for a weekend of gambling and were worried that you might lose all of the $1,000 you intended to wager, you wouldn't be able to insure against that risk. You clearly have a possibility of a gain or a loss (although you may argue about the chances of your winning). Insurance is not designed to protect against these types of risks. What else could you do? This is when you should consider other risk-management alternatives, such as avoidance or hazard reduction.

Insurable Pure Risks

A pure risk is potentially insurable. Life insurance protects against the loss caused by death. There is no gain or potential for gain. There is either a loss or no loss—i.e., death or no death.

For example, when you insure your home against fire, you will either not have a fire, or you will have a fire that creates a loss. You won't have a fire that improves the home's value (no matter what your neighbors think of the color of your house).

What Else Do Insurers Require?

In addition to the pure risk requirement, insurers have strict standards that must be met. The loss must be:

➤ *Important.* The loss must be significant enough to warrant the insurance company's involvement. This is primarily because there are expenses associated with insurance, including the expense of the paperwork, communications and commissions, salaries, and other administrative items. It's impractical and uneconomical for an insurer to issue a policy that covers items that are worth less than the expense of providing the coverage itself. For example, the insurer wouldn't want to insure a $5 teapot if the expense of issuing the policy was $100.

➤ *Accidental.* The loss must be accidental, from the insured's point of view. For example, life insurance companies exclude coverage for suicide within the first two years of the inception of the policy. A suicide is clearly not accidental.

➤ *Calculable.* The insurance company must be able to calculate the possibility and extent of the loss. The chance of an individual loss may be impossible to estimate, but the likelihood of loss in a larger sampling of insureds is predictable. This is known as *the law of large numbers*, which is the mathematical foundation of insurance. The larger the sampling, the greater the degree of predictability.

Bet You Didn't Know

WOW!

According to one statistical table used by insurers, in a population of adult males, 4.55 males out of every 1,000 45-year-old men die each year. (Please note that those applying to be the .55 of a death are not taken seriously.)

➤ *Definite Loss.* The insurance company must be able to determine whether the loss occurred, and if so, how much money was lost. This figure could be arrived at by appraisal, estimation, or, in the case of life insurance, by prior agreement.

➤ *Not Excessively Catastrophic.* The insurance company must protect itself against losses so catastrophic that it cannot absorb the loss. Insurers would not, for example, try to insure every home in a particular fire-prone area.

Not all five of these requirements are always met every time a company issues insurance. However, the guidelines do give you an idea of how insurers evaluate risks.

Insurance is about protecting you against those losses that are significant in dollar amount, accidental in nature, calculable in large numbers, measurable at the time, and not so catastrophic as to bankrupt the insurer. *For you, the importance and measurability requirements are the most relevant.* As you learned in Chapter 1 with the big mistake/small mistake concept, you need to concern yourself with the potential losses that will cause you the most harm.

Will the Real Insurance Agent Please Stand Up?

The financial services industry is composed of the various institutions that handle your money, such as banks, savings and loans, insurance companies, stock brokerages, and mutual funds. During the 1970s and 1980s, the financial services industry began to change in ways that have—and will continue to have—a major impact on you. The lines between the various institutions have blurred and in some cases disappeared. As a result, you're no longer likely to look to an insurance agent for insurance only, or to a stockbroker just for stocks. Almost everyone in the financial services industry is in someone else's business. Only time will tell whether you'll be better served by these changes. Still, you need to be aware of these changes and their impact on your security.

Here's a look at the various parties involved in the sale of insurance today.

Insurance Companies

The organization that assumes the risk you choose to hand off is the insurance company, also known as the *insurer* or the *carrier*. Its size (in assets) can vary from under a million dollars to over a hundred billion dollars. Size shouldn't be the determining factor in which carrier to select, but size is an important consideration in choosing a stable and reliable company. A company needs adequate assets to diversify its investments and fund its future growth. Solvency issues will be discussed in the next chapter.

Bet You Didn't Know

WOW!

Of the approximately 6,000 insurance companies in the country today, most of the policies are issued by 900 companies. On the property and casualty side of the business, over 40 percent of net new premiums are issued by the top 10 companies.

Insurance Agent

The individuals who solicit your business on behalf of the insurance company are known as *agents*. They can be employees of one company or work as independent agents. In both cases, an agent technically represents the insurer, not you. This means they have an obligation to sell their company's products, although some agents may also sell products from other companies.

Insurance Broker

A broker represents *you* rather than the company. Generally, a broker will research and gather quotes from several companies to find the best insurance product for you. This doesn't mean that a broker will necessarily serve your needs better than an agent. A well-trained, experienced agent is better for you than an inexperienced broker.

Watch It!

An agent for one product can be a broker for another. For example, a life insurance agent who represents only one company for life insurance products may represent numerous companies for health insurance because his primary company does not sell health insurance. Ask the salesperson who they represent and in what capacity.

Insurance Consultant

Unlike agents and brokers, who are paid a commission by the insurance company, consultants are usually paid fees by you. This can mean less expensive insurance coverage, if commissions are not charged as part of the premium. However, this doesn't mean you always avoid the expense of a commission. There might still be a commission paid to someone other than the consultant—for example, if an agent or broker is involved in the purchase of the insurance. Before hiring someone in the capacity of a consultant, make sure you understand whether a commission will also be charged.

Financial Planner

A more recent addition to the scene, the planner purports to evaluate your overall finances. As part of this evaluation, the planner may recommend insurance products. Planners work for fees or commissions, but usually not both. State laws may dictate the ability of planners to receive double compensation. Many insurance agents and brokers likewise evaluate your overall financial needs.

Stockbroker

This is the traditional seller of stocks and bonds through a firm registered with the NASD (National Association of Securities Dealers) and the SEC (Securities and Exchange Commission). Stockbrokerage firms now sell insurance as well as traditional investments. In recent years, a number of experienced life insurance people have emigrated to securities firms, making it possible to receive good advice from these firms.

> *OOOH...* **Insider Tip**
>
> The securities industry, along with most of the financial services industry, has grown enamored with sophisticated-sounding titles. Today, a broker might be called an investment representative, a financial consultant, or a financial advisor. Look behind the title. Ask for the person's credentials and find out who they work for.

Bank Teller

Although a teller may have a different title, bank personnel are selling insurance products throughout the country. Some aggressive institutions are selling all types, while others are selling only *annuities*. Annuities are contracts between insurance companies and the insured that allow the insured to accumulate monies or receive income payments for long periods of time, often for life, usually on a tax-advantaged basis. Annuities are the subject of Part 3.

Direct Seller

A number of organizations, including credit unions and associations such as the AARP (American Association of Retired Persons), offer insurance products to their membership directly, through mailings or advertising. This eliminates the agent or broker, which is not always a good thing for you. There are times when you need the counsel and advice as much as the product, because the products can be complex and your needs can be complicated.

Who Do You Trust?

With all these people and companies selling insurance, what's a shopper to do? A life insurance agent for one company may sell health insurance for another company, mutual funds through his company's brokerage arm, and also charge fees to give you retirement plan advice. A typical stockbroker today can offer you stocks, bonds, mutual funds, annuities, life insurance, and disability insurance. Even *trust services*, such as the administration of wills and trust documents, once available only through banks, are now readily available elsewhere. It's not surprising, then, that banks want to be in the insurance and securities businesses.

Bet You Didn't Know

A major insurer recently agreed to a settlement of $1,000,000 for not controlling the marketing practices of its agents. The agents at fault made representations about the policies in order to increase sales. Most of the policies were less secure than explained by the agents.

As a result of the rush to get into everyone else's pocket, there are too many poorly trained people selling products they don't really understand and can't explain to you. Recent litigation against sellers of life insurance and annuities illustrate that point.

Where does that leave you? Do you need someone to help you with your insurance and annuity needs? And if so, how do you find the right person?

Foremost, you need to find someone you trust. This is more important than whether he or she is an agent, broker, planner, stockbroker, or teller. So how do you do that? You have to know the ingredients that make for a trusting relationship.

➤ Experience is the first factor you should consider. Unfortunately, it isn't always easy to measure. Some people truly have 20 years' experience in the business, while others with the same tenure have one year's experience 20 times over. You need to ask what these people have accomplished in their time in the business.

➤ Ask about the person's integrity. Has the individual or agency ever been punished or cited by a regulatory agency for misconduct, misrepresentation, or mishandling of funds? You'll get this information from the regulatory agencies themselves. The State Insurance Commissioners are listed in the Appendix.

➤ Look at a person's continuing education. Today's products and planning tools are complex and confusing. Competition is driving this complexity, and you need a representative who can keep on top of the latest developments and communicate them so you understand them. Your representative must have a commitment to continuing education.

➤ Finally, you must consider a less tangible ingredient—empathy. Because insurance frequently involves matters concerning a painful loss, you'll want to work with professionals who are more concerned with your welfare than their earnings. In fact, this is the best definition of a professional: One who places your needs above their own. Looking them in the eye and listening to your gut may be the best barometer here.

In this book, you'll learn more about the products, prices, and providers of these insurance products. After you've read the entire book, you'll be in a better position to select the right person for you.

Bet You Didn't Know Most states now require agents to attend courses or classes as part of a program of continuing education in order to renew their licenses. All states require agents to be licensed.

The Least You Need to Know

In summary, not all risks are insurable, but the ones that are should be considered by using the "big mistake/small mistake" test. You will need to find the insurer and representative who will most closely meet your needs. Choose from the list provided earlier. And select your adviser on the basis of trust gained through their experience and professional development.

➤ The insurance industry, like most industries, is driven by sales. Agents and brokers get paid when they sell something. Not all salespeople care what they sell, as long as they sell something. You need to assume the primary responsibility for securing the right coverage at the right price.

➤ There are many financially-sound, quality-conscious insurance companies that can satisfy all your insurance needs. Choose among the most stable and secure, with the tools you'll acquire in the remainder of Part 1.

➤ There are many competent, conscientious, and caring professionals selling insurance. You need to find the right person for your insurance needs, using trust as the cornerstone, premised on the person's experience, education, and empathy.

A Brief History of Insurance

History Lessons

Historians trace insurance roots back to ancient traders among the Babylonians, Phoenicians, and Chinese. More than four thousand years before the fax machine, some shippers pledged their cargoes as collateral for loans to make overland or overseas passages. The extra sum traders paid on loans to protect their cargo was called a *premium*. The term stuck. Today, *premium* refers to the payment made to the insurer to keep the insurance in force.

Still other traders devised schemes to ship only a part of each trader's cargo on any one of the caravan's barges, so that if one barge broke loose and sunk, the trader didn't sink financially along with his shipment. This is an early example of *risk shifting*.

During the rise of the Roman Empire, fraternal societies paid death benefits to the survivors of its members. This early form of life insurance survives in a somewhat more scientific form today.

Property Insurance

Property insurance as you know it today emerged from the needs of commerce in the 13th century. *Property insurance* is insurance designed to protect the insured against the loss of an asset caused by certain perils—for example, by fire. *Marine insurance* refers to the coverage of risks on or around the water.

Individuals, rather than companies, issued marine insurance to protect merchants shipping their goods. After drafting a document describing the ship and the cargo, the ship owner invited wealthy individuals to assume part of the risk. Accepting individuals wrote their names on the document, under the description, and therefore became known as *underwriters*, a term still in existence today.

Jargon Alert

An *underwriter* is the company that assumes responsibility for the risk and in turn receives the premium. An individual within the company who decides whether the company should accept the risk is also called an *underwriter*. The term has also been extended to sales personnel. A life insurance agent is alternatively called a *life underwriter*.

The earliest marine policies in this country were issued by British companies in the middle of the sixteenth century. American underwriters started issuing policies around 1750. And in 1752, Benjamin Franklin and the Philadelphia Contributionship for the Insurance of Houses from Loss by Fire started a fire insurance company.

It Was an Accident, Really

Casualty insurance was originally designed to protect against loss or liability as a result of an accident.

In 1848, the British Parliament granted a charter for the Railroad Passenger Assurance Company to protect travelers. In 1859, James C. Batterson of Hartford, Connecticut, founded an American company to provide similar protection, the Travelers Insurance Company. It also was one of the first companies to offer medical expense insurance.

Industrialization spawned the railroad, as well as most of the other causes of losses and liabilities that would become the driving force behind the casualty insurance industry. For example, in 1866, the Hartford Steam Boiler Inspection and Insurance Company was created to protect against boiler explosions. The rise in industrial accidents led to a public outcry for liability legislation. These new laws aimed to protect workers and punish negligent employers. In response to this legislation, insurers developed policies to protect the employer from these new areas of liability. Even accidents outside the workplace, such as in elevators and automobiles, fueled the demand for insurance protection.

Today, casualty insurance has a broad scope, including accidents, theft, and public and professional liability. And yet, there are companies that specialize to the extent of protection for amusement parks and mountain climbers, for example.

Bet You Didn't Know
The first automobile policies in this country were issued in 1898. In 1994, there were approximately 33,900,000 automobile accidents reported in this country with a total cost of $110.5 trillion, according to the Insurance Information Institute.

You Bet Your Life

The first life insurance company in America was The Corporation for Relief of Poor and Distressed Presbyterian Ministers and the Poor and Distressed Widows and Children of Presbyterian Ministers. The company is still in operation, although one could speculate that its low profile is directly related to its inability to print its name on direct mail reply cards. The company was formed as a *stock insurance company*, as opposed to Ben Franklin's fire insurance company, which was a *mutual insurance company*. The first mutual life insurance company was New England Mutual, created in 1835. That company also exists today.

The differences of ownership still remain today between stock and mutual companies, the latter being owned by the policyholders.

Jargon Alert

A *stock company* is owned by stockholders, individuals, or institutions that invest in the company's stock, with the hopes of profits being returned in dividends on the stock. A *mutual company* is owned by its policyholders and managed by a Board of Directors elected by the policyholders. Profits are shared with these policyholders, also in the form of dividends, but they are dividends on the policies themselves.

Life insurance also prospered from the demands of the Industrial Revolution. As more Americans and immigrants moved to the industrialized cities, families left at home were less able to step in and care for newly created widows and orphans. Without the traditional familial support group, workers turned to insurers for financial assurances. Insurance companies responded to this increasing demand.

The Right Wright and Mr. Armstrong

Life insurance grew rapidly in the middle 1800s—perhaps too rapidly. By the 1870s, the intense competition among the new companies led to serious abuses of the buying public. The disclosure of the abuses by the press led to a dramatic falloff in business. More than a third of life insurers failed between 1870 and 1877. Surprisingly, new state regulation of the insurance companies helped their demise. At the relentless urging of a determined pioneer named Elizue Wright, most states enacted severe legislation regulating the industry. A byproduct of the increased oversight was the forced closing of many companies that had heretofore been unsound and unwatched.

Bet You Didn't Know

One of the most famous insurers is Lloyd's of London. It has been known for insuring difficult risks, such as movie stars' legs and singers' voices. But Lloyd's of London is not an insurance company at all. It's an association of individuals and companies that underwrite insurance individually. Lloyd's itself functions as the organizer and facilitator between the individual underwriters and the party seeking coverage. This means the underwriters have personal liability for their promises to insure. This is the reason so many of Lloyd's underwriters lost fortunes during the great catastrophes of the last decade, such as hurricanes, earthquakes, and nuclear accidents.

After a resurgence of sales and sales abuses during the 1880s, life insurers again attracted the close scrutiny of the regulators. In 1905, the State of New York appointed the Armstrong Investigating Committee to probe the alleged abuses. The recommendations of that committee set the stage for the regulation of insurance as you know it today. The new regulations required tighter state supervision, forbade investment in common stocks, and limited expenditures for the acquisition of new business.

This severe reining in of the industry slowed sales. However, when the public realized they could again trust life insurers, sales boomed. In 1900, life insurance in force was $7.5 billion. By 1930, in-force business exceeded $100 billion. Today, life insurance in force exceeds $11.5 trillion.

Déjà Vu All Over Again—More Abuse

History tends to repeat itself in the insurance industry. Unfortunately, a new wave of abuses has again tainted the industry. It began with the highly publicized failure of several annuity companies in the 1980s, such as Baldwin United. Then came the severely damaged or failing insurers with disintegrating real estate or depressed junk bond portfolios, such as Executive Life.

Recently, there have been widespread and costly class action suits against some of the largest insurers, alleging misleading and fraudulent sales practices. One insurer has already settled one of these suits with a $20 million payment to policyholders. If it sounds familiar, it is. And the response is predictable: a call for better regulation. The lesson for you is that you need to be responsible and careful in selecting your agent and your insurer. (Insurance company solvency is covered in Chapter 4.)

Litigate, Litigate, Dance to the Music...

The final chapter on regulation has yet to be written. In fact, it's a topic in Congress today. The issue was first addressed by the U.S. Supreme Court in 1868 in the famous case of *Paul v. Virginia*. The court held that the insurance industry was necessarily and properly regulated by the states, rather than the federal government.

That judgment remained in effect until 1944, when the U.S. Supreme Court faced the issue of the adequacy of state regulation. The court this time reversed its position and said that insurance was a form of interstate commerce and therefore subject to federal laws. This decision prompted Congress to enter the fray. It passed the McCarran-Ferguson Act, which reestablished state regulation of the insurance business. This is the law today.

Insider Tip
The significance of state regulation for you is that each state determines how it will interpret that responsibility. As a result, the rules and regulations of the various states are not the same. Even though the state insurance commissioners occasionally agree to standardized regulations, it's still up to each state to make its own rules.

The Insurance Commissioners

Each state has a department of insurance, although the exact title may differ. (You'll find a listing of the state offices in the Appendix.) The department has the responsibility to regulate both the solvency of insurers and the marketing of insurance. Specifically, each state has responsibility for:

➤ Issuing rules and regulations

➤ Licensing and supervising insurance companies chartered and residing in that state (known as *domestic* companies)

➤ Licensing and supervising salespeople in that state

➤ Deciding what types of insurance can be sold in the state

➤ Regulating the level of *reserves* that insurance companies must keep in order to sell in that state

➤ Supervising marketing practices

➤ Handling consumer complaints

Jargon Alert

Reserves are the dollars held by the insurance company to ensure the capability to pay future claims. They are one of the important elements in a company's solvency and safety.

As you might expect, some states are tougher regulators than others. The tougher they are, the better for you. New York has long had a reputation as a tough regulator, undoubtedly surviving from the Armstrong Investigation Committee days.

Bet You Didn't Know

If your state takes the same stance as New York on a particular issue, you're probably being well represented at the Insurance Commissioner's office. For years, admission of an insurance company to sell in New York was a reasonable assurance of its solvency and reserves. And while this is not necessarily true today, New York remains one of the most consumer-oriented regulators.

The State of Disunion Address for Financial Services

The financial services industry is in a state of great flux, characterized by the mad dash to get into everyone else's business. A second front of legislation is very much at the center of the controversy over who can sell what financial products.

Following the Depression of 1929, Congress provided for the separation of insurance, banking, and securities companies and their right to sell each other's products. This *firewall* approach to financial services made for sound policy in the 1920s and 1930s. Its viability today is questionable. Today, insurance companies own stockbrokerage firms, banks, and savings and loans; they sell insurance and annuities; and stockbrokers offer

CDs. One has to wonder what the best limits are, if any. The life insurance lobby, for example, has strongly resisted the notion of banks selling insurance. The question is before both the appellate courts and the Congress. The issue is especially acute because of the reported abuses and misleading sales practices by bank personnel presenting insurance products and mutual funds.

The free-for-all that has evolved in financial services will have significant impact on your insurance options. More competition should mean lower premium rates and more innovative policy provisions. However, it will likely result in a greater number of poorly trained representatives and more complicated products. All the more reason to protect yourself by reading this book.

A final word about state regulation. Each state has created a fund to protect policyholders against the insolvency of insurers doing business in that state. In some states, there's a *guaranty fund*, and in others, a *guaranty association*.

In either case, if an insurer fails to honor claims, the fund or association will assume the responsibility up to prescribed limits. They do this through assessments of solvent insurers in the state.

The question, then, is how do you know if a company is safe—that it has adequate assets and adequate reserves to pay its claims? Read on.

Jargon Alert
A *guaranty fund* or *association* is a state vehicle for reimbursing policyholders against financial losses suffered when an insurance company fails in that state or with specific insureds in that state.

Watch It!
While this backup protection gives you an extra measure of safety, you should never rely on the availability of the state guaranty funds as a rationale for doing business with a weak or unsound company. The process of recovery from the guaranty association or fund or new insurance company is at best slow and aggravating.

The Least You Need to Know

History tends to repeat itself in the insurance industry, meaning periods of closer or looser regulation, depending on where you are in the cycle. As of this writing, the movement is toward tighter state regulation. And while there is some debate about how insurance should be regulated, the regulatory responsibility clearly lies in the hands of the individual states.

➤ The two basic types of insurance companies, stock and mutual, have very different objectives, depending on whether you're a stockholder, policyholder, or a policyholder in a mutual company.

➤ Insurance is regulated by the states. To find out how to contact your Insurance Commissioner's office, see the Appendix.

➤ The current wave of company failures and class action lawsuits should serve as a warning to pay close attention to your choice of a sales representative and an insurance company.

Chapter 4

How Does the Company Rate?

In This Chapter

➤ Why you must find financially sound companies to insure you and your property

➤ Who analyzes and rates insurance companies

➤ How you translate the ratings into recommendations

This chapter discusses the reasons for doing business with financially sound insurance companies, and how to find them. Over the recent decades, many policyholders, of life and annuity companies particularly, have lost money and been inconvenienced by the failure of their company. In this chapter, you'll learn how to avoid the same fate.

Why Soundness Matters

It pays to buy your insurance from financially secure companies. In the case of some coverage such as life insurance, the day you may need the protection can be decades away. Unless you have access to a crystal ball, you need to find some way to select a company that will be there to write the check when you need it. Not all companies will.

If that sounds a little scary, it's meant to. There are approximately 6,000 insurance companies in this country. Between 1984 and 1993, an average of 70 companies failed each year. The combined assets of these companies was in the billions of dollars. By comparison, from 1976 to 1984 the average was 20 failures a year.

An insurance company's failure isn't your only concern—you also need to worry about the company's overall financial health. With many of the new products in the market today, particularly in life insurance and annuities, the performance of the product is tied to the performance of the company. Mediocre performance can cost you thousands of dollars over the life of a policy.

Fortunately, you won't need either psychic training or a financial analyst's degree to choose the right company. There are reputable rating services that study the financial condition of insurance companies for you. You'll take a look at them in this chapter.

The Best—A. M. Best, That Is

One organization that specializes in the analysis of the insurance industry is the A. M. Best Company. For many years, it has been the primary source of opinions as to the financial condition of insurers. Because insurers are heavily regulated, they're required to publish financial statements with the appropriate governmental agencies. A. M. Best gathers this information and rates the companies according to size, type, and financial soundness. They charge a small fee to the insurer to be rated.

In the past, A. M. Best's analyses have not always warned policyowners quickly enough to let them get out of failing companies. However, as a result of several recent failures, A. M. Best has made changes to help it become more reliable. It is not foolproof.

Bet You Didn't Know
According to the A. M. Best Company, most property and casualty insurers fail because they have inadequate reserve, their premiums are too low, or they grow too fast. Life and health companies fail most often because they price their products too low or they grow too fast.

A. M. Best rates more insurers than any of the rating services, and its history of rating life insurers goes back almost to the turn of the century. In their publication, *Best's Insurance Reports*, they provide an annual analysis and rating of the larger U.S. companies. They evaluate the financial strength of the insurer, including its ability to honor its promises to pay claims. Best's assigns a letter rating to the company, ranging from A++ to F, just like in school. Some companies are classified as Not Rated. This could be because the company is too new, too small, or for other reasons.

The top ratings from Best's are A++ and A+, both of which they consider Superior. The next two ratings are considered Excellent, noted as an A or an A-. These four top ratings are assigned to insurers who have consistently met their obligations. There are eleven other ratings, ranging from B++ to F (Liquidation).

> **OOOH...** **Insider Tip**
>
> You should only do business with companies rated A- or better. Let someone else do business with newer, weaker insurers, even if someone you know is making the sale. Remember, your friend or relative (the salesperson) will not be writing the check to cover your loss. And do not let an agent tell you not to worry about the size of the company because the state has a guaranty fund or association. Would you buy an inferior car because the dealer had a good repair department?

Other Rating Services

Insurers are likewise rated by traditional credit analysts, such as Standard & Poor's Rating Group, Moody's Investors Service, and Duff & Phelps Credit Rating Company. These companies also rate non-insurance companies on their credit-paying capability. For an insurance company, the most significant part of the credit equation is the capability to pay its claims. That should be your primary concern.

A relative newcomer to the field is Weiss Research. Its ratings are more severe in describing financial soundness, and it has been criticized for overstatement. They have less of a track record during the more difficult decades of rating, but if you want another opinion, they're a player today.

How Do I Contact an Agency?

The addresses and phone numbers of the rating agencies are:

A. M. Best Company
Ambest Road
Oldwick, NJ 08858
(908) 439-2200

Duff & Phelps Credit Rating Company
55 East Monroe Street
Chicago, IL 60603
(312) 368-3157

Moody's Investors Service
99 Church Street
New York, NY 10007
(212) 553-1658

Standard & Poor's Rating Group
25 Broadway
New York, NY 10004
(212) 208-1527
Internet: http://www.insure.com/ratings/define.html

Weiss Research, Inc.
P. O. Box 2923
West Palm Beach, FL 33402
(407) 627-3300

A call to the rating service will give you an opportunity to check the rating for a particular company. However, you should also check with your public library for reports and information. And, since most proposals for insurance are generated by an agent rather than you, the insured, ask the salesperson for the latest reports from the various services on any company recommended.

How Do I Interpret a Rating?

Naturally, the rating services all use different grading scales. So, what do you look for? You should only consider companies that are rated very good to excellent. This might mean AAA to Standard & Poor's, or A+ to A. M. Best. Whatever the letter grade, don't settle for anything less than "very good." Your future financial well-being may depend on that claim check.

Here's what to look for from each of the services:

A. M. Best Company

Superior = A++ and A+
Excellent = A and A-

Duff & Phelps Credit Rating Company

Highest claims paying ability = AAA
Very high ability = AA+, AA, AA-

Moody's Investors Service

Exceptional = Aaa
Excellent = Aa

Standard & Poor's Rating Group

Superior = AAA
Excellent = AA

Weiss Research, Inc.

Excellent = A+, A, A-

If you're unable to get a rating of a particular company from one of the services besides Best, it may be because the service charges the insurance company a great deal of money to be examined and listed, and not all companies are willing to pay to be rated by all services. However, you will find the healthiest companies rated by all of the agencies in this chapter. A major disparity from one service to another, aside from the tougher grading Weiss, should prompt you to dig a little deeper to find out why.

The Least You Need to Know

There is usually a great deal at stake in insurance—too much for you to rely on financially unsound companies. Because claims may arise well into the future, it pays to do your homework at the time of the sale, not when the insurer collapses. Use the rating services to check on the financial condition of your insurer or proposed insurer.

➤ The safety of your insurance carrier is critical to meeting your needs now and in the future.

➤ Insurance companies are examined and rated by several services, and the information is readily accessible. A. M. Best is the oldest and most recognized.

➤ You should only do business with the top-rated companies, assuming you have a choice.

➤ Premium savings will be little consolation if your carrier goes bankrupt and you lose money and/or time. Do not try to save premiums by doing business with anything less than the most secure companies.

Chapter 5

Evaluating Risk

In Chapter 1, you learned that risk is the uncertainty of loss. But that doesn't go far enough in helping you decide what to protect with insurance and when. In this chapter, you'll learn about making those tough decisions: which risks to insure and which risks to assume yourself.

Emotional and Financial Losses

At some point in your life, you've probably lost a friend because of an argument. While it was probably a painful experience from an emotional perspective, it probably wasn't a financially painful experience. Unless, of course, your friend was also your "pal" in a palimony suit stemming from the argument.

Insurance covers financial losses, which are measurable in dollars and cents, not emotional losses. But you shouldn't gloss over the emotional loss just yet—frequently emotional and financial losses are interrelated. For example, assume you're in an automobile accident and suffer a disability that prevents you from working in any meaningful capacity. This can be emotionally devastating to you and your family. But if the disability also means that you lose all of your income, then the impact of the disability is even greater. Insurance is usually available to protect your income, and if it is affordable, you would be acting responsibly by purchasing the coverage. The insurance may even help soften the emotional blow by addressing the financial need.

Not with My Money

The first challenge in evaluating your insurance program is deciding what should be insured. In Chapter 1, you read about the big mistake/small mistake approach. Another way to approach the issue is to ask "Which of my assets are so valuable that I would suffer great financial loss if they were destroyed?"

Immediately your home comes to mind, as well as your car and other expensive physical assets. But the most important asset in most families is *you*, the wage earner, parent, homemaker, or caretaker of the lives of others. Without you and your ability to earn a living and/or raise a family, others suffer financially as well as emotionally. Notice that the non-employed homemaker/parent is included in this classification. There is no question that a surviving spouse will suffer additional expenses when a working-in-the-home spouse/parent dies. Whether you choose to insure that loss is another matter, but you do need to realize that there will be an economic loss.

The Worth of a Life

The concept of *human life value* is not new. Solomon S. Huebner is the person usually recognized as the creator of the concept earlier in this century. He measured a person's life by estimating that person's future earnings and then subtracting the amount that would be expended on that individual's personal needs. This approach is still viable today.

Jargon Alert
Human life value is a concept used in measuring the value of one's future earnings as a way to decide how much insurance to buy to protect those future earnings.

Another approach to deciding how much life insurance to buy is a compilation of what you want to provide. If you want mortgages and bills paid, education funded for your children, and income for some period to your surviving spouse, these are ascertainable amounts, and the sum of the items is the total needed at death, from insurance or other assets you may own. You'll study life insurance needs in greater detail in Chapter 8.

Where's My Paycheck?

As previously mentioned, income replacement is another major need for most people. This is true because expenses continue whether income stops or not. And most people don't have adequate reserves to last very long without a steady stream of income. Workers' Compensation and Social Security are inadequate alternatives to insurance and savings. You'll learn more about disability income insurance in Chapters 16, 17, and 18.

Bet You Didn't Know

The reason Social Security cannot be counted on lies not just in the fact that the fund may be bankrupt when needed; Social Security's definition of disability is so restrictive that it may be difficult to qualify for it in the event of a disability. The Social Security definition of disability is the complete inability to engage in *any* "substantial gainful activity" because of either a mental or physical impairment that is expected to result in death or will last more than 12 months.

It's easy enough to calculate the income you need, especially if you're living on all of your current earnings. Otherwise, add all of your current expenses each month and that's what you need.

Medical Expenses—Not for the Unhealthy

Medical expenses is another area that demands attention in any insurance program. Fortunately, most people are covered by a group health plan through an employer. In most cases, you pay part or all of the premium. You may also have a choice of several types of coverage, and that choice will impact your out-of-pocket expense.

You should approach health insurance as you would any other coverage—by asking how much of this potential expense you're willing to accept on your own, and how much you should transfer to the insurance company. Obviously, the trade-off between coverage and cost is important. Health insurance alternatives are discussed in Part 4, starting with Chapter 20.

A Crash Course for Automobiles

Automobile and other property coverage is approached in the same way. What is the financial value of the asset to be insured? Are you willing to assume some of the expense personally, and thereby reduce your premium? As you learn in later chapters, some auto insurance is required by law and some is discretionary. If you can assume some of the risk of loss on your car and other personal belongings, you can save significant premium dollars. As always, use of the big mistake/small mistake test will help you decide how much of the risk you can assume yourself. Property insurance is discussed in Part 6.

Litigation Protection—Here Comes the Judge

Casualty coverage guards against potential exposure to losses due to litigation. If you have anything worth protecting, then you need to purchase coverage that will keep your assets safe from the awards of outrageous juries. Anyone who reads a newspaper or watches television today knows the absurdity of many of these jury awards. Juries frequently rationalize excessive awards because they know an insurance company will pay for the awards. They apparently never stop to think that excessive awards contribute to the increase in premiums that you and they experience almost every year. You should have insurance to protect yourself and your assets from this risk. Liability insurance is detailed in Chapter 33.

Who's Responsible for This?

Deciding whether to buy insurance is an exercise in responsibility, but being responsible seems to be a dying art.

In this country, there was a time when someone who drove away from a fast-food restaurant with a cup of scalding coffee in their lap would be considered negligent, if not downright stupid. But not today. When it happened recently to a driver who spilled the coffee and got burned, the jury blamed the restaurant for serving their coffee too hot and decided to scald the fast-food restaurant and their insurance company to the tune of millions of dollars. We've placed a greater value on behaving like morons and then suing someone else for our stupidity, than on being responsible.

WOW! Bet You Didn't Know
The last quarter of 1995 was the most costly fourth quarter in history for insurers. With a blast from Hurricane Opal, insured losses exceeded $2.6 billion for the three-month period. Total losses for the year were $8.3 billion, the third worst year on record. There are enough demands on insurers without irresponsible lawsuits.

The point here is that considering insurance is part of a *process*, a process of assuming responsibility for yourself and your own welfare. And looking for windfall profits from litigation should not be a part of that process. Adequately insured individuals adopt the attitude that they're responsible for themselves and their families, and they exercise that responsibility by maintaining appropriate levels of personal assets and purchased insurance.

Please, I'd Rather Do It Myself

Self insurance is that portion of a given risk you're willing to assume personally. For example, if you drive a $20,000 automobile and are concerned about the expense of replacing or repairing the car in the event of an accident, you can protect yourself against financial loss with insurance. However, because most accidents cause only minor losses, the insurance company could greatly reduce its premium if it didn't have to worry about smaller claims. In other words, the insurance company reduces its exposure to risk and therefore is able to charge you less of a premium.

Your goal should be to restrict your coverage to just that amount of loss that you cannot assume yourself. If your $20,000 car needs $10,000 worth of parts and labor after an accident, it's not the first $1,000 of out-of-pocket expenses that hurts the most—it's the last $1,000. And if you have adequate savings to assume that first $1,000, then do so, and reduce your premiums. This same process applies to health insurance, life insurance, and almost all other types of coverage. The objective should be to cover with insurance what you're unwilling to cover yourself.

The Least You Need to Know

You should consider all of the areas of risk in your life as serious, but only the financial as potentially insurable. The survey of needs will be covered in greater detail throughout this book, but be aware of your responsibility and potential for self-protection.

➤ Buying insurance is about being responsible for your own affairs, which includes financial responsibility to yourself, your family, and your neighbors.

➤ The process of deciding what to insure involves an analysis of your assets and their importance to you.

➤ The process also involves a realistic assessment of your ability to assume responsibility for some of the loss by yourself. Take a hard look at your existing assets and income to be used to self insure and reduce your premiums.

Chapter 6

Everything Has Its Price

In This Chapter

➤ How to distinguish between needs, objectives, and wants

➤ Why you're motivated to seek safety, security, and many of the other needs in your life

➤ How insurance companies put a price, called premiums, on your needs and wants

Before you begin to delve into the specifics of insurance, you should understand a bit more about your own nature—human nature—especially as it relates to this risk business. It's your very humanness that drives your demand for protection against risks.

This chapter explores the concept of need as it relates to insurance. Most people buy insurance to satisfy a "need" that they feel for safety and security. Very little insurance is mandated by law. Instead, you protect yourself and your assets because it is consistent with your sense of what is right, or expected. The cost of the protection is part of the decision-making process as well. Read on to find out more about your insurance needs.

Maslow's Hierarchy of Needs

Human hopes and creeds
Have their root in human needs.

Eugene Fitch Ware, *The Rhymes of Ironquill*

The psychologist Abraham Maslow, one of the deans of the study of human motivation, developed a well-known theory of man's actions, referred to as the *hierarchy of needs*. He explained why man is so concerned about his economic security. He believed that man's actions reflect his basic needs. He found that a person will concentrate on loftier needs only when lower needs are substantially met. His hierarchy is as follows:

1. *Physiological needs*—These are the most basic and include food, clothing, and shelter. If your need for food isn't met, you won't be concentrating on your need for self-esteem, for example.

2. *Safety needs*—This is the need for protection from bodily and psychological harm. It's at this level that insurance begins to have great appeal. The amount of risk you're willing to assume on your own is a function of how safe and secure you feel.

3. *Love and acceptance needs*—Man's social needs include a sense of belonging, of being loved and accepted by one's family, and then by one's peers and community. This is a powerful motivator, but only if you feel safe enough to turn your attention to these needs.

4. *Esteem needs*—Maslow anticipated man's need for self-esteem and the esteem of others at this level. Neither are ever completely satisfied, but if a person has high self-esteem, great respect, and prestige, he can concentrate on the most lofty of the needs in the hierarchy (as shown at the top of the pyramid in the following figure).

5. *Self-fulfillment needs*—Maslow referred to the highest need as a need for *self-actualization*. By that he meant the development of one's personality and capabilities, making the most of one's self. Again, a person struggling to find food and shelter will not be able to concentrate on reaching his full human potential. Many people never reach this stage.

A triangle representing Maslow's hierarchy of needs.

Economists Have Needs, Too

Maslow's hierarchy of needs represents the psychologist's perspective on human motivation. But other sciences have perspectives of their own. For example, economists see man as driven by economic needs, including the need to work, produce, save, and consume. They recognize the need for security, but see it as being more in the background.

The economist's view complements Maslow's. Your pursuit of security can be viewed as a journey upward through the various levels of the psychologist's hierarchy. At the physiological level, man is driven to work, beg, or, if necessary, commit crimes to meet the basic needs for food, clothing, and shelter. However, when a person has satisfied his basic needs, the drive for security (and perhaps memories of more difficult days) motivates him to put money aside for future needs. These are the motivations at the safety level.

From an economic perspective, man works in order to eliminate the threats to his safety and security. This includes buying health, disability, and property insurance. These policies could be the very protection he needs to keep him and his family from slipping back into the first level's struggle for survival.

You also need the love and affection of your family and want to satisfy your need for self-esteem. You may purchase life insurance to ensure the well-being of your family and to make them feel good about you as the provider and protector. This is an unselfish act, and one usually not taken unless you're beyond the struggle for basic needs. It's difficult to worry about the future when you can't even make do in the present. Likewise, retirement planning is a priority only after adequate food is on the table.

At the self-actualization level, you have a different perspective on money. It becomes a means of self-expression. Here the emphasis could be on giving to charity, establishing foundations, and working for the welfare of others.

Do You Need It or Just Want It?

With all the talk about needs, you're probably wondering when a "need" becomes a "want" or a "must have" becomes a "nice to have." And how does that relate to Maslow and the economists? The answer to the question is important because we tend to create problems for ourselves. By overbuying under the guise of meeting our needs, we are in fact only giving in to our wants.

You must be able to distinguish between a need and a want, and not just for your teenager's sake. In the strictest sense, you need to eat, breathe, avoid the severe elements, and so on. A nutritious meal at the local cafeteria can be differentiated from dinner at The Four Seasons in New York. And yet, it's consistent with human nature to upgrade one's requirements as one moves up the economic ladder. But an upgrade in taste should not be confused with a "need." At some point, the need becomes a "want." It's a matter of priorities—a big mistake or a small mistake.

"Needs Selling"

Here's another very important point to understand. In the last few decades, most insurance sales training courses have shifted their emphasis from product selling to "needs selling." Under the former, the salesperson's goal was to sell you the product they were told to sell. Your specific needs were of little or no concern. A salesperson going door-to-door selling burial policies is an example. The sales pitch would proceed without much interest in whether you even need such protection. On the other hand, *needs selling* is just what it sounds like. The salesperson sells by focusing on your individual needs.

Jargon Alert
Needs selling is a sales philosophy that is based on putting the customer's needs at the forefront of the sales process. The goal of the sales interview is to find out what the prospect needs, and then to solve that need with the appropriate product.

The salesperson is interested in finding out who you are and what you need. Then the salesperson recommends the appropriate product for you based on your situation. Unless you have performed your own analysis and know exactly what you need, you should do business only with people who understand this kind of needs selling. That's true of any product—you should buy what you need based on your actual situation, not based on the community's needs or the needs of the average 40-year-old man. Find an agent who's experienced enough to know the difference.

And what is the role of money in the equation? Buy what you need *at a price you can afford*. Unless you have unlimited funds, you should match your needs with your premium-paying ability. Most insurance policies have deductibles, or the equivalent of a deductible, such as a waiting period, an exclusion, or copayment. These options are means of lowering the premium enough to make the coverage affordable, and will be discussed later.

Jargon Alert

A *copayment* is the sharing of an amount due between two or more parties. A common example is the sharing of medical expenses under a health insurance policy between the insurer and the insured, such as 80 percent paid by the insurance company and 20 percent by the insured. A copayment has the effect of lowering premiums by reducing the insurance company's exposure to a claim.

Your Buck Starts and Stops Here

Now let's talk about rates. You learned about rating services in Chapter 4, but that's something different. The rates I'm talking about here are the funds you pay to the insurance company to keep the policy in force.

You've seen how your basic needs drive your decisions. And you've had the opportunity to consider the differences between real needs and mere wants or wishes. You're now ready to put these concepts to work in a buying scenario—that means having to make decisions that balance coverage alternatives and premium costs. The options are usually more complicated than a direct trade-off between coverage and premium.

Jargon Alert
A *rate* is the dollar cost of the insurance, usually cited on a per-unit basis, such as per $1,000 of death benefit for life insurance or per $100 a month of disability income insurance.

The Coverage/Cost Balancing Act

As an example, let's examine some choices in the health insurance area. Assume you're convinced that you need health insurance and you have no coverage where you work.

Assume further that you have almost no savings and you're a young family. A broker has recommended a policy that covers your basic health expenses almost completely, with very little out-of-pocket expense to you. The premium is $175 a month. It covers up to $25,000 in total expenses. Another broker proposes a major medical plan with less coverage on the front end of a claim, but coverage up to $1,000,000 in total expenses. This coverage is $250 per month.

How do you decide which coverage is best for you? If you started with the big mistake/small mistake analysis, what could you learn? Let's take a hypothetical claim of $4,000. You find that the basic hospitalization plan for $175 per month covers all but $100 of the claim. But, the major medical plan requires you to pay $400. You save $300 on the hypothetical illness and subsequent hospitalization under the basic hospitalization plan, and the premium is less than the major medical premium. It looks like an easy decision so far.

But what about a claim for $50,000? These days, this is a relatively easy bill to accumulate. The basic hospital plan pays $25,000. The major medical pays $49,500. With the less expensive plan, you would be faced with a $25,000 unpaid bill—a big mistake.

Most people would be better off with the major medical plan, even though they will in all likelihood pay more for less costly illnesses and accidents. The question you should ask yourself is whether short-term savings are worth the risk of financial ruin.

You can take this example to a different level. What if the choices included a third policy that covered all of the expenses of the $50,000 claim, but had an even higher premium than the major medical plan—say, $350 per month? Now there's a trade-off of out-of-pocket cost for a higher premium. The big mistake/small mistake test is less helpful here because both of the major medical plans protect you from the excessive bill. Now the issue is dollars and cents. Is the extra $100 a month or $1,200 a year worth the first dollar protection? You weigh the likelihood of using the policy against the extra premium.

You face these types of trade-offs and decisions with almost all of your insurance purchases. And there's nothing like the sound of your internal cash register ringing you back to reality on the difference between needs and wants.

The Least You Need to Know

You act on your needs. This is natural and healthy. Most people crave safety and security. But you know it carries a price. Make sure you understand the price and are sure that it is a reasonable one for you. Shop around.

➤ You're driven by a hierarchy of needs that begins with the fundamental desire for food, clothing, and shelter. These should be your first priorities.

➤ Your need for safety and security follow. You pursue these needs when you consider insurance to help protect yourself from life's risks.

➤ While satisfying your safety needs, you're also addressing your economic priorities. Don't let your craving for security blind you to the economic realities of reasonable coverage for affordable premiums.

➤ The weighing of alternatives in coverage and cost of insurance is an example of analyzing your needs and differentiating your wants from your needs. You can make good choices if you are armed with the information in this book.

Chapter 7

Shopping for Insurance and an Agent

In This Chapter

➤ How to tell when you need an agent and when you can wing it on your own

➤ The keys to finding the right representative and the right company

➤ How to decipher the designations after the agent's name

This chapter discusses the problem of deciding when to use an agent (or broker) and when to try to find the right coverage on your own. This is not an easy decision. Most people are better served when they have a professional working with and for them. And in these cases, the problem becomes one of finding the right agent and insurance company. They are out there, and this chapter will help you find both.

But I'm Not Very Good with Relationships...

In most cases, insurance agents call you before you call them. Experiences with pushy salespeople can make you even more reluctant to go out in search of insurance. This is unfortunate, because you may choose to defer the purchase of sorely needed coverage just to avoid the pressure. If this has happened to you, it's time to pay attention to the concept of *relationship selling*.

No, this is not about falling in love. But it *is* about building a relationship of mutual trust and honest dealings, based on *your* needs—not the agent's.

Over the last three decades, consistent with a move toward *needs selling* (explained in Chapter 6), there has been a continuing movement toward *counselor selling*. Enlightened companies teach their salespeople to build relationships with their customers. And the way they're taught to do this is by putting the customer first!

Jargon Alert
The *close* is the attempt to complete a sale, characterized by one or more attempts to get the prospective customer to agree to make the purchase. A *hard close* is uncomfortable pressure applied by the salesperson.

If you decide to deal only with a salesperson who puts your needs first, you can eliminate many of the salespeople you meet right off. Many amateurs and old-timers alike live for the action of the sale, the challenge of closing the deal. A trip to your local used-car dealership should provide plenty of examples. It's like walking into the lion's cage. If you do manage to find a car salesman who actually tries to find out something about you and what you need from your transportation, you'll never buy a car from anyone else again. You're theirs forever.

Counselor or *relationship selling* is about a salesperson helping you make the best decision. Old-school sales training involved 10 percent understanding needs and 90 percent closing techniques. But the *close* is no longer the key to sales. Problem-solving is the key.

OOOH... **Insider Tip**

If you feel that you're being sold to rather than helped, either change the relationship or change the salesperson. This doesn't mean that the salesperson shouldn't ask you to make a decision. After your situation has been explored and the appropriate product found and explained, the salesperson would not be doing her job if she didn't ask you to make a decision. But you should feel that your needs have been met and that your needs are paramount.

But I Don't Need Counseling

Some buyers may not need a salesperson to help them decide what they need. Those who understand the analysis process, insurance products, and their own needs, may want to make their own coverage decisions without the aid of an agent.

This is more common if the need is simple rather than complex. For example, say you borrowed $10,000 from the bank and they want you to provide life insurance to pay off the loan in the event of your premature death. This is a straightforward need for a $10,000 policy for a limited period. Therefore, a term insurance policy is the best solution. If you knew that much, you could shop around for the cheapest premium with a sound company.

The best of all worlds is to have a professional relationship with a broker or agent you can call for any insurance products you need. (In all likelihood, that will actually be two persons, because most agents for life and health insurance are not licensed for property and casualty insurance.) It is rare to find insurance that is significantly less expensive because there is no agent involved in the sale. Insurance companies have found that, usually, insurance does not sell itself.

When to Wing It on Your Own

The ingredients to making a sound purchase are:

➤ The right amount of protection

➤ The proper type of protection

➤ The appropriate duration of protection

➤ The ability to find and compare the insurers' financial strengths

➤ The ability to compare premiums

The rule of thumb, then, could be that if you understand how to calculate the need, and understand the types of contracts well enough to make the right product selection, and understand how to research the solvency of the insurance company, then, *and only then*, should you find the coverage on your own. Otherwise, you're better served if you have an experienced, trustworthy, professional agent or broker who will find the right coverage at a competitive price. This is not what many people want to hear in this do-it-yourself world, but more often than not, professional insurance advice pays for itself.

You're Judged by the Company You Keep

Many of you remember that old admonition from your parents, "You're judged by the company you keep." They were, of course, referring to your friends and acquaintances. But the old saw has teeth in the financial arena as well. In the 1980s, many honest, well-meaning insurance professionals put their customers in financial jeopardy by recommending products, especially deferred annuities, in companies that were later declared insolvent. These were supposed to be "safe money" vehicles. But the companies pursued an investment strategy that included a *portfolio* of *high yield bonds* (also called *junk bonds*, for good reason).

> ### Jargon Alert
>
> A *portfolio* is the total investments of an insurance company. Analysis of the portfolio in relation to its obligations reveals the financial condition of the company. The term portfolio also applies to the investments of an individual or trust. *High yield bonds* are bonds that are of inferior investment grade and therefore must pay a higher yield to investors in order for them to assume the risk of buying the bond. They're called *junk bonds* because they're rated below investment grade by some of the same rating services discussed in Chapter 4.

You should ask your broker or agent about the company recommended. The best way to do that is to ask for a Best's Report, a written analysis provided by the A.M. Best Company, which was discussed in Chapter 4. Most companies reprint small, pocket-sized reports to distribute to the public. Then, you should call Moody's or Standard & Poor's for their ratings. Remember to apply the acceptable guidelines listed in Chapter 4.

This will not guarantee that the company will never experience problems, but at least you know at the point of sale that the company is rated well by these services.

The Right (Wo)Man for the Job

The insurance business is not a man's business, and the fact that there are far more men than women in the industry should in no way affect your decision of who to choose to represent you. Select the right person, regardless of gender.

And how do you do that, particularly in an industry where you're usually approached first rather than vice versa? Well, you can always go shopping for your own team first. And there's no reason why you can't assume the initiative after a more traditional approach has been made by an agent, whether by referral, cold call, or direct mail response.

In Chapter 2, you learned the ingredients of a good agent—trust being the most important. But where do you start finding the person for you?

The best way to start is by asking your friends (and acquaintances whom you believe have good financial sense) who they use—and why. The "why" part of the question is important because you may end up being referred to someone because she's the referrer's cousin or he's a son-in-law. That may be the reason the referrer does business with them, but should not be a reason for you.

The second place to look is almost too obvious, and that's the telephone book. But what is less obvious is what you're looking for in the yellow pages. Reading the ads can provide good clues. For example, an agency that states it has been in business for 30 years probably can boast of experience. Agents and companies are usually listed together so you can look for names of insurers who are financially sound according to A.M. Best's. Finally, the insurance agents often list their designations after their names.

What's in a Name?

CLU, CFP, CPCU, RHU...? What do all those letters mean?

The leaders in the insurance industry recognized the importance of continuing education decades ago, and encouraged their agents to seek higher levels of professionalism in the business through independent study and examinations. Many states have since joined in requiring that agents complete continuing education courses on a regular basis to maintain their licenses. These continuing education requirements are similar to the requirements for lawyers and CPAs in most states.

The states do not issue designations or evidence of courses attended and passed for insurance professionals. They act punitively only, suspending or revoking licenses for noncompliance. The letter designations after an insurance salesperson's name are a different matter. They represent a significant commitment of time and energy beyond the state's continuing education requirements.

The American College in Bryn Mawr, Pennsylvania, issues four designations. The Chartered Life Underwriter, or CLU, is awarded to those individuals who complete 10 courses in the life insurance area. The selection of courses could include topics on life insurance, health insurance, retirement planning, Social Security and social insurance, estate planning, group insurance, and employee benefits, to mention a few. The CLU designation is the premier achievement for life underwriters. The courses are college-level in difficulty and credit.

The American College also issues a Chartered Financial Consultant designation, known as a ChFC. This course is of the same caliber as the CLU, but the curriculum is broader, encompassing financial planning (of which insurance is but a part). Two newer designations now issued by the American College are the RHU (Registered Health Underwriter) and the REBC (Registered Employee Benefit Consultant).

Another widely respected financial planning designation is the CFP designation (Certified Financial Planner). This curriculum is also geared toward the broader scope of total financial planning, and most of the CFPs have a working knowledge of insurance, at least life insurance. The College for Financial Planning in Denver, Colorado, issues the CFP.

Insider Tip

When shopping for an insurance professional, the CLU designation is more important. If you are shopping for a financial planner with broader experience, the CFP and ChFC designations are preferable.

The premier designation for property and casualty agents is the CPCU (Chartered Property and Casualty Underwriter). Again, an extensive series of courses and exams is required.

Does the designation automatically qualify the agent as a good fit for your needs? Of course not. But at the very least you know they've been in the business long enough, invested in their future enough, and are intelligent enough to be considered.

Bet You Didn't Know

The American Society of CLU & ChFC in Bryn Mawr will make available a list of CLU and ChFC designees. The address is The American College, 270 Bryn Mawr Avenue, Bryn Mawr, PA 19010. The telephone number is (610) 526-2500. For a listing of CPCU designees, write The CPCU Society, 720 Providence Road, P.O. Box 3009, Malvern, PA 19355-0709. The telephone number is (610) 251-2728.

The Least You Need to Know

You can shop for insurance on your own, but the planning and purchasing process may be more than you feel comfortable pursuing alone. Find a professional or group of professionals to help you meet your insurance needs using the characteristics in Chapter 2 and the guidelines in this chapter.

➤ There are many professionals waiting to serve your insurance needs. Use the resources outlined in this chapter to find them.

➤ You need to find those who believe in needs and counselor selling, who will be putting your insurance needs before their income objectives. Ask your friends and associates for recommendations.

➤ Professional designations such as CLU and CPCU will not guarantee that an agent is more professional, but chances are the individual will exhibit a better knowledge of the industry and your needs.

➤ Finding the right agent should precede finding the right coverage. Find the right person or persons for all your needs.

Part 2
Life Insurance

Almost everyone owns or relies on life insurance. And yet, almost no one understands what they own.

Part 2 gives you the information you need to understand the different life insurance alternatives in the marketplace today. You are probably your family's most important asset. Learn how to protect yourself wisely and adequately after you learn all about your choices.

You'll also learn how to read the policy insuring your life or the life of another. Life insurance plays a role in not only your personal life, but also your business. Taxes are also a consideration when contemplating life insurance.

Chapter 8

What's the Risk?: The "Not Me" Syndrome

In This Chapter

➤ The likelihood of death at various ages

➤ The advantages and disadvantages of owning life insurance

➤ How to measure the value of a human life in dollars

➤ How to identify and quantify the needs for life insurance

➤ Why an agent should be involved with most life insurance sales

All men think all men mortal but themselves.

Edward Young, *Night Thoughts* (1742-1745)

Edward Young's words ring truest when the subject is life insurance. Especially in our younger years, we dismiss death as an affliction that affects only the old and others. And statistics do support the notion that fewer people die at younger ages than at older ages. But when you approach the matter of death from the standpoint of a big mistake or a small mistake, weighing the cost of dying with or without coverage, you're less likely to gamble on death's only striking down someone else. In this chapter you'll learn about the likelihood of death striking at various ages and the viability of life insurance as a way of shielding your loved ones from financial hardship in the event of a premature death.

How Do You Figure?

Any discussion of death rates, mortality tables, or other such statistics requires explanation. The old saying about "figures lying and liar's figuring" underscores the importance of understanding the statistics to avoid making judgments based on the wrong conclusions.

Jargon Alert
Mortality tables are statistical studies that show the death rate at different ages. *Morbidity tables*, on the other hand, show the rate and duration of disability. Both state the rates per thousand people. The tables are composed by *actuaries*, who are professionals trained in the mathematical sciences of insurance and related areas.

In the year 1915, approximately 14 people out of every 1,000 people died. Men were more likely than women to die. By the year 1940, the number of deaths in the U.S. shrank to 10 per 1,000. Today, the number of deaths per 1,000 is roughly 5. This decline in the death rate over the century has important implications for you, your family, and your insurance company. Undoubtedly, medical advancements, nutritional gains, and an overall awareness of factors that increase longevity have contributed to this trend.

One of the more common actuarial tables is the Commissioners 1980 Standard Ordinary Table. There are several tables designed for different purposes, but this one relates most closely to life insurance. Table 8.1 shows a sampling of rates from the larger Standard Ordinary Table. It's a summary of the table that actually lists the expected number of deaths per 1,000 persons at every age.

Table 8.1   Commissioners 1980 Standard Ordinary Table Summary

Age	Male Deaths Per 1,000	Expectation of Life (Years)	Female Deaths Per 1,000	Expectation of Life (Years)
0	4.18	70.83	2.89	75.83
10	.73	61.66	.68	66.53
20	1.90	52.37	1.05	57.04
30	1.73	43.24	1.35	47.65
40	3.02	34.05	2.42	38.36
50	6.71	25.36	4.96	29.53
60	16.08	17.15	9.47	21.25
70	39.51	10.96	22.11	13.67

Age	Male Deaths Per 1,000	Expectation of Life (Years)	Female Deaths Per 1,000	Expectation of Life (Years)
80	98.84	6.18	65.99	7.48
90	221.77	3.18	190.75	3.45

Note: These rates were derived from experience from 1970 to 1975.

So what does the table purport to teach you? For one thing, women outlive men. Not every woman, of course, but in a population of 1,000 50-year-old women, 4.96 women will die at that age as opposed to 6.71 men. Likewise, the table tells us that women who survive to age 50 will live an average of 29.53 years more—that is, almost to age 80. Fifty-year-old men, on the other hand, will live on average 25.36 more years, to age 75.

More recent updates of the mortality tables show that the trend toward longer lives is continuing. More people will live to be 100, placing greater stress on the health care industries and insurers, as well as your retirement assets. You'll revisit this subject in greater depth when you read about long-term care insurance in Chapter 25.

Glancing at Table 8.1 may give you a false sense of security. You might be tempted to say that your chances of dying at age 40, for example, are very slim—less than 5 chances out of 1,000. While this may be true, it distorts the picture because of the severe consequences of being one of those five. It's one thing to risk being one of twenty people exposed to a flu bug. Death is decidedly more final. Again, weigh the outcomes on the big mistake/small mistake scale.

Watch It!
If you're a married woman, you should prepare yourself for the likelihood of outliving your husband. Don't wait until widowhood to learn about finances, insurance, and investments. Take courses now and a more active role in the financial management of your family.

The Pros and Cons of Life Insurance

There are many reasons to buy life insurance, and only a few reasons not to. This section looks at the arguments for and against life insurance.

What are the advantages common to all types of life insurance?

➤ Cash is paid to the beneficiary at the death of the insured. This is the primary reason for owning life insurance. The *death benefit* (the amount payable to the beneficiary) is usually significantly greater than the premiums paid.

Jargon Alert

The *death benefit* is the sum payable upon the death of the insured, or later if the policyholder made other arrangements before the date of death. The death benefit is also referred to as the policy *proceeds*.

➤ Policies allow for a flexible payout of the proceeds. There are many options for the payment of proceeds to the named *beneficiaries*. The flexibility could be exercised by the beneficiary or the owner.

➤ The proceeds can avoid *probate* and public scrutiny after the insured's death. If you care about the privacy of your affairs after your death, do what you can, within reason, to avoid probate. Naming a beneficiary other than "the estate of the insured" on your insurance policy will avoid probate. Will and trust planning, by attorneys trained in this field, is the best way to avoid probate for your overall estate.

Jargon Alert
A *beneficiary* is the person or party named by the owner of the policy to receive the proceeds at the insured's death.

Probate is the legal process of submitting the decedent's will to the court for verification of validity and to establish the administration of the estate. Most of the probate records are open to the public.

➤ Death benefits are received income-tax free. This is an immense tax benefit for beneficiaries who will receive the policy death proceeds without the shrinkage associated with most other sources of funds.

➤ Life insurance is usually protected from the claims of creditors. This is a matter for state regulation, but the vast majority of states do insulate death benefits from creditors.

➤ Some life insurance policies likewise have a savings or investment element that can increase your financial security during the insured's lifetime.

As you can see, the compelling reasons in favor of life insurance are many, assuming there is a need. But there are some negative aspects to be considered as well. The disadvantages of life insurance are few, but include the following:

➤ The premiums divert dollars from your personal use. Insurance is not inexpensive, and the money spent on premiums reduces your funds on hand to spend on yourself and your family. Even if you have enough money for living expenses, the premiums reduce the amount available for investment.

➤ Life insurance products have become extremely complex. Competition and tax preferences have combined to make insurance a fertile ground for ingenious product design. Unfortunately, the actuaries who build these products are not responsible for describing them to an untrained audience. Many licensed life insurance salespeople don't even understand the products.

➤ Not everyone can qualify for life insurance. Because of the significant gap between the premiums and the death benefit, insurers require the insured to be in good health. Not everyone is.

What's It For?

In Chapter 7 you read that you can shop for your own insurance if you understand and can quantify your needs. This is often a matter for computer programs and important decisions involving assumptions. Some of the most common uses for life insurance include:

➤ To provide an income for survivors, whether spouse, children, or business associates. The cash death benefit can be invested for the survivors to provide a continuing stream of income.

➤ To pay off debts, such as mortgages, credit card balances, bank notes, margin loans, or family loans. Some creditors offer insurance to cover their loans. As a rule, you can beat the rate offered by lenders by purchasing the coverage on your own.

➤ To fund a child's education.

➤ To pay federal and state estate taxes. Care must be taken in planning beneficiary designations to make sure insurance proceeds do not increase the estate tax by increasing the estate by the amount of the proceeds.

➤ To fund the transfer of a business interest, ensuring continuity of the business without the interference of the surviving spouses or their lawyers.

➤ To fund a commitment to a charity—for example, to your alma mater or your church.

All of these traditional uses of life insurance should be considered again in light of the needs test. Apply the big mistake/small mistake test to decide what to insure and for how much.

How Much Is the Right Amount?

There are several methods for determining how much insurance you should own. One mentioned earlier is to make assumptions about your future earnings and reduce those earnings by the amount you personally consume (because you will no longer be consuming). Another approach is to simply multiply your current income by the number of years you want to continue the income flow to your beneficiaries. But the approach that makes the most sense is the "needs" approach.

The primary question is what do you want to provide? Good life underwriters can give you all the guidelines in the world, but it's up to you to decide what you want to leave to your beneficiaries. Or, in the alternative, if *you're* the beneficiary, what you want to have for your ongoing needs.

Income Needs

Let's start by considering income needs. An income-producing head of household provides income for the family. The end of that stream of income will usually reduce the amount of money the family has to live on. If that's a concern, as it should be, the question then is how to replace that income. Can a surviving spouse find a job and make the same income? If so, will there be child-care expenses to consider? What if the surviving spouse is disabled in the same accident that takes the other's life? Is there a need to insure both lives? These are all the questions you need to ask yourself in arriving at the right amount of protection.

Assume you're a male head of household and your spouse is full-time mother and homemaker (easily the toughest job around). With three children ranging in age from 1 to 5, there are quite a few years of child-rearing ahead. Assume further that you currently earn $36,000 a year, and with $30,000 net after taxes, that it's enough to get by on, but not enough to allow you to save any money. At your death, Social Security will provide a benefit to your children up to age 18 and to your wife until the last child reaches 18. If those benefits totaled $18,000 per year, there's still a shortfall of $12,000 annually ($30,000-$18,000), and we haven't made any provision for inflation yet.

Jargon Alert
The *principal* is the sum of money on hand that's to be deposited in order to earn income. If you received a $100,000 lump sum from a policy and deposited it in an interest-bearing account, that $100,000 would be considered the principal.

How much cash would it take to guarantee that $12,000 per year? Using a conservative approach, you would ask how much it would take in principal, earning at, say, 5 percent, to provide $12,000 annually in interest. The answer is $240,000 ($12,000 divided by 5% = $240,000). But what if you didn't care if there was any money left over at the end of that period of time? Without regard to insurance, you would need $12,000 times the number of years of income you wanted to provide. In this hypothetical scenario, the answer is 17 years: $12,000 × 17 = $204,000.

But, wait a minute. The money won't be sitting in a shoebox for those 17 years. Hopefully, it'll be in some interest-bearing account where annual or monthly withdrawals can be made. Therefore, the amount of money you'll need will be even less than the $204,000 computed above. With the use of compound interest tables and discounted dollar tables (and the company's computer), your insurance agent will be able to tell you exactly how much will be needed on day one at various interest-rate assumptions.

Income needs continue beyond the college years for surviving spouses. And with the increases in life expectancy well into our 80s, you should think in terms of providing an income your survivors can't outlive. This entails providing sufficient capital to provide an income that doesn't eat into the principal, and to prevent for the gradual erosion due to *inflation*.

> **Jargon Alert**
> *Inflation* is the gradual increase in the price of goods and services that we purchase. If a loaf of bread costs $1.00 this year and $1.04 next year, inflation is 4 percent. Inflation's impact is harmful to you because your income may not be increasing as fast as the rise in the cost of the products you purchase every year.

Education Needs

Funding for college education poses the same type of problem—providing adequate funds today so that when the money is needed for school it will be there in adequate amounts to pay the bills. Unlike funding an income, however, fewer dollars may be needed at the time of death. This is because monies can accumulate at interest without income depleting the earnings, until needed for tuition in the future. Again, the rising cost at most schools makes it difficult to know just what tuition will be at a particular school. And, of course, you won't know for sure where your child will go to school, if at all. Flexibility, then, is important in your planning.

The Mortgage

Mortgage protection is another possible need. Most mortgage lenders offer life insurance to pay off the mortgage in the event of the primary wage earner's premature death. Usually, the policy proceeds are payable directly to the lender. You're usually better off buying your own policy and naming the surviving spouse as beneficiary. This gives the survivor the flexibility to remain in that home, pay off the mortgage, refinance, and so forth. You'll likely find a lower premium than the lender's as well.

These are just three of the more common needs addressed by life insurance. As you can see, the factors you need to consider are many and sometimes complex. All the more reason for a good life insurance professional to assist in the analysis.

The Best Kind of Insurance

The best kind of insurance is the insurance that is in force the day you need it. This principle should be remembered as you begin to learn the different choices available in the following chapters.

The Least You Need to Know

Life insurance is based on the actuarial estimates called mortality tables. But don't rely on the tables to give you a sense of security. Death is final. Consider whether the advantages of life insurance outweigh the disadvantages in your particular situation.

➤ The lower risk of death associated with the younger ages is misleading because of the severity of the consequences.

➤ The advantages of life insurance far outweigh the disadvantages, as long as it is affordable.

➤ The reasons for owning life insurance are varied; you need to approach the subject of needs based on your situation and your ideas about how to leave your heirs.

➤ A good life underwriter can help you crystallize your needs and put a dollar figure on them as well. Some computer programs can quantify your needs too. Unless you're well versed in the process and the products, you're better off with a professional life underwriter.

Chapter 9

Term Insurance

In This Chapter

➤ The difference between term and permanent insurance

➤ The types of term insurance you can choose from

➤ How to choose among alternate options

➤ How to comparison shop for term insurance

This chapter introduces term insurance, which was designed to meet temporary needs. You will also learn to distinguish term insurance from permanent insurance. Term insurance needs vary widely. Consequently, there are many different term insurance products to meet these needs.

Term Insurance or Permanent Insurance

One of the great debates in the insurance and investment arena over the last two decades, but especially since the early 1980s when interest rates spiked dramatically, has been the viability of *term insurance* versus *permanent insurance*. At the heart of the controversy is the question of whether life insurance should be considered an investment at all.

Term insurance products provide a death benefit. Permanent insurance provides a death benefit and a savings/investment benefit. The premium charged for permanent products is higher than the premium for term products because of that savings element in the policy, referred to as the *cash value*.

> ### Jargon Alert
>
> *Term insurance* is life insurance for a specified period of time, such as 1, 5, 10, or 20 years. It provides only indemnification—only a death benefit—in the event of death of the insured while the policy is in force. *Permanent insurance*, on the other hand, is designed to cover a longer period of time, perhaps even an indeterminate length of time, because the date of death is rarely known in advance. Unlike term, permanent plans also provide a *cash value*—that is, a savings or investment element.

The debate revolves around the competitiveness of the rate of return on the savings or investment element of permanent policies. That issue hinges on the lower premium charged for term insurance, because it's strictly indemnification and only for a limited period of time.

Those arguing against permanent insurance claimed that an individual was better off "buying term insurance and investing the difference" themselves, in stocks or mutual funds, for example. Those arguing to defend permanent plans claimed that "termites," those in the pro-term category, ignored long-term trends and the application of tax rules.

The debate has lost steam because the insurance industry recognized the need to develop new products that would provide a better rate of return reflected in the cash value. These new products will be explained in Chapters 11–13. The new products are more responsive to fluctuations in the economy and investment returns in general, as you will see.

> OOOH... ### Insider Tip
>
> The general rule of thumb is to buy term insurance for temporary needs, and buy permanent insurance for permanent needs. The exception is if you can only afford the less expensive term insurance. You are better off with term insurance protecting a permanent need than no protection.

Basic Policy Provisions

All policies of insurance, including term insurance, have certain information in common in each policy. The death benefit is always stated on the *Policy Specifications Page* of the policy. The Policy Specifications Page is a page the insurance company always includes in the policy. It states the key information about the policy, such as the policy number, name of the insured, policy date, type of policy, premiums for the policy, and any additional provisions or benefits. These are usually itemized in a *rider*, which is an amendment to the original policy adding another provision.

Jargon Alert
The *death benefit* of a policy, also known as the *face amount*, is the amount of proceeds the life insurance company agrees to pay at the death of the insured.

Types of Term Insurance

There are three basic types of term insurance: level term, decreasing term, and increasing term. Each has its own pros and cons, and each is appropriate for its own specific situations.

Level Term Insurance

The *death benefit* of a level term insurance policy remains the same during the term of the contract. Level term was designed to meet a constant need. The premium is also constant during the life of the policy.

Level term can be represented graphically, as shown in the figure below.

Level term insurance was designed to meet a constant need.

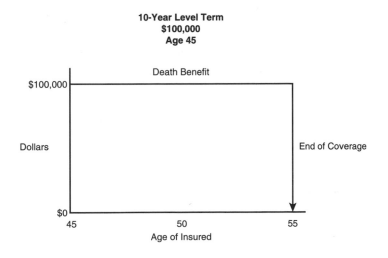

**10-Year Level Term
$100,000
Age 45**

Decreasing Term Insurance

Decreasing term insurance was created to provide a decreasing amount of protection over a specified period of time. The death benefit usually decreases at a constant rate. For example, a 10-year decreasing term policy with a face amount of $100,000 would usually decrease $10,000 each year, until the end of the tenth year, when the benefit would be zero.

> **OOOH...** **Insider Tip**
>
> Decreasing term policies have traditionally been used to cover mortgage loans, which by nature decrease with time. While mortgage lenders offer policies that provide the exact balance due on the mortgage in the event of a premature death, a regular decreasing term will possibly be better for you, both from a cost and a flexibility standpoint. Make sure to buy enough term to match the remaining principal due on the mortgage and make your heir—not the lender—the beneficiary. Your heir, usually a surviving spouse, will be able to decide at the time of receipt of the death benefit if it is advisable or not to pay off the mortgage loan.

The figure below shows what a graphical depiction of decreasing term would look like.

While decreasing term death benefits decline, the premium traditionally stays level.

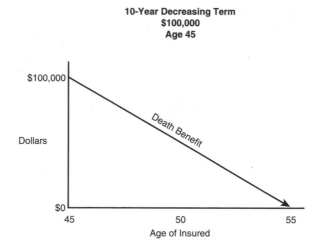

Increasing Term Insurance

Increasing term insurance is usually a rider to another policy rather than a separate policy. Premiums are higher than the other forms of term because there's a *greater* death benefit as you get older. And because premiums are calculated on the basis of age, you'll pay more. (Remember from Chapter 8 that the number of deaths per 1,000 increases with age; therefore, the insurance claims will also increase.)

Some of Your Options

In addition to the three types of term plans just explained, there are two types of options that are common to term contracts. The two options are the right to renew and the right to convert the policy. They allow the insured to extend his or her policy, without having to submit to another physical examination.

Wait a minute! *Physical examination?* Is this life insurance, you may be asking? It is, it is. But before an insurance company is willing to assume the risk for a life insurance policy, it will make sure you're insurable. You learn more about physical examinations later in Chapter 15.

Renewability

The first common option on term policies is the right to renew a policy. Remember, one of the characteristics of term insurance is the fact that the coverage lasts for a specified term of years. At the end of that 10, 20, or however many years, the policy stops.

Insurers realize that sometimes there's a need for continuing coverage beyond the original term period. The option to renew the policy guarantees that you'll be able to continue the contract—although it might be at a higher premium. This is fair, because you'll be older then, and premiums increase with age. (That's because mortality increases with age. This was the lesson in Chapter 8, with the number of deaths per 1,000 increasing at each older age.)

The most popular term insurance in recent years has been a level term for one year that renews annually. This plan is called YRT, yearly renewable term, or ART, annual renewable term. There's usually a limit on how long the policy can be renewed, such as to age 65, or 20 years, or some such time frame. However, some policies will renew to much more advanced ages, although at quite high premiums.

> **Insider Tip**
> People who need life insurance beyond age 65 or 70 are usually trying to solve permanent needs, such as to replace estate taxes, to fund trusts or charities, or to provide sufficient liquidity to fund business buyouts. Term insurance provides a temporary solution at an increasing cost. If the funds are available to pay permanent premiums, you're probably better off locking in the lower premium for the permanent plan sooner rather than later. The premium for permanent insurance is fixed at the time of purchase.

Table 9.1 illustrates an example of an annual renewable term plan. The policy is for a nonsmoking male, 40 years old, for $250,000. Now, before you start screaming about the death benefit, remember that $250,000 invested at 5 percent will provide only $12,500 per year in income.

Table 9.1 Annual Renewable Term with Premiums Illustrated in the First Six Years

Year	Current Premium	Guaranteed Premium
1	$297.50	$297.50
2	$382.50	$382.50
3	$487.50	$487.50
4	$580.00	$580.00
5	$695.00	$695.00
6	$807.50	$2,407.50

Wait a minute. What just happened in year 6? Notice the disparity between the Current Premium and the Guaranteed Premium? This particular company guarantees the lower premium for only five years. After that, the premium could take a large hike—but not just for you. The company would have to raise everyone's rates in a similar situation. They can't single you out because of poor health, late premiums, or any other reason.

This difference between *current* and *guaranteed premiums* doesn't exist in every ART policy. That's why it's very important for you to understand what's being proposed to you. There's nothing wrong with this provision, as long as you understand it. Table 9.2 continues with the premiums at five-year intervals.

Table 9.2 ART Continued with Premiums Shown Every 5 Years for 50 Years

Year	Current Premium	Guaranteed Premium
10	$1,315.00	$4,100.00
15	$2,265.00	$6,557.50
20	$3,810.00	$9,375.00
25	$5,247.00	$12,327.50
30	$7,455.00	$18,210.00
35	$12,487.50	$29,675.00

Year	Current Premium	Guaranteed Premium
40	$19,917.50	$51,655.00
45	$31,725.00	$96,720.00
50	$50,440.00	$144,655.00

What becomes apparent in this policy is that if you had to settle for the higher guaranteed premium in column 3, at some point you would be better off putting the premium in a savings account. At the 35-year mark, which is age 75, the higher premium is $29,675.00. It increases each year thereafter up to $51,655.00 at age 80. You can't see the intervening years' premiums, but they total more than $180,000.00—for a death benefit of $250,000.00. Not a very good deal, especially if the insured is in good health.

The figure below shows a graphical depiction of ART.

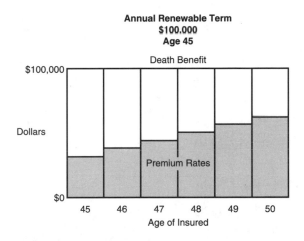

Annual renewable term, shown as a graph.

Watch It!

You must look at all the policy provisions to make sure you're getting what you need. Each company has its own variation to make its product more attractive. Study the proposal. Get it in writing, and make sure you have footnotes to explain the guarantees on the proposal.

Convertibility

The second common option is the right to convert a term policy into a permanent policy without new evidence of insurability. If you're healthy and insurable, the right to convert is of limited value. It would only save you the time it takes to get a medical examination, which is paid for by the insurer anyway. But, if your insurability changed…

This protection of insurability involves risk on the insurance company's part, and there's a cost associated with that conversion privilege. Many term plans are convertible as a right of the policy, and the premium is built into the overall term plan premium. Others show the cost of the right of conversion as an optional rider. Whichever way is used, this is an important option to have. Things have a way of changing, and often in ways you can't anticipate. A policy purchased to fund one need could end up being used for a different need. The right to convert is valuable built-in flexibility.

The right to convert usually can be exercised in one of two ways: *attained age* or *original age* conversion.

The *attained age* conversion allows you to purchase the new permanent policy at the premium rate, applicable at your currently attained age. *Original age* conversion, on the other hand, allows you to go back to the premium rate charged for the permanent plan at the younger age when you first bought the term. However, an additional sum is paid in to make up for the premium differential over those years.

Generally, because of the larger sums of premium due with the original age conversion, you're better off with the attained age approach.

Side-By-Side Comparisons

A recent advertisement in *The Wall Street Journal* offering term insurance quoted the following rates for various plans (see Table 9.3). No claim is made that these premiums are competitive, with quality carriers or carrier, or any other representation. The numbers do, however, illustrate the difference in premium rates as between the various alternatives.

The ad offered $1,000,000 of death benefit for a nonsmoking male.

Table 9.3 $1,000,000 Term Insurance

Age	1-Year Increasing Term	5-Year Level Term	10-Year Level Term	15-Year Level Term	20-Year Level Term
30	$520	$650	$645	$715	$875
40	$560	$885	$935	$1,100	$1,395

Age	1-Year Increasing Term	5-Year Level Term	10-Year Level Term	15-Year Level Term	20-Year Level Term
50	$1,050	$1,940	$2,060	$2,510	$3,314
60	$2,600	$4,540	$4,850	$6,290	$7,600
65	$4,730	$7,495	$8,355	$10,455	$13,554

Which is the best policy? It's the one that's in force at the time of death. The trick, then, is to guess when the time of death is going to be, and insure accordingly.

The following factors can all have a bearing on the type of coverage that's best for you:

➤ *The length of the term.* If your need is for a 30-year period of time to cover a mortgage, for example, then a decreasing term with a level premium might be the least expensive. If you have a very short-term need, an ART might be best.

➤ *The death benefit needed.* Companies traditionally encourage larger policies so they can take advantage of *economies of scale*, an economic term meaning they have the same issue expenses for a $10,000 policy as they do for a $100,000 policy—so why not aim for more premium? Some companies are more competitive at the higher face amount, so you need to shop around to see who's best at different levels of protection.

➤ *Your health and habits.* Nonsmokers pay less in premium than smokers, and some companies have preferred rates if you're a nonsmoker. Other companies reserve preferred status for nonsmokers who also meet other criteria for height, weight, blood pressure, and so on.

➤ *The desirability of conversion.* If you know you'll convert the policy to a permanent plan in the near future, you may want to select the company with the more competitive permanent policies, even though their term rates may be initially higher. If conversion is out of the question, shop for the lowest premium with a company that'll be in business when you need them most.

➤ *Available dollars for premiums.* There are times when a permanent plan might be a better solution to your needs, but the premium is too high. Having the coverage is more important than the long-term expense of the term versus the permanent plan. If you need the protection, and all you can afford is low-cost term, you're doing the right thing to buy it. It's a big mistake to die without protection; it's a small mistake to temporarily buy term insurance for a permanent need. Again, the best coverage is the coverage in force at the date of death.

The Least You Need to Know

Term insurance is designed for limited term needs. Permanent insurance such as whole life, explained in the next chapter, is designed to meet permanent needs.

➤ Term insurance is ideal for temporary needs, measurable in time as well as death benefit. Temporary needs could include a term mortgage, education funding for four or more years, or provide income for a spouse until retirement.

➤ Different types of policies meet different needs, whether level, decreasing, or increasing. Begin by defining your needs, then look for the best solution. Don't be afraid to ask a professional agent for help at both stages.

➤ Selecting the right plan is usually easier with a qualified professional. Remember the lessons in Chapters 2 and 7 about finding the right agent.

➤ Covering the need effectively is more important than covering it efficiently. Buy term insurance if it is all you can afford at the time—even if you have a permanent need. Just find a policy convertible to a good choice of permanent plans.

Chapter 10

Whole Life Insurance

In This Chapter
➤ Whole life insurance versus term
➤ Participating versus nonparticipating policies
➤ The alternatives to whole life within the whole life policy form
➤ Understanding combination plans

This chapter discusses whole life insurance, the most common form of permanent insurance in this century. It is the product most often compared to term insurance in the argument over the best form of insurance—term or whole life. This chapter will explain the basics of whole life, and in Chapters 11 and 12 you'll see the evolution of whole life into products with greater responsiveness to changes in the investment environment.

When Is a Whole Life a Whole Life?

The most popular form of permanent insurance in this century has been *whole life insurance*. As you may have guessed by now, it was designed to last for your whole life, which hopefully is a long time. But as is usually the case with labels, the name can be misleading. Whole life really only provides true insurance protection to age 100, although you could argue that age 100 is close enough to a whole life. This is obviously a big distinction from term insurance.

Bet You Didn't Know

WOW!

This oversight on the actuary's part might be more important than you think. In the design of the actuarial tables, everyone was assumed dead at age 100. But the current projections for older Americans show that the number who live beyond age 100 will actually double in the next decade. This is important, because when a policy matures at age 100, it triggers a taxable event. More on taxes later in this chapter.

Characteristics of Whole Life

The characteristics of whole life that follow will help you understand this form of permanent insurance as well as the more modern permanent plans that have built upon or improved upon this product. The three ingredients to compare are premiums, death benefits, and cash values.

Premiums 'Til When?

One of the important characteristics of whole life is that premiums can be paid to age 100. This doesn't mean you actually have to pay the premium all those years to receive a benefit. However, this is one of the ways in which whole life differs from term insurance, where premiums are paid for a stated number of years.

Premiums are level, and guaranteed not to increase to age 100. The younger you are at the time you purchase the policy, the lower the premium will be each year. As you learned in Chapter 8, premiums are higher each year because the rate of deaths per 1,000 increases each year.

Death Benefits to 100

The second important characteristic of whole life insurance is that the death benefit remains level to age 100. Take a look at this graphically in the following figure. Using the conventions you saw in Chapter 9 on term insurance, time will be shown on the horizontal axis, in years to age 100. The vertical axis is dollars—dollars of death benefit to the insured's beneficiary.

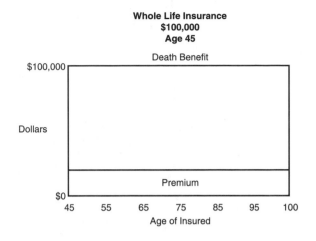

Whole Life Insurance
$100,000
Age 45

Death Benefit

$100,000

Dollars

Premium

$0

45   55   65   75   85   95   100

Age of Insured

A graphical depiction of whole life insurance.

Cash Values

The biggest difference between the term insurance and whole life insurance is the introduction of the *cash value* into the equation.

When whole life insurance was originally designed, a death benefit to age 100 was not the only need the insurers sought to meet. There was also a need to create a savings vehicle. Individuals needed a way to set aside funds for retirement, emergencies, and countless other purposes. Adding a savings element to the policy made this possible. A portion of each premium payment goes toward the savings element of the policy, called the *cash value* or *cash surrender value*. It belongs to the policyowner and may be used in various ways to benefit the owner.

You will notice in the following figure that the cash value grows gradually over the years until it equals the death benefit at age 100. This is called the *maturity* of the contract. (You'd ordinarily think of "maturity" as taking place a little earlier than age 100—although while you're raising teenagers, that seems to be the timetable they're on.) A policy *matures* when its cash value equals its death benefit. This is also called the *endowment* of the policy.

Jargon Alert
Cash value is the savings or investment element in the policy. The accumulated values grow annually as premiums are paid. Guaranteed cash values are stated on the Policy Specification page.

Jargon Alert
The *maturity* or *endowment* of a whole life policy is when the accumulated cash value equals the death benefit. At this point, the policy has no true mortality or death benefit element, just a return of all cash value.

A typical whole life policy with cash values.

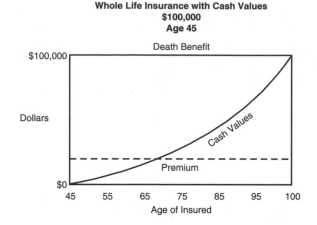

Whole Life Insurance with Cash Values
$100,000
Age 45

The significance of the endowment of the contract is twofold. At that time, you can stop paying premiums. Plus, the death benefit will be paid to you as a taxable cash settlement. At that point, the policy ceases to exist. See what you have to look forward to?

Cashing In Your Policy

Up to this point, you've seen what happens if you live to 100 or die before that age. But there's a strong possibility that you'll decide to stop paying the premiums before death or age 100. What are your alternatives then?

WOW! **Bet You Didn't Know**
When you mention life insurance, most people think of death benefits. But the monies paid out to policyowners as living benefits are greater than death benefits paid to beneficiaries. In 1993, for example, $28 billion was paid out to beneficiaries, while $30 billion was paid to policyowners. Over $40 billion was paid to annuitants.

The primary reason to purchase whole life insurance instead of term insurance is the living benefits, which are tied to the cash values in the contract. You'll notice that the words "policy" and "contract" are used interchangeably. That's because the policy is in fact a contract between the policyowner and the insurance company. In return for the payment of the premium, the insurance company promises to pay the death benefit, accumulate a cash value, and make available certain options called *nonforfeiture options*. These are rights in all permanent contracts to use the cash values in various ways to the benefit of the policyowner.

There are three traditional options: *surrender* the policy for its cash value; use the cash to purchase *paid up insurance*; use the cash value to purchase *extended term insurance*.

The cash surrender option is the right to discontinue life insurance in force in return for its cash value. The policy lists the guaranteed cash values at each policy anniversary, assuming all the premiums have been paid. This option makes sense when the need for any additional coverage under this policy has ceased.

The second option, paid-up insurance, assumes there's a need for continuing coverage, but at a reduced amount. Frequently, this option is a default option in that the policyowner no longer wants to pay the premium, but recognizes the need for some ongoing protection. The available cash value purchases a single premium paid-up policy for as much death benefit as the cash value will buy. The protection continues for life.

The third option, like the second, allows for the continuation of coverage—not at a reduced face amount for life, but rather the full face amount for a specified period of time. This extended term insurance is most appropriate for a situation where the need for the protection will end in the future, but the policyowner would prefer not to pay any more premiums.

Again, it's the cash value that drives these three options. The greater the cash value, the greater the surrender value, the paid-up insurance, or the term of years that the extended term insurance remains in effect. All three options are spelled out in the policy under the nonforfeiture options section.

Need a Loan?

Another important option in whole life policies is the right to borrow the cash value. Because you'll be taking dollars that are already being used to make the values grow, you'll be charged interest on the loan. In newer policies, the rate is determined by a formula or index stated in the policy. In older contracts, before interest rates spiked upward in the early 1980s, the borrowing rate was fixed, usually at 5 percent. Today, the rates will approximate favorable bank rates.

Participating Insurance Policies

So far, whole life insurance sounds pretty straightforward. A table of values, guaranteed premiums, guaranteed death benefits, and nonforfeiture options. Nothing too complicated there. In fact, the graph of the typical whole life contract in the preceding figure is very straightforward. Unfortunately, it isn't necessarily typical of your actual policy.

In Chapter 3, you learned about mutual and stock life insurance companies. Stock companies return profits to stockholders in the form of dividends on their stock. Mutual companies are owned by the policyowners, and profits are returned to them in the form of dividends on the policies they own.

The policyowners "participate" in the profits of mutual companies through policy dividends. Stock company policies that don't share in the profitable operation of the company are called *nonparticipating*. Things would be fine if the lines were this clearly drawn all the time; alas, they are not. The newer generation of policies introduced in the next chapter continue the trend toward obscuring the differences between stock and mutual company products. Nevertheless, you should try to understand the impact of dividends on a whole life policy.

Again, participating policies will have a dividend, a way of sharing company profits with policyholders. Dividends can be used by the policyholder several different ways, depending on need.

Dividends to Reduce Premiums

One way a policyholder can use a dividend is to reduce premiums (see the figure below). Notice how the premium line decreases, while the death benefits and cash values continue. This is similar to the case of the nonparticipating policy illustrated earlier.

Dividends can be applied to reduce premiums.

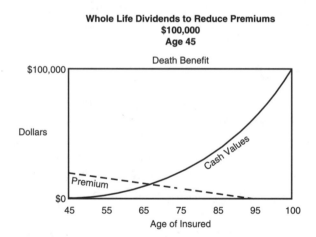

Whole Life Dividends to Reduce Premiums
$100,000
Age 45

Dividends to Accumulate at Interest

A second use of the dividend is to leave it with the company to accumulate at interest. This has the effect of increasing the cash value and the death benefit. Compound interest can make the accumulation significant over time, as shown graphically in the following figure.

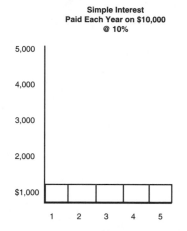

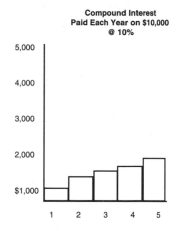

A comparison of simple vs. compound interest.

If you had $10,000 to invest and could receive 10 percent interest, you would have $11,000 at the end of the year ($10,000 principal × 10 percent interest = $1,000). If the interest is simple interest, in year 2 you would receive another $1,000 ($10,000 principal × 10 percent interest). However, if you are receiving compound interest, you receive

$1,100 ($11,000 principal × 10 percent interest). The difference over time is dramatic. In 10 years, you will have $20,000 under the simple interest method and $25,937 under the compound interest scenario. In 30 years, you would have $40,000 with simple interest, the original principal of $10,000 plus $10,000 each decade. But with compound interest your original $10,000 is now worth $174,494.

This is the most important lesson in saving and investing money today. And it's as applicable to insurance products as to mutual funds (see the following figure). Invest or save regularly and for the long term. The dramatic gains are in the later years.

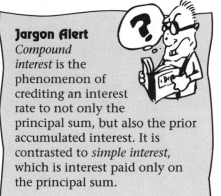

Jargon Alert
Compound interest is the phenomenon of crediting an interest rate to not only the principal sum, but also the prior accumulated interest. It is contrasted to *simple interest*, which is interest paid only on the principal sum.

Accumulating dividends can substantially increase the cash value.

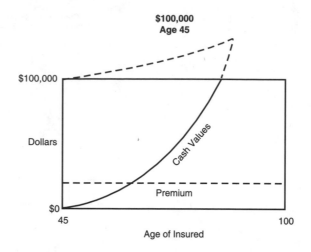

Dividends to Purchase Paid-Up Additions

The third alternative with dividends is to reinvest the dividends in the policy by purchasing paid-up additions. This has the effect of buying more permanent insurance and therefore increasing the cash values. Notice the impact on the policy in the following figure. Some contracts also allow the owner to purchase one-year term insurance. This significantly boosts the death benefit.

Paid-up additions increase cash values and the death benefits.

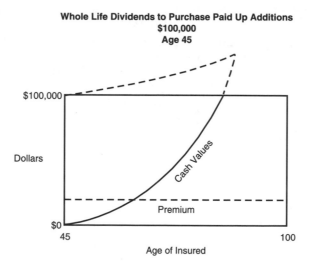

Variations on Whole Life

Whole life has spawned several other insurance vehicles, each better suited to a particular market or a particular need. For example, limited payment whole life policies appeal to owners who understand the need for protection for life, but who don't want to be burdened with premiums for life. The whole life policy can be reconfigured to allow a shorter premium-paying schedule and yet still have the contract endow at age 100 (see the following figure).

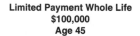

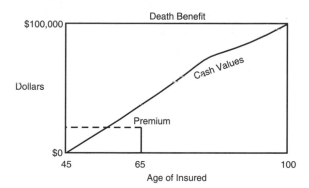

Limited Payment Whole Life
$100,000
Age 45

Limited payment whole life provides death benefits for life, and premiums for a chosen shorter period.

Notice how the cash values grow faster as you shorten the premium-paying period. This makes sense because the insurance company has more of your money and is investing it (and accumulating compound interest on it).

Single Premium Life

The most severe form of limited pay whole life is a single premium whole life. This was a popular form of investment vehicle sold during the 1980s, usually for its tax-free accumulation of cash values rather than its death benefit. Congress passed the Technical and Miscellaneous Revenue Act in 1988, which dramatically changed these products by redefining life insurance. The net effect of the redefinition was to reclassify single premium life as a *modified endowment contract* (MEC). These MECs were denied the favorable tax treatment accorded life insurance.

The mechanics of MECs are less important today than in 1988, because insurance companies now have a clear understanding of what will and will not qualify for favorable tax treatment of life insurance under IRS rules. You shouldn't see any policies sold that even skirt the line drawn in the sand by Congress. You should be aware, however, that if you own one of the older contracts, you own a valuable antique. And, in all likelihood, your policy is *grandfathered* for tax purposes. This means you still get the favorable tax treatment because you owned the contract before the date specified by Congress as the effective date of the new MEC provisions. Check with your tax advisor if you have any doubts.

Modified Life

The limited payment life policy resulted in higher premiums for a shorter time period. *Modified life* is just the opposite. It allows the insured to purchase permanent insurance today even though he or she cannot pay much in premiums at first. Such policies have a modified premium structure during the first several years, with premiums closer to term rates. Thereafter, the company charges a premium for life that is just a little higher than traditional whole life. The extra premium in the later years pays back the company for the lower premiums earlier. The usual period of lower premiums is five years. As you can see in the following figure, the cash value buildup during the reduced premium period is slower.

Modified premium whole life allows for a lower premium in early years.

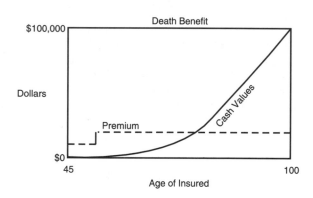

Modified Premium Whole Life
$100,000
Age 45

Graded Premium Life

This policy form is similar to modified premium, except the lower premiums are step-rated to permit a gradual transition to full whole life premiums. The following figure shows a graded premium life policy form. Notice that it ends at the same place as any other whole life, endowed at 100.

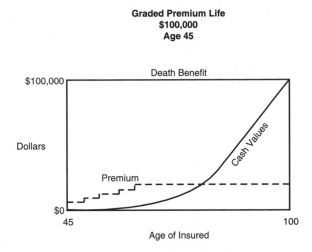

Graded Premium Life
$100,000
Age 45

Graded premium life allows for a gradually increasing premium in early years.

Combos

There's an entire series of policies that are a combination of term and whole life. These *combination policies* are typically designed with the younger insured in mind, for a time when more coverage is needed than financial circumstances permit. The term portion of the policy can be a rider or built into the permanent portion of the policy. The term can be level, decreasing, or contingent on some future date.

Family Income policies are common examples of combination plans. A decreasing term policy is sold atop a whole life plan. The term generally runs for 10, 15, or 20 years. Note that the death benefit can be paid in monthly income amounts. Another variation in the combination family is the Family Maintenance Plan, which employs level term in combination plans.

The Tax Man Cometh

There are many tax advantages to owning life insurance, including term and whole life insurance. And while this treatment appears in this chapter, understand that the tax rules apply to all life insurance, except as noted where the specific product is discussed.

➤ Life insurance death benefits are received by the named beneficiary income-tax free.

➤ Cash values accumulate income-tax deferred. There is no tax payable during the accumulation period even after cash values exceed total premiums paid.

➤ Loans against policies are not taxable income at the time of the loan.

➤ Gains in the policy are taxable only when a policy is surrendered for its cash value. If a policy is never surrendered, meaning a death benefit is paid instead, the gain of the cash value in excess of premiums paid is never taxed.

The Least You Need to Know

Whole life insurance was created to meet the long-term needs of individuals, needs of a "permanent" nature. It is characterized by guaranteed premiums to 100, level death benefits, and a cash surrender value. By altering either the premium structure or death benefit, whole life can be rebuilt to meet a wider variety of needs and situations.

➤ Whole life has been the most common policy choice in recent decades and should be considered if you have the ability to pay the higher premium and if your needs are "permanent" in nature.

➤ Whole life comes in various sizes, shapes, and configurations. Choose the one best suited to your needs.

➤ Cash values differentiate term from whole life. Learn how to use your cash values and your rights under nonforfeiture options.

➤ Participating whole life policies, most often issued by mutual companies, usually give you more for your dollar than nonparticipating whole life policies.

➤ There are a number of variations on the theme of whole life that give the buyer flexibility as to death benefits and premiums. Again, choose a policy designed to meet your particular needs.

TICK TICK TIC

Chapter 11

Interest-Sensitive Life Policies

In This Chapter

➤ Understanding the newer versions of permanent life insurance

➤ Why assumptions in the contract are just that, and not guarantees

➤ How to recognize the important differences between the plans

➤ How to select the type of policy that will most likely be best for you over the years

The trend in the last decade and a half has been toward more life insurance alternatives and more complex policy forms. This shift means greater flexibility in planning and meeting your needs. But it also has resulted in the creation of plans that are difficult to understand. The insurance industry has sacrificed simplicity for flexibility. In this chapter, you will learn about interest-sensitive policies, created to make permanent insurance more responsive to change in investment environments.

A number of factors contributed to the trend. First, unusually high interest rates in the late 1970s and early 1980s made traditional whole life policies relatively unattractive as savings and investment vehicles. In fact, almost all investment alternatives were out of whack, but insurance looked especially bad with its 4.5 percent returns when the world was going by at 12 to 15 percent.

The Evolution of Interest-Sensitive Products

At the same time, in the late 1970s and early 1980s, some insurance companies were concentrating on single premium life and single premium annuities investment-oriented products, the former with almost no insurance death benefits. These products captured the spotlight, and otherwise rational insurers began to make more and more speculative investments (with your money) to compete.

But not only was there competition within the insurance industry, there was also extreme competition from other financial services areas. Stockbrokerages, banks, and savings and loans all got into the annuity arena. It was just a matter of time until they added life insurance.

WOW! **Bet You Didn't Know**
Insurance companies invest your premiums in a variety of investment vehicles, including bonds and mortgages. They make a profit by earning more on their investments than they credit on their policies, after deducting the cost of insurance and the expenses of doing business. This is called the *spread*. And banks, for example, are in the same business—managing the spread.

Individual insurance company response varied from outright war to an attitude of "If you can't beat 'em, join 'em." New, flexible, interest-rate-sensitive products were designed to compete for your insurance dollars *and* your investment dollars.

The dramatic changes in the insurance and financial services industry continues today. While there is considerable dialogue about the problems, there hasn't been much commitment to resolve the issues. The implication for you is that there are many good financial-planning tools available to you today, but you probably need someone competent and up-to-date to help you find them and understand them.

New Age Alternatives

There are times when you'll wonder whether to consult a professional life underwriter or a psychic. Most insurance companies sell insurance using illustrations or proposals; they "illustrate" the results of the policy under "guaranteed" provisions and "assumed" conditions. And if you rely too heavily on the current assumptions rather than the guarantees, you may need the psychic. Keep in mind that assumptions are just that. The failure to illustrate and/or explain the difference between the two prompted the class action lawsuits that have cost insurance agents jobs, insurance companies tens of millions in fines, and policyowners frustration in not achieving their goals.

Interest-Sensitive Whole Life

The first policy you'll see is what is called *interest-sensitive whole life* or *current assumption whole life*. The insurance company makes assumptions about your policy with regard to mortality, investment returns, and expenses. If the company is accurate in its assumptions, then the policy performs as expected.

If its results are below expectations, then you must increase your premiums. Conversely, if the company does better than expected, your premiums drop and your cash value increases. The figure below illustrates this type of insurance. The broken lines in the figure indicate the variable elements in the policy—the premiums and cash values.

> **OOOH...** | **Insider Tip**
>
> You don't have to worry about these adjustments every year—it takes time for the variance between projected and actual rates of return to make a difference. But they will make a difference. Pay attention to the illustrated values and the labels "guaranteed" and "current assumptions."

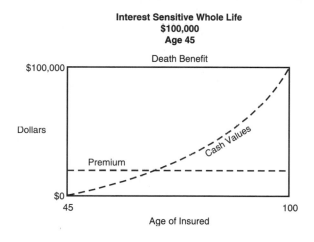

Interest Sensitive Whole Life
$100,000
Age 45

Interest-sensitive whole life, with assumed premiums and cash values.

This is the time to restate one of the most valuable points in this book: Assumptions are just that—assumptions!

The insurance industry has withstood (and paid for) a barrage of complaints from policyowners who bought policies with high expectations based on the illustrations used to market and sell the products.

Jargon Alert

Illustrations in the life insurance business are numerical depictions of the performance of the policy over a period of time, typically 20 years or to age 65. A typical illustration shows the premiums paid, death benefits payable, and the cash surrender values, at the very least. But the performance of a particular policy depends on the interest rate credited, the cost of pure insurance, and the expenses of the insurer. If the results are something other than what is assumed, then the results will be different from those shown in the illustration that the company provides.

As an example, a highly rated and well-respected life insurance company has an interest-sensitive life plan with the following footnote in its illustration:

Current values are based on the Company's current cost of insurance and the credited interest rates shown above. These rates are not guaranteed, and are subject to change by the Company. The guaranteed minimum interest rate is 4.00% in any policy year, and 5.00% cumulative. See your…representative for information on the current interest rates.

Watch It!

Never buy any life insurance that relies on assumptions without clearly understanding what the assumptions are and whether they're reasonable. If their significance is not obvious to you, demand an explanation before you purchase the policy. It is not reasonable, for example, to assume that current rates of return or interest will stay the same or grow. Rates fluctuate.

This is not only a straightforward and honest attempt to notify the prospective purchaser of the assumptions, but also a commitment to reasonable assumptions.

The problem that arises is that sometimes the disparity between what was illustrated and what was achieved can be quite large. You must know what the underlying assumptions are in the contract. Even then, you may not be in a position to judge them as to reasonableness. Ask for help.

An agent proposing the plan should be able to explain the assumptions and speak to the issue of reasonableness. He or she may have to get the company involved and perhaps ask someone in the actuarial department. But you should feel comfortable with the basic assumptions underlying the plan before purchasing any policy that relies on anything beyond written guarantees.

Indexed Whole Life

Inflation erodes the purchasing power of your dollar. When prices for the basics in life rise faster than your earnings, you're losing ground because the value of your dollar is shrinking. To prevent inflation from eroding your life insurance death benefits, insurers introduced *indexed whole life*. Indexed whole life increases your benefits in proportion to a given measurement of the economy. The index used most frequently is the Consumer Price Index (CPI).

The death benefit under an indexed policy increases in conformity with the rate of inflation as measured by the CPI or some other widely recognized index. There can be an annual increase in your premium to pay for this gradual increase, or the insurer may build in enough extra premium in the basic rate to cover the anticipated additional death benefits.

The figure below shows the schematic of an indexed whole life policy.

> **Jargon Alert**
> *Inflation* is a general increase in prices of goods and services in the economy. Because it's impossible to include each and every product or service in the entire economy, a representative sampling of goods—a hypothetical basketful—is used. That basket is referred to as the *Consumer Price Index* or *CPI*.

**Indexed Whole Life
$100,000
Age 45**

Indexed whole life fluctuates according to a defined index.

Adjustable Life

No, the product is not sold by behavioral psychologists or chiropractors. Adjustable life insurance is the next step in flexibility (see the following figure).

Adjustable life with variable premiums, cash values, and death benefit.

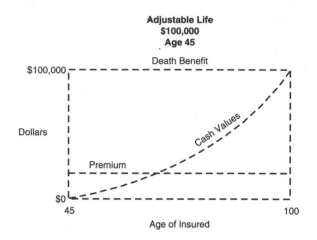

You might wonder what there is to rely on, because everything seems adjustable in the figure above. It's true, the product is very consumer driven. You just need to make sure you're the right customer for the product.

With adjustable life, you can adjust the premiums or the death benefits. Any changes are prospective only, affecting only future benefits. This is a great plan for a young head of a family whose needs are likely to be heavy for a period of years, and then perhaps taper off. However, if your needs are likely to remain relatively level, then you may be better off with a different policy selection.

If you wanted to increase the amount of death benefit or shorten the premium-paying period, you could increase the premium. By decreasing the premium, on the other hand, you could reduce the cash value, reduce the length of coverage, or stretch out the premium-paying period.

Insurance company computer illustrations should be available to help you weigh various alternatives—another reason for the services of and relationship with a professional life underwriter. Changes in interest rate assumptions will impact the values. Assume a worst-case, only guaranteed values, scenario. If you can live with that scenario, the product will not underperform to your expectations.

An Example of Projected vs. Guaranteed Values

Take a look at some representative numbers. Assume a 45-year-old nonsmoking male needs $100,000 of protection.

One insurance company quotes a preferred premium rate of $977.59 per year. This is a nonparticipating policy—that is, one with no policy dividends. The death benefit is shown at $100,000. The "Projections" section of the illustration assumes a 6.0 percent interest rate. At that rate, the policy endows for $100,000 in 50 years, at age 95. However, the *guaranteed* interest rate is only 4.0 percent. And if the credited interest rate is only 4.0 percent, the policy would only survive at the current premium level for 23 years. In other words, the policy cannot carry itself any further than 23 years without some adjustment of premium, death benefit, and/or cash value.

Here's what the insurer states in a footnote:

> *The calculation of premiums, the ability to stop premium payments, the duration of coverage, and the ability to take surrenders and/or loans from policy values are sensitive to interest and mortality rates. It is important to understand that current and/or assumed values, reflecting nonguaranteed rates, are illustrative only. If actual values vary, additional premiums may be required for the policy to perform as originally intended. It is also possible that coverage will expire prior to the date shown if premiums are not received by the dates assumed, or if future mortality costs are higher or interest rates lower than projected…*

This is a fair disclosure because it tells you in comprehensible language the difference between the guarantees and current assumptions. Again, it shouldn't be relegated to a footnote, but it is up to the state insurance commissioner to require a more prominent showing.

What if your agent downplays the guaranteed rate or promises the higher rate? Get a second opinion, and while you're at it, get a second agent. The footnote disclosure is there for a reason. It is a great deal more than just window dressing. The state regulators insist on the layout of both the illustrations and the policy. They require a separation of the "Projections" from the "Guarantees." You should understand the basics of your policy.

Bet You Didn't Know Almost all companies now distinguish between smokers and nonsmokers. The impact of smoking on mortality is so well established that insurers offer lower premiums to nonsmokers.

The Least You Need to Know

The reaction of the insurance industry to rising rates of return on investments, increasing competition from other financial services, and the blurring of the lines between insurers and other financial sources has driven the spread of interest-sensitive adjustable policies. The focus is on flexibility.

➤ Interest-sensitive life is just that—sensitive to interest rate changes.

➤ Indexed life prevents the erosion of the dollar due to inflation. Select this product if inflation is your primary concern.

➤ Adjustable life is highly sensitive and flexible to the changing needs of the young family.

Universal Life

Universal life (UL) takes the insurance company trend toward flexibility to the next level. In fact, it's the ultimate in flexibility today; it allows the policyowner to change the policy whenever he or she wants.

The following figure shows a graph of a universal life policy. The dotted lines indicate factors that the insured can change. The lack of permanent fixed lines indicates complete flexibility. One of the great advantages of UL is the ability to make the alterations without issuing a new policy. It's like buying a dress or a suit that you never have to replace. You just bring it in for alterations whenever you feel the need.

Universal life is the ultimate plan for flexibility.

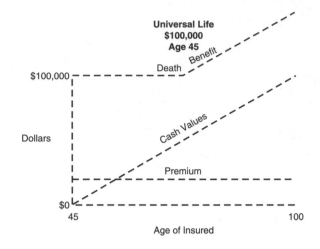

Source: The Tools and Techniques of Life Insurance Planning, 1993.

However, there are limits. In the clothes analogy, you would be governed by the amount of cloth you had; with the universal life contract, you would be limited by the amount of cash you've been depositing. For example, if you've been paying a premium of $500 a year for four years and decide you need the maximum amount of death benefit, you won't be able to purchase $50,000,000 of protection for the same premium.

The Mechanics of the Policy

When you pay a universal life insurance premium, the insurance company deposits your premium into a cash value account. It then siphons off mortality charges and administrative expenses. The remainder is credited with an interest rate based on the investment results of the company, or the guaranteed rate, if higher. The figure below shows this concept.

The UL bucket, with its fluctuating cash values.

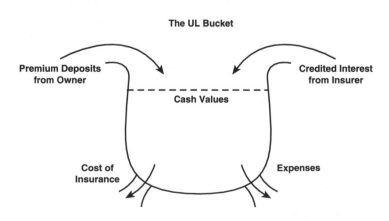

You can see that lower charges and expenses will mean more in the bucket to be credited with interest. And the higher the credited rate, the more cash in the cash value account.

The expenses deducted include commissions and administration costs. The cost of the death benefit, called the *mortality expense*, is the cost of the pure protection. These charges are usually reasonable, or the company is unable to remain competitive. But reasonableness is not always easy to determine item by item, because the expenses are not always itemized in the policy. However, one company states in its footnotes that expenses will be 7.5 percent of each premium paid. The companies must charge for expenses as they exist, not as they would like them to be. This is why some of the larger, more established companies have lower expenses—economies of scale.

Jargon Alert
The mortality charge or expense is the amount the insurance company charges for the actual death benefit. It is like a term insurance premium for the upcoming year based on the actual death benefit in the policy.

The remainder of the premium is credited to the cash value account at the *current rate*. The *guaranteed rate* is the interest rate the insurance company promises will be the lowest rate it will credit on the cash value portion of the contract. It provides a guaranteed floor of earnings inside the contract. The *current rate* is the rate the company actually credits based on its own investment experience.

Insider Tip
As with the policies studied in the prior chapter, you must understand the difference between *current* and *guaranteed* rates.

All computer-prepared illustrations that you receive from an underwriter or agent should show columns for both the current and guaranteed rates. If both are not shown, ask for them. If the agent balks, find a different agent.

By now, you should realize that the options you have at any point in time relate to the values in the policy. The higher the credited rate, the more the cash value and the greater the flexibility.

Construction Models

There are actually two models of universal life to choose from, referred to in the insurance industry as Options 1 and 2. The first was shown above. You decide on the amount of death benefit you want, and the company constructs the policy with a combination of cash value and pure insurance (term insurance). With time, the amount of term insurance decreases and the amount of cash value increases. However, because the tax laws require a minimum corridor of death benefit in excess of cash values, the death benefit will actually begin to increase as the policy approaches maturity.

Option 2's picture is a little different (see the figure below).

UL Option 2.

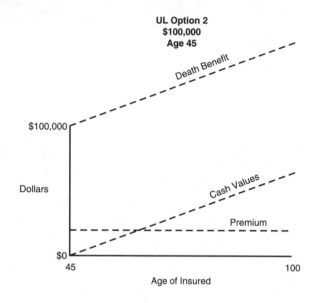

With Option 2, you're concerned with the cash levels, and you can see that there's a proportionate increase of the corridor of death benefit over the cash value. In effect, there is a level term policy on top of the cash portion of the contract. This satisfies the tax law rules enacted in 1984 that sought to eliminate the use of life insurance as purely investment contracts.

What Can You Change?

You may be from Missouri and wondering why the fuss about flexibility. What are the changes that can really be made? Let's look at them in the following sections.

You Don't Like Your Premiums

You may increase your premium.

There are, however, limits on the amount of the premium increase you may initiate yourself. In certain circumstances, you may have to increase your premium to keep the insurance in force. For example, a company may issue a contract that guarantees a 4.5 percent interest rate credited to the cash value account. But the premium actually charged may be based on a current rate assumption of 5.75 percent. If the actual rate credited is closer to the 4.5 percent rate over the years, at some point you'll need to increase the premium to continue the same level of benefits.

You may decrease your premium.

This option will likewise result in a day of reckoning if actual results are less than projected results. However, if the interest rate credited exceeds the projected rate, say of 5.75 percent, you could decrease premiums without adverse long-term effects.

You may discontinue premiums.

The ability to continue coverage while discontinuing premiums comes in handy when jobs are changed or lost, emergencies arise, basements leak, children go to college, or parents need support. The length of time you can discontinue the premium will depend on how long you've owned the policy and how much cash value is intact to draw against.

Change My Benefits, Please

Death benefits may be increased.

Within the limits of *insurability*, you may increase the amount of the death benefit. You might want the increase because you have added to the size of your family or have added significant debt.

There are several ways you may increase the amount of coverage. You could increase the term element within the policy itself. If, for example, you were using Option 2, you could request an increase in the term corridor. Or, you could request an actual term rider like the ones discussed under combination policies.

You could decrease the death benefit.

This would have the obvious advantage of increasing your cash values because less money would be allocated to mortality charges. A change in family obligations or an elimination of debt could give you reason to decrease the protection levels in the contract.

Benefits could be pre-funded.

If the cash values are sufficiently large, the death benefit could be prepaid by using cash values. This option is rarely invoked because it does tend to restrict flexibility, which should have been part of the reason for buying universal life in the first place.

Jargon Alert
Insurability relates to a determination by the insurance company that you are a risk they're willing to assume. In the case of life insurance, it means you're healthy enough to meet their standards and that your avocations and occupation are not overly risky. Insurability is covered in greater depth in Chapter 15.

The ATM Option

Cash may be borrowed from the policy.

Typically, the loan limit is 90 percent of the cash value fund. The primary reason for the holdback of 10 percent is to ensure enough to pay interest on the policy loan and continue the contract in force. Again, this is an asset that should be considered a part of the liquid portion of your financial statement. Consider it in the same category as bank accounts, CDs, and money market funds.

Cash may be withdrawn from the policy.

As opposed to a policy loan, withdrawal is a permanent removal of cash from the contract. You will be required to leave enough in the contract to keep it in force.

The policy may be surrendered for cash.

The "cash out" option is always available, so long as you have cash left in the contract. Most companies impose a *surrender charge* against the contract in the early years, which is a charge levied against the cash value at the time of surrender, and designed to reimburse the insurer for expenses it chose to amortize over several years and which have not yet been recovered.

Let's Look at the Numbers

To get a better feel for the way UL operates, take a look at numbers extracted from an illustration provided by a large, highly rated mutual company for a nonsmoking 45-year-old male with a death benefit of $100,000 (see Table 12.1).

Table 12.1   Sample UL Policy Summary Illustration for Male Age 45 ($100,000)

			Guaranteed 4.50%		Current 5.75%	
End of Year	Age	Annualized Payment	Cash Value	Net Cash Value	Cash Value	Net Cash Value
1	46	$1,350	$970	$0	$970	$0
5	50	1,350	4,778	3,418	5,229	3,869
10	55	1,350	9,737	9,057	11,378	10,698
15	60	1,350	14,319	14,319	19,230	19,230
20	65	1,350	17,449	17,449	29,546	29,546
25	70	0	8,962	8,962	35,305	35,305

			Guaranteed 4.50%		Current 5.75%	
End of Year	Age	Annualized Payment	Cash Value	Net Cash Value	Cash Value	Net Cash Value
27	72	0	$2,435	$2,435	$37,776	$37,776
30	75	0	——	——	41,374	41,374
35	80	0	——	——	46,078	46,078
40	85	0	——	——	44,357	44,357

The Rates

The first thing to notice in any interest-dependent product today is the current interest rate and the underlying guaranteed rate in the illustration in Table 12.1. This policy guarantees 4.5 percent. The current rate is 5.75 percent. Is that the whole story? Not by a long shot. Every illustration from a reputable life insurance company will have a statement or direction to an accompanying *Supplemental Footnote Page,* which is just a separate page for footnotes. The language may vary from policy to policy, but the concept is the same. There should be a page or at least a note on the bottom of proposal pages that states clearly the rates assumed in the projections.

A check with the Supplemental Footnote Page of this illustration reveals the following statement:

> *The CURRENT Column is based upon current interest plus current cost of insurance rates. The GUARANTEED Column uses the current mortality costs for the first year and current interest rate guaranteed for the initial premium. Thereafter, this column uses the guaranteed minimum interest rate and guaranteed maximum mortality costs. Current values in this proposal assume an interest rate bonus of 0.85% beginning in policy year 11 which increases to 1.25% beginning in policy year 16.*

What does all that mean for you? Well, the first part states what you would expect, that current rate columns are in fact based on current rates. And what you would hope is that after the first year, the illustration shows the worst-case scenario for interest rates and mortality expenses. So far, so good.

The hooker is the last sentence, about interest rate bonuses. What are interest rate bonuses and how do you earn them? The answer is not to be found in the illustration, even though they're illustrated. One would assume that these bonuses would be paid if interest rates and expenses continued at the now current rate that allows for a crediting of 5.75

percent. But—and this is big—this bonus is not guaranteed. With this caveat in mind, let's explore the numbers.

The Premiums

The illustration in Table 12.1 shows an annualized premium of $1,350.00. This premium is the same under both guaranteed and current interest rate scenarios.

Does this mean that this premium will keep the policy in force no matter what happens to interest rates? No.

This premium will keep the policy alive for 27 years at the minimum guaranteed rate of 4.5 percent. At 5.75 percent, the policy will stay afloat much longer. But notice that the policy is beginning to lose its value even at this 5.75 percent rate level in the later years. This particular illustration states that the *guideline annual* premium is $1,904.25. In fact, this is the premium recommended to cover all the demands of the contract and keep it afloat to maturity at the guaranteed rate of 4.5 percent.

Cash Values

There are two columns, cash value and net cash value, for both the guaranteed and current set of numbers in Table 12.1. The first year the cash value at the end of the year is $970 for both. Remember the footnote previously cited said that values in the first year were assumed current. What is the $970 and how did it get there?

The footnote states that expenses are 7.5 percent of premium.

Premiums × Expense Rate = Total Annual Expenses

$1,350.00 × 7.5% = $101.25

This means that $1,248.75 remained after expenses ($1,350.00 Premium– $101.25 Annual Expenses).

The cost of insurance brought that $1,248.75 down to $970.00. This cash value amount will be credited with interest in the following year. The second year's cash value is $1,899 guaranteed and $1,976 based on the higher 5.75 percent current rate.

The lower net cash value is the value available for surrender of the contract. The gap between the cash value and net cash value gradually narrows as the surrender charge decreases to zero in the 15th year.

Table 12.2 Increased Popularity of UL

| Year | Universal Life Insurance | | Variable-Universal Life Insurance | |
	Policies	Amount (billions)	Policies	Amount (billions)
1983	1,185	$ 92.449	——	——
1984	2,551	205.583	——	——
1985	3,545	289.926	101	6.807
1986	3,949	301.951	259	20.736
1987	3,726	273.148	410	37.198
1988	3,508	269.811	343	37.430
1989	3,437	275.207	320	35.933
1990	3,058	261.446	345	37.919
1991	2,659	248.284	329	40.057
1992	2,393	220.203	402	53.056
1993	2,471	249.896	563	73.103
1994	2,776	295.499	553	81.996

Source: American Council of Life Insurance, 1995 Life Insurance Fact Book Update

By age 65, in the 20th year, the cash values are $29,546 on a current assumption basis and $17,449 guaranteed. By this time, you will have paid in $27,000.00 in premium. In essence, if you had $29,546 cash after paying $27,000 in premium, you would be about breaking even. To look at it a little differently, the cost of the $100,000 protection over the 20 years would be the cost of the use of your money each year. That's the amount you could have earned if you had invested the $1,350.00 each year instead of buying life insurance.

Surrenders

The insurance company provides a comparison figure for you on the bottom of its illustrations. The commonly accepted index is the 5 percent Surrender Cost, which is the example outlined above. It assumes you could've invested your premiums at 5 percent. It gives you a reference point if you want to comparison shop your cost of coverage.

Watch It!

The 5 percent Surrender Cost Method isn't the only means of comparing the cost of coverage. There are probably a dozen methods utilized for comparing policy costs. All are complex and beyond the scope of this book. You can rely on the numbers given in the illustrations as to cost and compare them, realizing that the numbers are only a part of the story and probably no more important than the quality of the agent or the solvency of the insurer.

The Least You Need to Know

Universal life is designed to be flexible and perform well in interest rate environments higher than the guaranteed rate. Because of its relatively transparent structure, it's sometimes easier to compare costs and benefits with other policies of the same type.

➤ Assumptions, assumptions, assumptions. These are the three keys to understanding universal life, or any other modern interest-sensitive life insurance product.

➤ Opt for UL when you need a great deal of flexibility in your insurance program and you're in a current position to pay the higher premium characteristic of permanent insurance.

➤ Give yourself leeway in purchasing UL by making sure you can pay the higher premium for at least five (hopefully ten) years before drastically altering the policy.

➤ Remember the value of a good agent in finding the right policy for you. The universal life policies, like all the permanent plans, can be complex and confusing.

Variable Life

Variable life insurance is an investment-oriented policy, and it is in fact registered with *securities regulators* because of its investment features. With whole life, adjustable life, and even universal life, the insurance company accepts your premium and assumes full responsibility for the successful investment of the portion not used to pay for expenses and for the cost of insurance. With variable life, however, the insurance company deducts these same mortality charges and operational expenses, and then puts you in charge of investing the funds wisely. You'd better know what you're doing, or have a great deal of confidence in those you select to manage those funds in your stead.

Jargon Alert

Securities regulators are governmental agencies responsible for the regulation of the investment industry and its salespeople. The SEC (Securities and Exchange Commission) approves insurance products for sale after it is satisfied the insurance company has complied with all the rules and regulations about securities (investments). The NASD (National Association of Securities Dealers) regulates salespeople and advertising. Approval by either organization does not imply the products will perform as illustrated or projected.

The Structure of Variable Life

The figure below shows the drawing of a variable life policy, in the same format as other permanent life insurance policies.

Variable life insurance driven by investment performance.

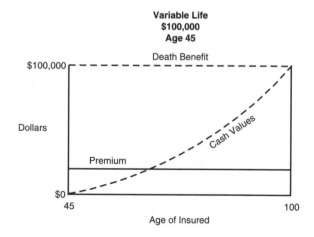

The premium is fixed, as you can see from the solid line. This means you have no flexibility to vary the amounts or frequency of the premiums. And the death benefit is likewise not changeable by the policyowner; it is dependent on investment results, usually with a minimum guarantee. Finally, the policyowner does not have the flexibility of partial withdrawals. Basically, the policy is designed to resemble a whole life policy while still being driven by the performance of the investments you control.

A minimum death benefit is guaranteed. The insurance company charges a level premium just as with the traditional life types. However, the cash values remaining after expenses are invested into *separate accounts* of the company, as opposed to the general account. This means that they are not a part of the general assets of the company and, therefore, are not subject to the general claims of creditors and policyowners. This is obviously an advantage if the company is experiencing financial difficulties. However, the biggest negative is that there can be no guaranteed cash value, because you're responsible for the investment of the cash value and not the insurance company.

Within the separate account, each policyowner must elect how their funds are to be invested. The choices are funds with different asset compositions and investment objectives. They're like *mutual funds*. And in fact, it is the popularity of mutual funds that has led to the increased popularity of variable life. (This was illustrated in Chapter 12, in Table 12.1, along with the increased popularity of universal life.)

The typical variable life policy also offers the policyowner a selection of equity, bond, and money market accounts. Most products offer in the neighborhood of 12 funds. The approach is analogous to a family of funds approach. A *family of funds* is a group of funds under the management of the same company. The funds usually have different advisors, but the parent company is the same. This allows for ease of moving from one fund to another and ease of administration. However, the latest wrinkle in variable life and variable annuities is to offer a variety of fund managers from different families under one contract.

> **Jargon Alert**
> *Mutual funds* are investment vehicles that combine the investment dollars of many investors with similar objectives into one fund that is under the professional expertise of a money manager or managers. For a fee based on the assets under management, the manager makes all the investment decisions as to what to buy, sell, or hold. The investor owns a number of shares in the fund, based on his or her contribution.

> **Jargon Alert**
> *Equities* are stocks or securities convertible to stocks. They are popular because of their overall investment success in the long run. *Bonds* are debt instruments issued by the borrower, which can be a corporate, municipal, or government agency. *Money market accounts* are cash vehicles usually invested in short-term debt instruments issued by banks or governmental agencies. They are very liquid and do not fluctuate in value as a rule.

Watch It!

Because this is an investment product, you must be given a *prospectus* before you make the purchase. This is a legal document explaining the contract and its inherent risks. As painful as it seems, it was created to be read. It is long, boring, and somewhat technical, but will explain important terms, changes, and objectives of individual funds. There is a movement to allow a summarized document, but until this happens, you should read it.

The investment results of the various funds determine the performance of the entire contract. This means that your cash value account could actually decrease from one year to another if your investments go down in value. This will likely happen sooner or later if you're invested in equities for the long term. Stocks do go up and down in value. Again, you, the policyowner, decide how to invest the funds. The insurance company is just the expediter of your decisions.

Is It Variable or Universal Life? Yes.

The next variation we need to talk about is variable universal life (VUL), shown in the figure below.

Variable universal life with greater premium flexibility.

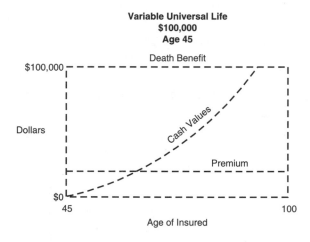

VUL offers the same kind of flexibility seen in adjustable life and universal life. The death benefit is guaranteed as long as the policy is in force. And the policyowner can increase or decrease the death benefits consistent with underwriting and policy guidelines. Premiums are flexible and can be varied as to amount and frequency by the policyowner. The cash values are a function of the investment results of the selected funds, and they may be accessed for partial withdrawals.

Who Needs This?

Variable life is most suitable for people who have a need for control over their cash values and a need for increasing death benefits. It's for people who have a better-than-basic understanding of investments and who are willing to assume the burden of the risk for investment results.

The opportunity for extraordinary growth of the cash values and the death benefit is the greatest appeal of the product. Most of the money invested in VL and VUL policies have been invested in equities, and equities over the long term have shown significantly higher returns than fixed asset investments characteristic of insurance company portfolios.

Watch It!

Some companies offer *asset allocation* plans that make automatic adjustments to your funds for you. This advisory service is designed to provide an extra level of investment expertise between you and the funds. The advisor recommends a mix of stock, bond, and cash funds consistent with that advisor's view of general market conditions. The insurance company makes the adjustments in the funds automatically, after you authorize such trading. Note that this does *not* mean the burden of investment decisions is no longer yours and has shifted to the insurer. You have simply delegated your responsibility.

Variable life and variable universal life should be viewed as long-range insurance policies with investment characteristics. They are not appropriate as a short- or intermediate-term solution to life insurance needs. The most important traits of successful investors are time and patience. And because this is an investment policy, the same two requirements are applicable.

The Benefits of Variable Life

There are many advantages to VL and VUL, but especially VUL:

➤ *Control.* You have control over the cash values, premiums, and death benefits, especially with VUL.

➤ *Free Switching.* Like a mutual fund family, you may switch between funds without incurring a charge. And because the product is a life insurance policy, the move between funds doesn't trigger an income tax, even if there is a gain within the fund family.

➤ *Increasing death benefits.* Assuming the investments perform well, the death benefits increase, too. And with VUL, you can change the death benefits to meet your needs, which will change with time.

➤ *Cash values are accessible.* They may be used to pay premiums, accumulate, and withdraw for emergencies or income.

➤ *Tax advantageous.* The products are considered life insurance and therefore enjoy a favorable tax treatment (as explained in Chapter 10).

The Drawback of Variable Life

The drawback of variable life is the possible consequences of shifting the investment risk to you. Poor performance means lower death benefits, cash values, and future income capabilities.

The Least You Need to Know

Variable and variable universal life were created to shift the burden of maintaining high levels of current interest inside the policy from the insurer to the policyowner. Their popularity comes from riding the coattails of mutual fund growth, especially equity mutual funds.

➤ Variable life and variable universal life are great products for the person with investment expertise, risk tolerance, and time.

➤ These policies perform best when given time to perform. They are not short- or even intermediate-term investment vehicles. Time is critical in order to smooth out the inevitable fluctuations in investment returns.

➤ The performance—and hence the cash values and death benefits—could be erratic and variable. If you need consistency, try another policy type.

➤ Read the prospectus before you accept the policy.

Chapter 14

What's All the Mumbo Jumbo?

In This Chapter

➤ Who the parties to the contract are—and why it matters

➤ The key provisions of a contract

➤ What are your rights under the contract?

Insurance contracts are special kinds of contracts that are approved by state regulators with your protection in mind. There are many features of insurance contracts that differentiate them from other types of contracts. Understanding these characteristics will help you better understand insurance itself.

Some Contract Terms You Should Know

The words used in contracts are legal terms with a great deal of history behind them, although some people would argue that the terms are still in use so that lawyers can perpetuate their own existence.

Life insurance policies are *contracts*. A contract is an agreement enforceable in a court of law. A contract must satisfy certain requirements in order to be valid and binding.

Contracts must have an offer and acceptance, consideration, legal purpose, and competent parties.

Jargon Alert
Competent parties are people who are capable of entering into a contract. The law presumes an applicant is competent unless he or she is a minor, mentally infirm, or under the influence of drugs or alcohol.

There must be an *offer* by one party and an *acceptance* by another. This is a fundamental principle of contract law. *Consideration* is something of value given in exchange for the promise of the other party. Your premium is the consideration in return for a promise to pay a death benefit.

When you fill out an application for life insurance and give the agent or company a check with the application, you're making an offer to the company. If they issue a policy, they have accepted your offer. If the application is not prepaid, the company makes an offer when they send a policy. You then accept by paying a premium.

Characteristics of Insurance Contracts

There are several characteristics common to insurance contracts. Understanding these characteristics will help you understand more about insurance in general.

➤ *Aleatory.* An aleatory contract depends on chance. An insurance contract is aleatory because there is the element of chance involved that the premiums paid over the life of the contract may not be enough to reimburse the company for the death benefit. If the insured dies shortly after paying a premium, the beneficiary will receive much more in proceeds than was paid in cash.

➤ *Executory.* A life insurance policy is executory because the death benefit is based on the occurrence of some future event, namely the death of the insured.

➤ *Unilateral.* The policy is one-sided. The insurance company is obligated to pay the death benefit if the premium has been paid and the claim is submitted with a proof of death. But there is no obligation on the part of the policyowner to pay the premium.

➤ *Valued.* A life insurance policy is valued because the contract owner agrees to pay a specified premium without regard to the potential loss.

➤ *Adhesion.* A life insurance policy is a contract of adhesion because the policy is a contract drawn entirely by one side, the insurance company. There is no negotiation; you can either accept it or reject it. Note that while you were not negotiating the contract, the state of residence probably was for you. All policy forms must be approved by the state insurance departments before being used with the public.

➤ *Utmost Good Faith.* The policy is a contract of utmost good faith, which means that both you and the insurance company are entitled to know all the important facts and information. There can be no attempt to hide, disguise, or distort the facts.

➤ *Insurable Interest.* The applicant must have an interest in the continued life of the insured. This prevents the policy from being a wagering or gaming contract. You can't take a policy out on the life of a stranger, hoping to receive more in benefits than you paid in premiums. The insurable interest range includes relatives, business associates, and the like.

The Party of the First Part...

There are four parties to a life insurance contract. They are important to know so you will understand the rights of each.

➤ *The Insured.* The insured is the person whose life is being insured. In other words, it is at the insured's death that the death benefit is paid.

➤ *The Insurance Company.* This is the company that has issued the policy to insure the life of the insured. It has the primary responsibility to pay the death benefit and cash values even if it has contracted to another insurer to share the risk, called *reinsurance.*

➤ *The Policyholder.* This is the party who has the right to exercise the rights in the contract, and it may be a different person or party than the insured. It may also be called the policyowner.

➤ *The Beneficiary.* The beneficiary is the person designated by the owner to receive the proceeds of the policy upon the death of the insured.

The Important Rights of Policy Ownership

Your life insurance policy should contain a paragraph about each of the important policyholder rights in the contract. The most important rights are explained in the following list.

➤ *The right to change the beneficiary.* This is one of the most important rights because the beneficiary receives the death benefit at the death of the insured. Why would you change beneficiaries? You may divorce and remarry. Your children may grow up and become financially independent of you. You may want to leave proceeds to a charity.

➤ *The right to decide how the death benefits will be paid to the beneficiary.* The most common form is *lump sum.* This means all of the death proceeds are paid out at once and in cash. There are other options available to the owner. For example, the owner worried about the frivolous spending habits of the beneficiary could select a payout over the years of a fixed amount, or a fixed percentage of the total sum. There is flexibility to help meet the circumstances at the time.

➤ *The right to surrender the policy.* The owner may also surrender the policy for its cash value at any time. This in effect terminates the policy and ends the promise to pay a death benefit on the part of the insurer.

➤ *The right to borrow against the policy.* Rather than cash in a permanent policy, the owner may make a policy loan, assuming enough cash value exists. With the new style policies, the owner may also alter the premiums, cash values, and death benefits wherever such flexibility exists.

➤ *The right to change the dividend use.* The owner has the right to use the dividend on participating policies to reduce the premium, accumulate at interest, or take the dividend as a cash distribution. In the later years of a contract's life, this can be a significant right.

➤ *The right to transfer the policy ownership.* The owner may assign the ownership of the policy to some other party. This may involve adverse income tax consequences, but the right is there nevertheless.

The Key Policy Provisions

There are standard insurance provisions, thanks to the cooperation of the National Association of Insurance Commissioners (NAIC). This group has helped standardize the important policy provisions in all life insurance contracts. While they do not agree on many other issues that could make the insurance business less parochial, this standardization is valuable.

Watch It!

Even though state insurance commissioners approve products for sale in your state, this does not mean that the products are good. It means the insurance company has met the minimum requirements to gain admittance in the state and has complied with the minimum required guidelines as to policy provision. Continue to rely on the standards of company soundness specified in Chapter 4.

Some of the most important policy provisions are explained in the following sections. You should take the time to read a life insurance policy from cover to cover. While the terms have a legal ring to them and it is easy to joke about lawyers, most states and insurers do try to make their life insurance policies readable. The same cannot be said of all insurance policies, as you will discover later in this book.

Entire Contract Clause

The *entire contract clause* states that the policy and the application for insurance that is attached makes up the entire contract. This is important to protect you, because the company cannot rely on any other documents (which you might not have) to make up the contract. With regard to the application that is stapled into the contract, the insurance company must regard the statements made as *representations*, nothing more. This means that the statements are true to the best of the applicant's knowledge. The applicant does not *warrant*, or guarantee, that the statements are true.

Insuring Clause

The *insuring clause* is the insurance company's promise to pay. The language may vary from state to state and policy to policy. Here's how one insurer wrote the clause on the front page in readable type:

> We will pay the proceeds of this policy to the beneficiary when we receive due proof that the insured died while the policy was in force. We will pay the Net Cash Surrender Value, if any, to you on the Maturity date if this policy is still in force and the insured is living on that date. The insured is named in the Policy Specifications. If not later changed, the beneficiary is as named in the application. We make these promises and issue this policy in consideration of the application for this policy and the payment of at least the Minimum Initial Premium. The Minimum Initial Premium is shown in the Policy Specifications. The provisions that follow are part of this policy.

Grace Period Provision

The *grace period provision* is one of the most important provisions in the policy. It protects you from losing the benefits of the policy just because a premium is late. The insurance remains in force for a period of 30 or more days after a premium due date. The 30-day time frame is most common, but the contract could specify 60 days, for example. State regulations usually require a 30-day minimum except in the case of insurance paid for on a weekly basis, such as industrial insurance. If the insured dies during the grace period, the insurer will subtract the premium from the death benefit before mailing the proceeds.

Reinstatement Clause

A third attempt by the insurance company to keep the insurance in force is the *reinstatement clause*. If the policy lapses (ceases to be in effect) due to a lack of premium, the company will allow the owner to reinstate the policy if they specifically request reinstatement; pay all the back premiums with interest; pay any outstanding loans against the policy; and submit proof of insurability of the insured. The contestability provisions discussed in the following section start anew, but not the suicide clause. (Suicides are usually not covered for two years as explained after the incontestable clause section.)

Incontestable Clause

The *incontestable clause*, also required by state insurance laws, states that after two years from the date of issue of the policy, the insurer will not contest the policy as long as the premium has been paid and the contract is in force. The company agrees to rely on your representations in the application unless it contests the statements during the first two years.

Suicide Clause

The *suicide clause* is a provision unique to life insurance that protects the insurance company against someone taking out life insurance and then committing suicide. Basically, the insurer will not pay the death benefit if the insured commits suicide during the first two years from the date of issue. The presumption is that no one will take out insurance contemplating suicide and have the patience to wait two years. The company will return premiums at interest if suicide is the cause of death in the two-year period.

Automatic Premium Loan

A related provision is the *automatic premium loan* provision, which is frequently referred to as the APL provision. This clause states that if the premium is not received during the grace period, then the company will automatically deduct the premium from the cash surrender value of the policy. Again, this is in the policy to keep it from *lapsing,* which occurs when the policy terminates due to a lack of premium, and it means the end of protection for the insured.

Misstatement of Age and/or Sex

The insurance company cannot use a misstatement of a person's age or gender as a grounds for not paying a claim or continuing the coverage. They may, however, make the necessary premium adjustments. Because women outlive men (actuarially speaking), life insurance premiums for women are lower than they are for men. This clause could mean a lowering of a premium if the insured is a woman rather than a man as originally listed in the application, or if the wrong date of birth given makes the insured older than in actuality.

Assignment Clause

The *assignment clause* allows the owner of the policy to transfer the ownership of the contract to another party. The assignment could be temporary, as when one collaterally assigns a policy to a bank to cover a debt in the event of death or loan default. All policies require that the insurance company be notified in writing of the assignment. The company will prefer you to use their assignment form.

Waiver of Premium

An optional benefit that must be applied for, and is found in most life insurance policies, is the waiver of premium provision. It is especially valuable in situations where the premiums are high. Basically, the clause prevents a policy from lapsing during a period in which the insured is disabled. The exact definition of disability varies from policy to policy, but generally, if the insured is unable to earn a living, the premiums will be waived until the insured returns to gainful employment. It is important to note that the policy continues in force as if the premiums had been paid by the insured, which means that the cash values continue to build and, in some circumstances, so do the death benefits.

The Least You Need to Know

No, the intention of this chapter was not to prep you for law school. But contracts are governed by law—and insurance contracts, not to mention claims, are very much in the legal environment.

➤ The insurance policy is a contract governed by the laws of the state where the insured resides.

➤ The contract is designed to protect the policyowner while still giving the insurance company the latitude to carry on a profitable business.

➤ The policy should be read for your general understanding of the concepts of insurance and to make sure you received what you applied for.

Chapter 15

The Underwriting Process

In This Chapter

➤ Understanding the underwriting process

➤ Knowing your rights in the process

➤ The insurance company's options for risks not considered standard

In Chapter 1, you learned that the term *underwriting* has several meanings within the insurance industry. In the context of this chapter, it means the process that the insurance company goes through for selecting risks acceptable to the company. At the heart of this process is an attempt to find out whether the insured is in fact insurable, and whether the applicant has an insurable interest in the insured.

The insurance company attempts to answer these two requirements through a series of information-gathering steps that the proposed insured has consented to in writing.

As with all contracts and written documents, it is important to understand what you have agreed to when you apply for insurance.

The Application

The application is the primary source of information for the life insurance company. Therefore, it is important that the application be as complete and accurate as is reasonably possible, whether it is filled out by the applicant or the agent. For some forms of insurance, such as direct mail offers, no agent will be involved.

The typical application has three parts. Part I is a general information section that requests names, dates of birth, addresses, and so on.

Part II is the medical information section. The size of the policy dictates the level of medical information required. In small life insurance policies, where the death benefit is not very large (say $100,000 or less), the company accepts questions asked by the agent or of the insured. The questions usually probe for ongoing medical problems likely to make the proposed insured an unacceptable risk. Large policies may require a medical exam by a paramedical professional or a physician. The insurance companies have become quite accommodating in this area and will usually have the medical personnel visit your home or your office.

The standard paramedic exam consists of a written medical questionnaire, a blood pressure reading, a blood test, and perhaps a urine specimen. In much larger policies, the insurance company may require an examination by a practicing physician, usually an internist. Additionally, the company may ask for an exercise electrocardiogram (EKG) and chest X rays.

Part III of the application is the Agent's Report, which includes observations and knowledge that the agent has about the insured—for example, the insured's financial condition, health habits, and character.

> **Insider Tip**
> During the application and underwriting process, you may be asked to reveal very personal information about your health, your credit history, your drinking and drug history, and avocations. Be honest without making yourself out to be a sick or a wild person. If the company finds out you are lying about your habits and history, you will find it difficult to get insurance.

Sources of Underwriting Information

There are several sources of information about you that an insurance company can call upon in order to underwrite the application for the policy.

Attending Physician's Statement

One of the forms that you sign during the application process is called the Attending Physician's Statement (APS). You are asked to authorize the insurance company to contact your personal physician and any other doctors you have consulted for information about your physical condition. You will be required to sign this form for all but *guaranteed issue* policies. If you want the coverage, you must authorize the opening of your medical records first.

> ### Jargon Alert
>
> A *guaranteed issue* policy is one that an insurance company agrees to issue to every one who meets the criteria for inclusion. For example, a company may make an offer to issue life insurance to all of the members of the AARP for up to $10,000 of life insurance, without regard to insurability. These are usually expensive contracts because they charge enough premium to every insured person to cover the high cost of those who would ordinarily be uninsurable or with health problems.

Medical Information Bureau

The Medical Information Bureau (MIB) is another potential source of information about you. At the time of the application, you should be given a form that states that the insurance company reserves the right to access a central computer bank, called the Medical Information Bureau (MIB). It collects information from your prior insurance applications. There are approximately 700 companies that are members. They have agreed to make note of medical impairments found or reported for all applicants during the underwriting process.

To protect your rights, there are strict rules regulating the use of this information:

➤ You must be informed in writing that the insurer may report your health information to the MIB.

➤ The MIB will share the information only with other insurers who are members.

➤ You must sign an authorization form so these companies can share this information.

➤ You're entitled to know what information is included in your medical file with MIB. However, the MIB will only disclose this

> **Insider Tip**
>
> OOOH...
>
> If you're ever declined for insurance for medical reasons, request that the MIB report be sent to your physician for his interpretation. It's important to remember that an insurance company's evaluation of your medical condition may be very different from your own physician's. A condition that could bar you from coverage may not alarm your physician. And the insurance company may have only made a mistake.

information to your personal physician. The rationale is that the information may well require interpretation and explanation by a qualified physician.

Special Questionnaires

Health issues are not the only ones that have a bearing on your insurability. Avocations and occupations are also relevant. For example, those on active military duty have a different risk classification than elementary school teachers; high-altitude steel workers are a higher risk than dentists. Insurance companies may request the completion of special questionnaires about your work.

The same is true of avocations, such as piloting, scuba diving, and spelunking. These can be hazardous avocations that increase mortality rates. Insurers have forms that ask for greater details when they become aware of these activities.

Inspection Reports

Large policies frequently call for even more information, and insurance companies request this information from independent investigators. You must be notified in advance of the investigation.

The interviewers will often consult neighbors, employees, and associates in order to build a profile of your character, morals, and finances.

Credit Reports

A final source of information frequently relied on by insurers is a retail credit report. Your credit may have a bearing on your insurability because poor credit risks are more apt to lapse insurance.

To protect your rights, Congress passed The Fair Credit Reporting Act of 1970. The following are the more important rights under this act:

➤ The right to be notified in writing that a report has been requested.

➤ The right to receive, if requested by you, the names of all persons contacted by the credit bureau on your behalf.

➤ The name and address of the consumer reporting agency that filed a report if you are denied insurance on the basis of the report.

➤ The right to the information in the report from the reporting agency, not the insurance company.

➤ The right to include a statement with your file disputing the reported information.

Declinations and Ratings

Sometimes, after evaluating all of the underwriting information, the insurance company decides it does not want the risk as applied for. In this situation, the company can decline the coverage in its entirety. You are then notified. If you've paid a premium with the application, it will be returned to you. Your rights to certain information involved in this decision are enumerated in the sections about medical and credit information discussed above.

But what if you die while the underwriting process is under way, and the insurance company would have turned you down given enough time? This is not just a moot question. People do die during underwriting (although not because of the process).

If you make a payment at the time of the application, the agent should give you a receipt for your payment. This receipt is called a *conditional receipt*. It is conditional because it states that the policy will be considered in force—even though not yet issued—*if* the policy would have been approved as applied for. However, if the insurance company would not have issued the policy because of medical or other reasons, no insurance is in effect, and in the event of death during underwriting, the premium deposit is returned. This is a very compelling reason to submit a premium with the application, rather than waiting for the policy to be issued.

Substandard Classifications

What if the company doesn't want the risk as applied for but will accept it on some other terms? This is not uncommon, yet it is largely misunderstood by the buying public.

Insurance companies have several alternatives to a *standard rating*. The company could rate a risk as a *preferred risk* if the insured is a better-than-average risk. Or the risk could be classified a *substandard risk* if the insured falls below the standard risk guidelines, but not so far below as to warrant a declination.

The following sections are alternate ways of classifying and issuing substandard policies. You should not interpret the term "substandard" as relating to anything other than the insurance company's perception of how you fit into its risk categories. The tendency is to take the classification emotionally, when it is strictly an objective rating without any regard to what kind of person you are.

Extra Percentage Tables

This is the most common approach to substandard underwriting. Each company applies its own standards, but the company generally assigns a numerical rating to certain conditions. These numerical ratings then are applied to the premiums charged. For

121

example, elevated blood pressure within a certain range may result in a 125 percent rating, which translates into a 125 percent premium for the same applied-for death benefit. The extra premium can go as high as 500 percent of the standard premium.

Temporary Flat Extra Premium

This approach calls for a level extra premium per thousand dollars of death benefit, on a temporary basis. The extra premium may only be charged for a fixed number of years or until the condition changes. Some cancers will not disqualify the insured for life insurance, for example, but the company may charge an extra $3.00 per thousand of death benefit for five years.

Permanent Flat Extra Premium

The insurer charges the extra premium per thousand for the life of the policy. It assumes that there will be no change in the condition that prompted the rating in the first place. Some avocations could draw an extra premium for the life of the policy or until you apply to have it removed.

Rated-Up Age

With this approach, the insurance company charges a premium at an older age, thus increasing the premium without an increase in cash values or other values. This approach is less common today.

Limited Death Benefit

This approach usually applies to a limited number of years during the early stages of the policy. Similar to a graded death benefit, the amount of insurance increases until the standard death benefit is payable. Sometimes the insurance company will only return your premium for the first three years, then it pays in full. Again, this is for conditions that insurance companies know will improve after the passage of some period of time.

The Least You Need to Know

The underwriting process is essential to good business practices by insurance companies. And while the process seems loaded in favor of the insurance company, you are not without your rights.

➤ Remember, you can be asked to reveal very personal information about yourself in the process. Don't try to hide unfavorable medical histories, dangerous sporting activities, or other information that might have a bearing on your insurability.

➤ The insurers have numerous options between acceptance and declination of the risk. They give the company flexibility to issue insurance in cases where the risk might be questionable. Remember, having needed coverage at a higher premium is preferable to no insurance.

Part 3
Disability Insurance

Disability has often been referred to as "the living death." Learn what disability can mean to you and your family, and how you can protect against the double threat of lost income and increased expenses.

There are several sources of protection against a lingering illness or long-term accidental injury. You will learn how to look for protection in the workplace first. Then you'll learn about individual protection. You'll also learn to shop for the coverage that gives you the best protection.

You'll also read about the uses of disability income insurance in business, whether it be for income replacement or to fund buy-and-sell agreements between business owners and/or key employees.

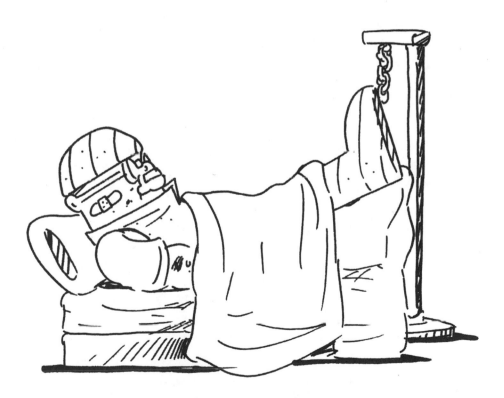

Disability Insurance— The Need for Protection

Disability is the least understood and least utilized of the major types of insurance. Similar to life insurance, it grew out of the necessities of the Industrial Revolution of the 1800s. In response to increasing accidents in the factories, disability income insurance took root in the mid 1850s. In fact, in 1847, the Massachusetts Health Insurance Company issued the first disability income policy in this country.

Workers' compensation laws were first introduced in 1911, offering job-related coverage. And in 1915, employer-provided group disability insurance was first offered.

The type of disability income policies offered today first appeared in the 1950s. These contracts have been improved over the last three decades. Still, fewer than one in every five workers in this country have long-term disability coverage.

Disability Insurance: Who Needs It?

This is not only the right question to ask, but unfortunately, it has also been the most prevalent attitude toward disability insurance. Because death is inevitable, everyone can accept the fact that sooner or later it will get us too. But deep down inside, don't you believe it will get the other guy first? No one wants to face the facts about dying. Well, if that's the way you feel about dying, imagine how most people feel about a disabling long-term sickness or accident.

This section examines the underutilization of disability income insurance and why you should consider it as an important part of your insurance program.

Bet You Didn't Know

The chances of becoming disabled for more than three months are greater than the chances of dying at every age. At age 30, the chances of disability are approximately 3.5 times greater than death. At 40, about three times greater, and at 50, two times as great.

Your Year-Long Vacation

Have you ever thought of taking a year off from work and traveling or writing or boating or whatever excites you? Why haven't you done it? If you're like most people, you haven't because you can't. Most people don't have the savings or the job security to just take a year off and play. If you can't take a year off to play, what happens if you miss a year of work because of an illness? You run a greater risk of suffering a disabling injury or sickness this year than dying. You undoubtedly carry life insurance. Why not disability insurance?

Your Most Valuable Asset

What is your most valuable asset?

If you had a machine capable of producing $30,000 or $50,000 or $100,000 a year, would you insure it against breaking down for a period of time? Naturally. You would want to guard against not only the total destruction of the machine, but also interruptions in production. And, in fact, most business owners carry insurance on their plant and machines that will replace the lost income caused by fire or flood or wind damage. These same business owners usually don't think as highly of themselves when it comes to replacing their income-producing value.

The "goose with the golden egg" analogy is a good one. You would insure a goose that produced the same income you do, wouldn't you? The fact that you haven't insured yourself probably has little to do with your preference for geese. If you're like most people, you just haven't given it serious enough thought.

The King Auto

The average household expenditure for insurance in 1993 was 6.8 percent of all household spending. Of that 6.8 percent, almost one third (or 2.2 percent) was spent on car insurance. Admittedly, many states now require insurance on your car, but the auto premium was almost twice what was spent on life insurance, and roughly four times as much as the homeowners premium.

You can dismiss the statistics as meaningless or rationalize them. But the fact remains that most of us panic at the thought of driving without car insurance, yet think nothing of working without income protection. And to make matters even more absurd, we are more concerned with the lack of coverage to replace our totaled car than the damage to others. The car is worth anywhere from one month's to six months' income. In a lifetime, you could earn enough to replace the car dozens of times over. Where should your priorities be?

You might be thinking that car insurance is required, and disability insurance is not. But this book addresses the importance of creating the best portfolio of coverage, not meeting the minimums that are mandated by the state.

The important point here is that an asset worth hundreds of thousands of dollars or more (your earned income) should have a priority greater than an asset worth $10,000–$40,000 or so (your car). Besides, if your car is stolen or damaged, it can always be replaced. You can't say the same about your income.

Bet You Didn't Know According to the Bureau of Labor Statistics, U.S. households spend 30.6 percent for housing, 15.6 percent for transportation, 14.3 percent for food, 10.5 percent for other expenses, 8.2 percent for retirement, 6.8 percent for all insurance, 5.5 percent for clothing, 5.3 percent for entertainment, and 3.2 percent for health care.

The Expense Crisscross

You suffer enough when you lose your income, but insult adds to injury in most cases because at the same time your income drops or disappears, your expenses increase, as shown in the figure below.

This crisscross chart shows decreasing income and increasing expenses after disability.

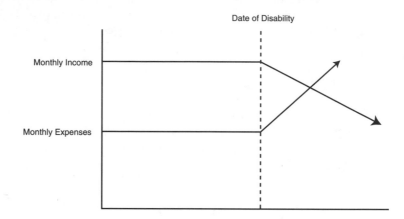

Despite the widespread coverage of health insurance, rarely will all of the medical expenses connected with a disabling injury be covered. For example, there may be additional clothing, diet, and educational expenses. With the high cost of *everything* today, it is not difficult to imagine a broader list of increased expenses.

The Alternatives to Disability Income Insurance

If you still aren't convinced of the need to consider income-replacement insurance, weigh your alternatives for dealing with the possibility of a disability.

Savings

How long could you live and pay your bills on a current basis if you relied on your savings? The first step in answering that question is to figure out your monthly expenses. If you spend everything you bring home after taxes and benefits, the calculation is easy. Otherwise, make up a budget, if you don't already have one. Use the outline suggested in Table 16.1.

Table 16.1 Household Budget Worksheet

Rent or mortgage payment	$ _____
Car payments	_____
Food	_____
Clothing	_____
Insurance premiums	_____
Utilities, including auto gas, phone	_____
Children, including tuition	_____
Debt, including credit cards	_____
Taxes, including real estate	_____
Additional expenses	_____
Total	_____

Now take your total monthly expenses and divide them into your savings. How many months can you last? Will you have to begin to deplete your retirement assets (if you're lucky enough to have any)? Most people who have adequate savings would rather protect those retirement savings dollars they worked so hard to accumulate.

Bargain Basement Sale

Another possibility would be to sell some of your assets. Your home is the first asset you might think about. But how feasible is it to sell your home under these conditions? If you need money fast, you'll be holding a fire sale. Then where will you live? You still need to pay rent and you may find your options more limited when you show no income on your housing application.

The other problem with selling your home is what you lose if the disability is not permanent. The thought of starting over is difficult for most people to face.

Charge It, Please!

Some people believe they can borrow the money they need. Either they have credit card limits most people can't get or their uncle owns the bank. Imagine yourself as a banker and a customer comes in for a loan and asks, "I'd like to open a line of credit, please?" You reply, "For how much?" "Well, I don't know exactly because I don't know how long this disability will last." "Disability?" you ask. "Yes. You see I'm out on disability and have no income and…" "No income?" you say, eyebrows arching.

You get the message. Bankers are notorious for lending when you don't need the money, not when you are at your neediest.

"I'm Covered by Workers' Compensation"

What if you're disabled in an automobile accident on the weekend? What if you contract a sickness not caused by the job (which is almost all illnesses)? You get the point.

You can't rely on a disability being job-related. To do so would be the same as having homeowners' or automobile insurance that covered damages on Monday, Wednesday, and Friday only.

"I Have Social Security"

You've got very little security if you are relying on Social Security. Forget for the moment that the monies may not be there in the future. That's a whole different issue of security. What *is* at issue is the likelihood of qualifying for benefits.

Bet You Didn't Know

In 1994, there were 42,883,000 people receiving benefits under the Old Age Survivors Disability Income (OASDI) program, affectionately known as Social Security. They received $316,835,000,000 in benefits.

Bet You Didn't Know

The maximum benefit payable in 1995 for a single disabled wage earner was $1,410.00 a month for a 25-year-old, which was scaled down to $1,219.00 a month for a 60-year-old. If the 25-year-old worker has a spouse and minor children, the benefit increases to $2,115.00 a month.

The definition of disability under the Social Security law is a total and permanent disability. That means that in order to collect any money from Social Security's disability coffers, you must be unable to engage in "any substantial gainful work which exists in the national economy." Furthermore, the disability must be a "medically determinable physical or mental impairment" that is either terminal (will likely result in death) or will last for at least 12 months. These stringent rules are in addition to having to qualify for the benefits by virtue of having worked long enough in the system, paying your share of the tab, and remaining disabled for at least five months in order to even apply.

The problem here is that if you're a manager, for example, and you suffer a disability that prevents you from supervisory work, you will be considered disabled only if you can't do anything in the job market, including janitorial work. You're not protected for your own occupation or even your own general level of achievement.

And, as you may have guessed, approval is not smooth and automatic. Approximately 70 percent of all applicants are denied coverage for Social Security disability benefits.

The Solution: Long-Term Disability Income Insurance

The solution is to rely on yourself to protect your earnings through long-term disability income insurance, often referred to as LTD coverage. The next chapter explores the coverage typically found with an employer-sponsored group disability income plan.

The Least You Need to Know

Disability has been referred to as "the living death" because it leaves your survivors in much the same position as death would, without the physical passing. Most people think they've protected themselves from illness and accident if they have adequate medical insurance, but that coverage will not replace your lost income.

➤ Disability income insurance is designed to replace your earnings. Don't overlook this protection because you believe the chances of being disabled are slim. They are higher than you think.

➤ If your budget permits only a limited expenditure for insurance of all types, you must prioritize your insurance protection. Consider the priorities using the big mistake/small mistake test.

➤ Don't rely on Social Security or workers' compensation insurance. The hurdles to qualify for this coverage are great. Find your own coverage that protects you under all circumstances.

➤ The higher your income, the greater the need for protection, especially if you consume most of your income.

➤ Check with your employer about group coverage, discussed in Chapter 17.

The Empty Pay Envelope

Disability is more likely to strike you during your working career than death itself. And yet, the vast majority of workers own life insurance and not disability insurance. The fault probably lies with the insurance industry for not educating the public. Insurance agents have targeted professionals—doctors, lawyers, and accountants—to the exclusion of the majority of Americans who need the coverage every bit as much as the higher earners.

Because disability income insurance replaces wages lost due to sickness or injury, the employer is a logical place to look for the coverage. Unfortunately, the coverage provided through the employer may be inadequate, as you'll see in this chapter.

I Gave at the Office

The first place to look for disability income coverage is through your employer. Often, an employer has a long-term disability plan as an option, but the employee looks right past the plan to other alternatives. This is especially true in groups with cafeteria plans. For those of you without a cafeteria plan, do not start your search in the company lunchroom.

A *cafeteria plan* is an employer-sponsored fringe benefit plan where the employee may select from a cafeteria-like layout of benefits. There are usually limitations as to the number of benefits and the dollar amount to be paid by the employer. The plan, for example, could offer disability income insurance, additional life insurance, dental insurance, and so on. Most employees, unaware of the need for protecting their income, will select coverage other than disability income insurance.

Most employer-sponsored disability income plans, where they exist, are group insurance plans. Group plans are usually funded by an insurance policy, although the employer may *self-insure* a portion of the benefits. For example, the employer may continue to pay disabled workers for the first 13 weeks, after which, insurance company benefits would begin. Many employee benefit plans condition eligibility on the length of time the employee has been with the company. Check the eligibility requirements carefully.

Jargon Alert
Self-insurance is funding the benefits without the help of insurance. The employer assumes the risk and responsibility without an insurance company.

The company plan could be short-term, long-term, or both. The short-term plan would provide an income for months rather than years. This is a start, but it isn't enough. If you lose $40,000 a year of income for 20 years, it won't be the loss of the *first* six months' worth that will hurt the most, but the loss of the *last* six months' worth.

Discrimination, Discrimination You Say!

Save your breath. Employer group disability income plans can discriminate in favor of the highly paid executives. As a result, most employees are not covered for long-term benefits. If there is coverage at all, it's usually short-term. If this is the case, you should seek your own coverage, dovetailed with the company plan. For example, if the company guarantees the continuation of your salary for up to six months of disability, you should find an individual policy that begins to pay benefits only after six months of disability. The six months is then your elimination period.

Don't try to buy double coverage. It usually won't work, because insurance companies usually insert a clause that coordinates benefits in such a way that you will not receive more than 100 percent of your income. This is just like the clause in health insurance policies that prevents double payments of health claims.

The *elimination period* in a disability income policy is a form of *deductible*, as in your health or auto policy. You are responsible for the expenses until the deductible threshold is reached. With disability income insurance, the deductible is expressed in time rather than dollars. As with the other deductibles, the larger the deductible, the lower the premium. Select an elimination period, if the choice is yours, to dovetail with your employer's coverage.

Typical elimination periods for group insurance are shorter than individual plans, such as 13, 26, or 52 weeks. The philosophy is to cover the employee sooner rather than later, because that is where most of the claims are, in the short-term range.

But I'm Sick, I Tell You!

It's all in the definition of disability. You don't want to end up like the occupant of the infamous grave whose marker reads "I told you I was sick." There is little consolation knowing you *are* right, that you *are* sick, but the company won't pay the benefits.

One common definition in employer-sponsored group plans is the "qualified for" definition. Under this variety, the employee is considered disabled if unable to engage in any gainful employment for which he or she is reasonably qualified based on training, experience, or education. This definition is not as severe and strict as the Social Security language introduced in Chapter 15, but it is restrictive.

The definition that provides the most protection for you is one that covers your "own" or "regular" occupation. Unfortunately, it is rarely used in long-term group plans. If you can get it without having to sacrifice all of your discretionary income to do so, then buy it. This is more like the definition used in the expensive individual disability plans.

You Mean You Don't Cover Sky Diving with Umbrellas?

Group plans do not cover every disability. Policies contain exclusions. An *exclusion* is a condition or result not covered by the contract. They are clearly spelled out in the policy or not allowed.

Typical exclusions include intentionally self-inflicted injuries, disabilities not under the care of a physician, and conditions that existed before you were eligible for the coverage. Note that the excluded self-inflicted injuries must be intentional. An injury that was the result of carelessness would be covered even though by your own hand. An example would be a gunshot wound caused by the mishandling of a handgun. You may have indeed shot yourself, but if it was not on

> **Insider Tip**
> Learn what the exclusions are under your policy before you need the benefits. If you are an avid scuba diver and will not be covered, you need to know this before you decide what to buy.

purpose, you are covered. These will be difficult questions for the insurance company. Just because you know what your intentions are does not mean the insurance company will know or agree.

What's the Formula, Professor?

It's not exactly advanced calculus, but there *is* some math involved in calculating your potential benefit under a typical employer-sponsored plan. Short-term plans, say up to 26 weeks of coverage, are usually more generous than long-term plans. The short-term plan may provide close to 100 percent of your income. However, the long-term plan will usually limit the benefit to 70 percent of your income or less. A benefit of 50 percent would be common. The idea is to discourage people from staying at home. Unfortunately, many people would do just that if they could receive as much money doing nothing as they do working. So, the reduced income is designed to encourage workers to recover and return to work.

Jargon Alert
Integration is a legal term that means that the plan's benefits are considered along with other plans so that the total benefit does not exceed your policy's limits.

Employer plans are usually *integrated* with other benefits.

For example, if your plan is integrated with Social Security and you're entitled to $3,000 a month in benefits, the insurance company will look to see what benefits are paid by Social Security before writing its check. If you're receiving $1,200 a month from them, your insurer will only pay the difference, which is $1,800 a month.

Typically, an employer-sponsored plan integrates its benefits with Social Security, workers' compensation, other insurance, and earnings from employment at that job or any other. As noted earlier, there are no double or duplicate benefits.

It's All Very Taxing, or Is It?

If your employer pays the premium, you will be taxed on the disability income payments you receive. The rationale here is that because the employer gets a tax deduction for the premium, you have taxable income.

Following this reasoning, if you paid the premiums, say by payroll deduction, then the income received under an insurance policy while disabled is not taxable income. If you paid part of the premium, a percentage of the disability payments will be tax free, on a pro rata basis.

For employees who are totally and permanently disabled, as under the Social Security test, there may also be a tax credit in the case of low-income workers. The credit calculation is beyond the scope of this book, but be aware of its existence.

OOOH... **Insider Tip**

In planning to take advantage of an employer-sponsored plan, try to select long-term disability income, if offered. If you can only select the insurance on your nickel, realize that the benefits will be received tax free in the event of your disability. Consequently, you can't tax deduct premiums you pay personally.

Not with This Job

If disability is not available with your employer, you need to look for the coverage on your own. You will have two other places to look. The first is for an individual policy. A good life underwriter should be able to show you alternatives. The second place is any association, especially a professional association, of which you are a member. Often, these career-oriented associations provide group plans for its members. The terms will most closely resemble employer-sponsored plans, but many are well designed and reasonably priced.

The variety of association plans cannot be covered here, but individual policies will be discussed in the next chapter.

The Least You Need to Know

Many employers offer disability income plans. Take advantage of them if you qualify, even if you have to participate in the premium payment. A report by the Menninger Foundation found that 9 percent of the more than 500,000 disabled workers each year will not return to work despite the availability of rehabilitation services.

➤ A long-term plan is more important than short-term coverage. While the short-term coverage is more likely to be used, the long-term coverage is more significant, because a long-term disability will more likely exhaust all of your existing assets.

➤ You need to know what is excluded before you are disabled. Do not wait until you are disabled to find out what conditions aren't covered. Plan ahead, don't just react.

➤ Even if Social Security is not bankrupt when you need it, the qualifications are so restrictive that you should not rely on it exclusively.

Chapter 18

Individual Disability Income Policies

In This Chapter

➤ How to know what is important in an individual policy

➤ Understanding the importance of the renewability provision in the contract

➤ How to read the definition of total disability and why you should ask for the best definition

➤ Why you need to have a residual disability benefit

➤ The disability income checklist and how to use it while shopping for your own coverage

Shopping for disability income insurance involves a realistic understanding of what the market offers. Unlike other forms of insurance, disability coverage is very much income- and job-classification driven. This means that different jobs carry different ratings, which translate into different benefit levels and different types of policies. But, as you read in this chapter about the variety of definitions and extras available in the contracts, remember that they will not be available to everyone.

Renewability Is Important

The issue of renewability is one of the most important in the contract you purchase. It has to do with your right to continue the policy in force under various circumstances.

Because the insurance company is assuming a potentially large liability if you're totally and permanently disabled, they want a definition that protects them as well as you.

The following sections discuss some of the renewability options you will encounter when shopping for a disability policy.

Noncancelable Policy Preferred

The best provision from your point of view is noncancelable. A *noncancelable* disability income policy can be renewed at the option of the insured at the same guaranteed premium each year. The insurance company can't cancel your insurance unless you fail to pay the premium. The insured exercises that option by paying the premium. The provision is usually applicable to renewals to age 65.

> **OOOH...**
>
> **Insider Tip**
> You want the most liberal terms for renewal you can buy. This means a provision that allows you to continue the policy in force as long as you choose with no increase in premium.

This provision is the most generous because it not only guarantees the right to continue the policy each year, but also guarantees a level premium. This is important for you because the insurer experiencing underwriting losses cannot turn to you to make up those losses. This is one of the few places in the insurance universe that you have some control over the premium.

You should be aware that disability income insurers have experienced heavy claims in recent years and many are reconsidering their involvement in the business. This usually means a change in the product offerings. Noncancelable policies are especially subject to review because of the generous benefit to the policyholder. As more and more companies try to come to grips with their unfavorable claims experience, you will find it harder to buy noncancelable policies.

Guaranteed Renewable

Guaranteed renewable disability income policies are easier for the insurance company to administer and less generous to you. The contract gives the policyholder the right to continue the policy in force until a specified time, such as to age 65. The insurance company does have the right to increase the premium. However, the insurer cannot increase *your* premium alone. The increase can't be a reaction to something you've done or said or experienced. The company must impose the rate increase on *all* of the policies that fall into the category selected for increase, such as a product type category or a category of occupations. Also, these rate increases for an entire class of policies must be approved by the insurance regulators in the various states.

> **Bet You Didn't Know**
>
> In a 1995 study performed by the Menninger Clinic and the Gallup Organization, researchers found that disabled individuals were more likely to return to work following an accident than an illness. Comparably, 68 percent returned from accidents and 56 percent returned following illnesses.
>
> *Source: 1995 Source Book of Health Insurance Data, HIAA*

The premium for the guaranteed renewable policies is up to 30 percent less expensive than noncancelable policies at the inception of the policy.

Conditionally Renewable

A third alternative is the *conditionally renewable* policy. It imposes certain conditions on renewability. Premiums may be increased or the contract canceled by the insurer. The most common condition required for renewal is employment. Under an association plan, for example, membership in the association may be a condition of renewability. This alternative is obviously less desirable than noncancelable or guaranteed renewable.

Other Developments

As insurers struggle with disability insurance claims, you'll see more innovative developments in the area of renewability. Remember that many insurance companies are trying to come to grips with huge losses suffered because of the extremely liberal concept of noncancelability.

One alternative being introduced is to offer different levels of benefits based on the degree of disability. Again, you can see how important the definitions are.

Income Replacement Policies

Another product surfacing is *income replacement*. Income replacement is *not* disability income insurance—which is not to say that income replacement is not of value in some circumstances.

Disability policies base the payment of benefits on being disabled, with heavy emphasis on the definition of disability. But income replacement policies revolve around a loss of income, presumably caused by sickness or accident. A statement of disability is not required. If the insured loses part of his or her prior income but returns to work full time, these new contracts will pay a partial benefit to encourage a speedy return. Again, this is a new development in insurance. The premiums seem to be less expensive than traditional disability insurance, but it is not as broad or liberal a coverage.

At least one state regulator has expressed concern about income replacement policies because of their lack of conformity to state requirements for disability income policies, and because of a lack of demonstration on the insurers' part that the products are properly priced.

Mean Accident or Accidental Means?

The definitions of injury and sickness are critical to the acceptability of a contract. The best definition of a covered accident or injury is one sustained while the policy is in force. This basically encompasses all accidental injuries. More restrictive language requires injury that results from *accidental means*. This refers to an injury that doesn't result from an activity knowingly entered into and hence possibly dangerous.

OOOH...

Insider Tip
Do not accept a policy with an accidental means definition, if you have any choice. You want a policy that covers all accidents and injuries sustained while the policy is in effect.

A person who races motorcycles will usually not be covered under an accidental means policy in the event of a motorcycle accident. An injured motorcyclist intended to ride the motorcycle.

Sickness should be defined as an illness that first manifests itself while the policy is in force. A sickness first *manifests itself* when it becomes known to the insured. The requirement is that the insured not be aware of the sickness or illness before the policy is applied for. Avoid policies that define a sickness or illness as a condition that exists when the policy is applied for.

Disability Defined

There are a variety of policies in the marketplace today that differ based on their definitions of disability. You may or may not qualify for all of them, but be aware of the policies that are most protective of you so you can pursue the best.

Own Occupation Policies

The most protective of your needs is the *own occupation* definition for disability. The contract requires that the insured is unable to perform the duties of his or her regular occupation.

You can easily understand the problem plaguing insurers who issued nothing but own occupation disability policies. Many professionals, such as surgeons, could suffer an illness or accident that prevents them from being surgeons—but they could still be doctors earning significant incomes. The insurance company is on the hook for the entire claim because the surgeon could not perform the duties of his specialty, surgery.

Many insurance companies compounded their own problems by making the coverage of disability for life. That meant that some who receive benefits, even though earning sizable incomes at different occupations, would continue to do so for their lifetimes. You will rarely see coverage today beyond age 65 or 70. The unfortunate reality is that lifetime coverage would be great to have under certain circumstances, but a few people who have taken advantage of the system have forced insurers to avoid the coverage altogether.

Insider Tip
If you can qualify for an *own occupation* policy and the premium is affordable, buy it. These policies will someday be extinct if the trend away from such liberal definitions continues.

OOOH...

Modified Own Occupation

Modified Own Occupation protects you for disability from your own occupation, only as long as you don't work at another occupation that is gainful or reasonable. Basically, the insurance company will pay the own occupation benefits unless you decide to work. If you do decide to work, and it is an occupation for which you are reasonably trained and experienced, the company will stop paying benefits.

OOOH... **Insider Tip**

If you can't qualify for or afford an own occupation contract, then the modified approach is the next best alternative. You might also find a contract with an own occupation definition for a limited number of years, followed by the "reasonable" and "gainful" language.

Any Gainful Work

The most restrictive definition of disability is the inability to perform the duties of any gainful occupation for which you are suited by reason of training, experience, or education. The list of jobs most people could qualify for by "training, experience, or education" is very broad and includes many jobs well below most people's current pay scales. If you have a choice, avoid a policy with this approach to disability.

What's Left Over? Residual Disability

One of the most recent and important developments in the disability field has been the introduction and expansion of the use of *residual disability*, which is a contractual promise to pay a partial benefit based on the loss of some of your prior earnings. This policy compensates you for a return to work even if it's on a limited basis. Residual disability can be sold alone or in conjunction with a total disability plan, such as a noncancelable policy.

Insider Tip

If you can buy residual disability income protection in combination with noncancelable renewal provisions, this is the best of both worlds—provided that you don't have to mortgage your home to pay the premium.

Again, the key to residual disability is a loss of income. Some policies require an inability to perform some of the duties of your occupation, while others require only that your earnings loss be at least 20 percent. Read the *specimen contract* to see what is being proposed to you.

Jargon Alert

A *specimen contract* is a sample policy of a particular coverage sold in that state by that company, except it is a copy or model of what will be sold to you. It is provided for you to read before making your decision.

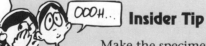 **Insider Tip**

Make the specimen contract a part of your study of the proposals for insurance. Request it if it isn't offered.

The Least You Need to Know

Disability income policies are measured by their definitions, especially in the areas of renewability, cancelability, sickness, and accidents.

➤ Buy a noncancelable policy if available. The next best alternative is guaranteed renewable.

➤ Look for a definition of a sickness as first manifested itself while the policy was in force. Avoid a requirement of accidental means.

➤ Choose as the definition of disability an inability to perform the major duties of your own occupation, if available.

➤ Opt for residual disability benefits, if available.

➤ Choose an elimination period based on the amount of savings you have on-hand. For example, if you always have enough savings to pay your expenses for three months, select a 90-day elimination period.

Chapter 19

Business Disability Insurance

In This Chapter

➤ Understanding the special problems created by the disability of a business owner or professional

➤ How to cover your business expenses when out with a disability

➤ When to insure the business against the disability of a key employee

➤ Understanding the need for an agreement for the purchase of a disabled owner's share of the business

➤ Understanding your options as a small business owner for a buyout, if you are disabled

This chapter is devoted to the small business owner, the professional with a small practice, or to employees who rely heavily on these owners. There are problems specific to this group of entrepreneurial leaders. If you are not a business owner or a professional, such as a doctor or lawyer, you will want to read this chapter anyway, especially if you work for one of these small business owners. You may have more at stake than you think.

The Entrepreneur and Risk

America encourages entrepreneurs. The American breed of free enterprise fosters a spirit of "ownership" unparalleled elsewhere in the world. This spirit of the small business may well turn out to be our most important export in the next century.

The small business owner creates, nurtures, encourages, supports, and lives the business out of a need to own and guide the destiny of his or her own career. There is great risk involved, and it extends beyond the commitments of dollars and cents. There is the risk of falling flat on one's face, unable to make the business a success. And, as it should be with any investment, the reward should be commensurate with the risk. Minimizing risk is a part of the business owner's challenge.

The rewards of owning a successful small business are many, and they are relevant to a discussion of insurance because disability threatens each of the rewards.

➤ *Freedom.* The owner is free to chart her own course in her career and business life. Freedom requires responsibility, however.

➤ *Responsibility.* The successful small business owner craves responsibility and interprets it to mean, "doing what others are unwilling to do." This is the hallmark ingredient of success.

➤ *Profits.* The small business owner gets what's left in the till after all the expenses are paid. This is only fair, because the owner pays all the bills until there's something left over.

Who's on First?

Just who is this small business owner? The answer may surprise you.

The small business owner is anyone who has a proprietary interest in a business small enough to be significantly impacted by their involvement. This involvement could be as the generator of revenues, such as a doctor, or a day-to-day operator of a retail store.

Who comes to mind? Think about the main commercial street in your home town. How about the professional office parks, the cluster of medical offices near the hospital? Is there a courthouse in your community? Are there any lawyers in the vicinity?

The list of people in any community who are truly small business owners is usually larger than you might originally think. Most professionals are included, such as doctors, lawyers, accountants, and related providers of services. There are also all those nonretail types of businesses that you don't see day to day unless you happen to be in their offices, such as consultants, shipping agents, counselors, contractors, and computer-related businesses.

Recognizing this expanded listing is important because these people have risks and exposures to disability that extend well beyond replacing personal individual income.

Back to the Golden Goose

You were asked earlier if you would insure a goose that laid solid gold eggs. Most people answer that question with a yes. And yet many of you are small business owners or professionals who have done nothing to protect the value of your business should you, the golden or potentially golden goose, suffer a long-term disability.

You read about replacing your personal income in the preceding chapters. Here is a different set of problems for you. If you're active in your business as a day-to-day manager or a professional, then your time, energy, and expertise produce revenue.

Ask yourself if your business revenue would suffer if you didn't work for the next six months. If it would, you need to consider business overhead expense insurance. If it wouldn't, you need to consider a more appropriate allocation of your time, leveraged to produce even greater revenue.

Paying the Bills with Business Overhead Expense Insurance

Business overhead expense (BOE) insurance pays the business bills when the business owner is disabled and unable to work in the business.

Just as your personal expenses continue (and frequently increase during a disability), so do your business bills. The following are expenses that are usually covered by a BOE policy:

➤ *Rent.* Most businesses have leases that extend beyond a month or two. This lease obligation is not premised on the health of the owner. BOE policies will pay the rent but often will not pay the full monthly rent bill if the business owner is the landlord.

➤ *Employee Wages.* With the owner out, paying the non-owner employees will be even more important. They'll be assuming at least some of the owner's responsibilities. Without income security, the employees could leave for other positions.

➤ *Taxes.* You just know that the IRS won't care if you're sick or out due to an accident. Taxes are still due, including income, payroll, real estate, sales, and so on. (That flat tax is beginning to sound good.)

➤ *Utilities.* The lights, telephone, heating, air conditioning, all must continue to run when you aren't around. BOE will pay these expenses.

➤ *Insurance Premiums.* I can't forget to mention this all-important category in a book about insurance and annuities. With you at home or in the hospital, the business

151

still needs property and liability coverage, autos need to be insured, health plans for the employees need to continue, and so on.

➤ *Supplies.* If the doors to your business are still open, there will still be office supplies, equipment repairs, and service fees, not to mention the continued payments for office product leases.

➤ *Janitorial Expenses.* Someone still needs to clean the joint up. You can't expect your employees to suddenly do windows just because you're out ill.

➤ *Dues and Subscriptions.* A disabled lawyer is still a member of the Bar association, and a disabled computer software designer still receives the magazines and papers as before the accident or illness.

➤ *Professional Fees.* You will still need an accountant, and you may have even *more* need for a lawyer, particularly if the disability will be long-lasting.

There may be more expenses peculiar to your business, too, but you understand the magnitude of the problem by now. Almost all of your bills will continue to come in, without regard to your presence or absence. Failure to meet these obligations could result in the closing of the business, or at least a backlog of expenses that will make it difficult to revive the business.

The solution is BOE, a policy designed to pay the bills when you can't.

BOE Policy Provisions

When you apply for BOE insurance, the insurance company asks you to itemize your current business expenses. They don't want to overinsure by issuing a policy for more than your actual expenses, and you don't want to pay the premiums that would go with excessive insurance.

Benefits

At the time of application, you apply for a specified benefit amount, stated in monthly terms. For example, you might itemize your monthly overhead as $8,500 per month. If the insurer accepts this figure, they will issue a contract to pay actual expenses up to this dollar amount each month.

What's most distinctive about BOE is the insurance company's agreement to insure 100 percent of the business expenses. With the other forms of disability protection, the insurer will only insure a percentage of the lost income.

Benefit Period

Naturally, the insurer will not insure the expenses forever.

The benefits will be paid for a shorter period than traditional disability policies: 12 to 24 months is typical. The rationale for the short period is that if the owner is to be fully disabled for more than two years, the business ownership should be restructured if possible. This means a sale or liquidation. The BOE payments will keep the creditors at bay long enough to make this a viable option.

In the prior section, you learned that actual expenses were the basis on which insurers pay benefits. Expenses can vary from month to month. This can be either because of infrequently occurring expenses such as annual dues to a professional association, or due to changes in usage, such as postage or utilities. In either case, the expenses actually reimbursed by the insurer will vary.

To overcome the problem of unused monthly benefits, insurers agree to pay the expenses "up to" the monthly benefit amount each month and to accumulate unused benefits for future use, even beyond the stated benefit period. Therefore, if your policy is for $10,000 per month for 18 months, you are entitled to $180,000 in benefits, assuming the owner is still disabled, even if it takes 20 months to use up the full amount.

> **Bet You Didn't Know**
> The Health Insurance Association of America reports in its 1995 *Source Book* that the Menninger Foundation's research shows that 48 percent of the more than 569,000 workers who become disabled each year will return to work without rehabilitation. However, 9 percent will not return at all.

The Elimination Period

Just as with the benefit period, the elimination period is short. Again, the elimination period is a form of deductible, a period of time of disability before benefits begin under the policy. Insurers offer 30-, 60-, and 90-day periods. Your choice should depend on the amount of cash flow the business will have to pay in expenses until insurance picks up the tab. If there is very little excess in the till at the end of each month, choose a shorter elimination period.

Your decision may also be impacted by the difference in premium. The shorter the elimination period, the higher the premium. However, the differences will not be as significant as with some other forms of disability coverage.

Renewability

Read the renewability provision in the proposal. What you want is a policy that is guaranteed renewable to age 65 or longer. This means you can continue the contract in force without an increase in premiums until that time.

Less than Total Disability

Most BOE policies will make some provision for a return to work on a less than full-time basis. This makes sense (and cents) because it's in the insurer's and insured's best interests to encourage a return to full capacity. Insurers who make no allowance for the gradual return of the disabled owner will encourage the owner to remain at home until benefits will not be compromised by the return.

Insider Tip
Choose a policy that encourages your return to work by gradually decreasing your coverage during the transition.

Other Provisions

There will be other provisions that can enhance the policy, but the basics have been covered. Make certain you understand any additional benefits and features of the proposed BOE policy, especially if there's an extra premium attributable to the coverage. Be slow to add extra benefits without really understanding the charge for the extras.

Non-Owners' Concerns

What if you aren't an owner, but you rely heavily on the owner and his involvement in the business for your future? If your future depends on a small business owner or professional, you should ask what provision has been made for the payment of business expenses, such as your salary, if the owner does suffer a disability. Without such coverage, long-standing employees will have to go to work for someone else rather than wait without pay for the boss to recuperate.

If you're the owner, you should think about the possibility of your best people going to a competitor because you can't pay their salaries while you're not working. This is especially the case with professional practices, such as law and medicine.

Key Employee Disability Insurance

Another problem for your business is the loss of revenue and profits if you lose the services of a *key employee* due to sickness or accident. The fact that you may not know when or even whether the key person will return makes the problem more difficult to solve.

Jargon Alert

A *key employee* is someone who is important to the overall productivity and profitability of your company. Loss of the services of a key person, whether by death or disability, usually impacts the bottom line of the business. A replacement can be found and trained, often at a higher cost, but this takes time.

The key employee may be your top salesperson, a critical manager, or hold some other position crucial to the success of your business. The knowledge this person has is almost irreplaceable, even if the person is not.

It's often difficult enough to continue paying this person income during a disability—out of revenues this person is not contributing to any more—but the drain on the business can be even greater if, for example, you need to hire one or more people to take up the slack. A company disability income plan would help by paying the key employee during the disability.

You should protect yourself and any key employees against disabling accidents and illnesses. The time period for the coverage should be relatively short, such as several months. This should be long enough to overcome the blow to the business and make adjustments in key personnel.

Disability Buy and Sell Insurance

The final business need covered in this chapter is the problem of how to deal with the disabled owner when there is more than one owner. As the business owner confronted with the problem of a disabled co-owner, ask yourself the following questions:

➤ Should a disabled and nonproducing owner share equally in the profitability of the business?

➤ Would you object to sharing the decision-making responsibilities with someone inactive in the business?

➤ Would you object to dealing with your co-owner's spouse on the management of the business?

If you're beginning to be uneasy about the direction of these questions, you're paying attention.

The Buy and Sell Agreement

In any business with more than one owner, the question of the sale of an owner's interest should be addressed before the need arises. The preferred way to do this is to draft and adopt a buy and sell agreement. The primary problem to resolve in the agreement is the right or obligation to sell an interest in a closely held business upon the death, disability, retirement, or termination of an owner. If you leave this question open until the triggering event occurs, you almost always end up in a painful dispute over one or more of the following issues:

➤ *The obligation to sell an interest.* The working owners will ultimately want the business to be owned by the ones active in the day-to-day operations. The disabled owner may want to hang on to the interest, as may the heirs of a deceased owner. This puts the old owners in the unenviable position of sharing profits and responsibilities with neophytes.

➤ *The price of the departing owner's interest.* This is the cause of the more well-known squabbles over ownership. The remaining owners want the interest at bargain prices, while the departing owner or the heirs want an inflated value.

➤ *The management of the business.* The representatives of the departing owner may want to run the business very differently than the active owners.

As you can see, there are compelling reasons for an agreement executed in advance that addresses each of these critical areas.

You can purchase disability buy and sell insurance to fund an agreement already in effect. The provisions of the contracts differ from personal disability insurance. They're explained in the following sections.

Extent of Benefits

The agreement should state an agreed-upon value of the business, at least for disability purposes. This makes it possible to insure that amount with certainty.

The insurance company will usually insure 100 percent of the agreed-upon value. Remember that individual disability insurance for income replacement will only insure a percentage of the lost income. Why the difference? In the case of individual insurance, the insurer is trying to encourage the individual to return to work to avoid malingering. That is not an objective in buy and sell situations because the insurer is obligated to pay the full sum upon the triggering of the benefit.

Elimination Period

The elimination period is longer than other disability policies, typically 12 months or longer. This allows ample time for a determination that the disability will be of a long enough duration to warrant triggering the buyout provisions of the agreement and, consequently, the benefits in the policy. You don't want an agreement that makes a buyout mandatory if the disabled co-owner will be able to return after a short time away from the business.

Benefit Payout

The most common payout is *lump sum*. This means that at the end of the elimination period, if the disabled owner is still disabled, the insurance company will pay the full benefit to the company so that it may in turn disburse the benefits under the agreement.

Payment could be made lump sum to the business, which could pay out the agreed-upon sum in installments. Or the business could opt to have the insurer convert the lump sum payment into installments, based on the agreement or by consent of the parties.

Jargon Alert
A *lump sum* refers to the payment of all benefits in one payment to the beneficiary. This is in contrast to payment of the benefits in *installments* or in smaller, time-separated amounts.

Professional Advice

Buy and sell agreements are legal documents, and they should be prepared by lawyers. Many insurance companies provide specimen documents to be used by your attorney. Don't be tempted to save the legal fees by copying the agreement and adopting it without a review. There are important tax considerations involved, and the cost of messing up those aspects will be far more costly than the attorney's fees.

The Least You Need to Know

There are several important business uses of disability income insurance above and beyond the replacement of the disabled worker's income. They are most appropriate for small business owners and professionals.

➤ If your business needs your involvement to help produce revenue, protect the business with business overhead expense (BOE) insurance.

➤ Design the BOE policy around your business' cash flow and reserves. If your business runs hand-to-mouth each month, select a shorter elimination period.

➤ If you have key employees who would be difficult and expensive to replace, consider key employee disability insurance to protect the business for their lost services during disability.

➤ If your business has more than one owner and they're active in the management and day to day operations, adopt a buy and sell agreement in writing that spells out the terms of a buyout in the event of death, disability, retirement, or termination of an active owner.

Part 4
Health Insurance

Most people are very aware of the need for adequate protection against the increasing expenses of medical services. And yet, there are 40 million Americans without health insurance. The uninsured are not just the poor. You need to know why it is important to protect against escalating health care costs.

The latest trend in health insurance is called managed care. Is it just a fad, or should you be looking for the latest alternative to traditional health insurance? And if you are considering managed care, just what is it that you should be looking for? What are some of the resources you can call on to make sure your choices are the best for you?

And what about the government programs? Are you covered by Medicare? Medicaid? And does government coverage mean you can abandon your personal policy?

A tremendous new area of insurance protection has been the increasing availability of long-term care insurance. Your chances of a long life are greater than ever. That's the good news. The bad news is the increasing likelihood of a need for nursing home care. Find out the myths and realities of long-term care alternatives.

Chapter 20

The High Cost of Health Care

In This Chapter

➤ The history of health insurance in this country

➤ Understanding the high cost of health care today

➤ How much of the burden of paying for health care you should be willing to accept

➤ Protecting yourself against the crippling expenses of health care—and the rhetoric of politicians

Never in the history of health insurance in this country has the issue of affordable care been more acute. Health care reform surfaces, sinks, and resurfaces like a drowning swimmer in the surf. We watch hopelessly from the shore as dozens of lifeguards fight among themselves to see who will attempt the rescue. The sight is discouraging.

It's the History Professor Again

The health insurance industry began in this country in 1847 with a medical care policy issued by the Massachusetts Health Insurance Company of Boston. In 1850, the first accidental bodily injury policy was issued by the Franklin Health Assurance Company of Massachusetts. The Travelers Insurance Company of Hartford offered medical expense insurance a decade later. The idea was so popular that over 60 health insurance companies offered similar policies by the end of the 1860s.

A gradual acceptance of the concept of insuring against accidental injuries led insurers to expand coverage to include disability in the late 1890s; they expanded to include surgical expense benefits after the turn of the century. By the 1920s, competitive pressures led the health insurance industry to expand benefits beyond a point that could be supported by the statistics and experiences of the industry. The excesses caused a subsequent pullback of benefits and coverage. This point is important because many insurers claim to be threatened with the same overexposure today.

Health insurance boomed again in the 1940s. The emergence of Blue Cross/Blue Shield plans spurred the expansion. Coverage become so widespread that Congress believed it to be a "birthright" for citizens over 65 years of age. Congress enacted the Medicare and Medicaid programs in 1966. In three short decades, the country dug a financial hole for itself that it can scarcely get out of, and you are at the center of the controversy, regardless of your age.

If you feel lost in the midst of the jungle of rhetoric, then you're part of the majority. The steamrollers that the various drivers in this "debate" are riding are threatening to flatten the very constituents they promised to represent. But this isn't a political treatise. It's a book written to help you help yourself. And there is no area where this is more critical than the health care area. Unfortunately, you cannot ignore the political and historical perspective any more than you can ignore current trends and present costs. They're part of the whole.

Statistics to Get Sick By

The most pressing problem in health care is rising costs. The statistics here help explain that problem.

➤ In 1972, the per capita expenditure for health care in this country was $387. In 1993, each American spent an average of $3,294 for health care. The figure is expected to be $5,712 by the end of the 1990s.

➤ In that same period from 1972 to 1993, health expenditures grew from 7.7 percent of the GNP to 13.9 percent. By the year 2000, the expenditures are projected to be 16.4 percent of GNP.

➤ From 1984 to the present, physician fees increased an average of 6.5 percent per year. The Consumer Price Index increased at a rate of only 3.7 percent during the same period. This is the same story for most health care expenses. They're rising faster than inflation.

➤ In 1993, a day in a community hospital averaged $880.52 per patient. Some states were more expensive than others. California was the most expensive in 1993, averaging $1,220.54 per patient per day.

➤ In 1993, the U.S. spent more than all other developed nations per capita for medical care, at $3,294 per person. And the rate of increase in expenses is likewise the highest among industrialized countries.

➤ More than 40 million Americans out of 260 million are without health care coverage. Of these uninsured, 12 million are children. Not everyone who is uninsured is considered lower-income. Many people who are uninsured simply gamble that they won't get sick or have an accident.

The most prevalent conclusion is that the system is broken.

The Current Situation—Rising Costs

Statistics can only tell part of the story, even if presented accurately and fairly. The conclusion reached by the Health Insurance Association of America is that rising health costs are *the* paramount problem in America today. In the 1995 *Source Book of Health Insurance Data*, they attributed the rising costs to three factors:

➤ Because coverage is so widespread, expectations and demand are great and increasing.

➤ Insureds are encouraged to over-utilize the system, while disregarding cost consciousness and accepting mediocre and marginal care.

➤ Technological advancements have improved quality, but often at a tremendous increase in the cost of treatment.

Potential Solutions

The response to the seemingly irreversible trend of rapidly rising costs has been threefold:

➤ A movement toward managed care, such as HMOs.

➤ A focused effort on prevention.

➤ Greater monitoring of claims and services.

What, then, are the implications for you?

Your health care costs are likely to continue to escalate no matter what you do. The trend toward a higher per capita outlay for health care is not likely to reverse itself overnight. This doesn't mean that you should do nothing.

Prevention

In the long run, you might be able to help your own cause most significantly by initiating preventive measures on your own or with the help of professionals. The Health Insurance Association of America reports that estimates of the dollars spent on health care that are due to "unhealthy lifestyles" is $188 billion. That's over 20 percent of the $884 billion Americans spent in 1993 for health care, research, and construction of health facilities.

Included in this category are alcohol abuse, drug abuse, smoking, unsafe sex, and the failure to properly use seat belts. If you find your behavior on this list, there's something you can do—and you already know what it is. What you might not know is how. The place to start may be your health insurance company.

> **WOW!** **Bet You Didn't Know**
>
> Alcohol abuse is a major problem in this country. It's measurable in a number of ways, including the burden on the health care delivery system. The American Medical Association believes that between 25 and 40 percent of all patients in hospital beds are there for alcohol-related problems.

Table 20.1 shows what percentage of health insurers offered specialized "wellness" programs, as of 1993.

Table 20.1 Insurers Offering Wellness Programs

Wellness Program	Percentage of Insurers Who Offer Program
Smoking cessation program	98%
Stress management program	97%
Hypertension screening	91%
Exercise/fitness program	91%
Alcohol/drug abuse program	87%
Periodic health exam	85%
AIDS education program	82%
Cancer risk reduction	71%
Prenatal maternity program	49%
Nutrition program	48%

Source: Health Insurance Association of America, Source Book of Health Insurance Data 1995

Monitoring Claims and Services

The industry regards wellness programs as one of their primary prongs of attack on rising health care costs, and to a lesser extent, it should be a concern of yours. There are a number of practical steps you can take to make your moral contribution, and at the same time even decrease your financial contribution.

First, check your bills for accuracy. The number and dollar amount of errors in billings must be staggering if the complaints of consumers are any indication. The problem is that insureds tend to gloss over bills because the insurance company is responsible for the payment. The company often pays submitted bills without challenging any expenses unless they're unreasonable. But a reasonable charge will often be paid even though it wasn't warranted.

Second, shop around for services when allowed by your insurance policy, particularly with elective procedures, such as cosmetic surgery. The weight of the charges doesn't necessarily signify the credentials of the provider.

Third, complain when you aren't getting the service and charges you're entitled to. Squeaking wheels often get better service.

What's Really at Stake in the Public Debate

Are health claims that are the result of nausea from listening to politicians covered under health plans? If they are, it will make it easier to drop in and out of the debate between the various interest groups.

Here's a summary of the current state of the debate over health care reform:

➤ The issues are real.

➤ The philosophical differences are great.

➤ The dollars at stake are enormous.

➤ The health of millions of uninsured Americans is in the balance.

➤ The quality of the health care you receive is an issue.

➤ The cost of health care for all Americans is at issue, and you're one of the people being proposed to foot the bill.

➤ There are no easy solutions.

This incomplete and abbreviated list illustrates why health care reform efforts are important to you. Join in however you see fit, or forever hold your piece of the bill.

The Future...

None of us has the right crystal ball to predict the future of health care. There's so much to be hopeful about on the technological front; however, the price tag for such innovation may be too great for us to assume.

The Least You Need to Know

The state of health care in this country has never been better for many Americans. Technological innovations and improved facilities have given great hope to millions of those with the insurance and private resources to demand the best services. For 40 million others, however, the health care system spells despair as they face rejection and frustration trying to receive care without money or insurance.

➤ Accept the fact that health care expenses will increase for you and your family before they decrease.

➤ Treat your health insurance as you would any other valuable asset.

➤ Be proactive in eliminating or reducing your unhealthy lifestyle choices. Join programs encouraged by insurers if necessary.

➤ Don't take the debate over health care reform lightly. You have a great deal at stake.

Traditional Health Insurance

Traditional health insurance is slowly becoming not-so-traditional. With the rapid growth of alternative coverage, traditional coverage is shrinking. But for tens of millions of Americans, it remains the best or only alternative.

Traditional health insurance includes the following plans:

➤ Hospital/medical expense insurance

➤ Major medical insurance

➤ Dental expense insurance

These policies will be explained in this chapter.

Private Insurance

One of the largest insurance groups is commercial insurance companies. They provide private insurance through numerous channels and vehicles. Without trying to make this sound too simplistic, insurers are in business to provide protection for a profit. Insurance companies are not charitable organizations. Anyone who has had to file extensive claims knows that. Understanding that fact makes it easier to work with them.

In 1993, according to the *1995 Source Book* of the Health Insurance Association of America, private health insurers paid $254 billion in claims for medical care and disability. Of this staggering total, $104 billion was paid by commercial insurance companies. It was one percent less than the amount paid the year before.

Besides commercial insurance companies, there are also the Blue Cross/Blue Shield companies. While they are not for profit, they are not charitable in the sense of giving away benefits. In 1993, the Blues paid $62 billion in benefits, roughly 60 percent of the amount paid by commercial carriers.

Private insurance also encompasses the HMOs and the self-insured plans. Their share of the benefits paid in 1993 was $144.7 billion.

Bet You Didn't Know

WOW!

The number of persons with private insurance in 1993 can be divided as follows:

Total covered by group insurance	$80.9 million
Total covered by individual plans	$7.4 million
Total covered by Blue Cross/Blue Shield	$65.9 million
Total self-insured and HMOs	$105.7 million

These numbers can include individuals and families covered by multiple plans, so there is some duplication.

The relevance of the number of persons covered by type of private insurer appears in Table 21.1, which compares the distribution of persons with private insurance in 1990 and 1993.

Table 21.1 Distribution of Persons with Private Insurance in 1990 and 1993 (in millions)

Type of Insurer	1990	1993
Insurance companies (net)	83.1	74.7
Group insurance	88.7	80.9
Individual	10.2	7.4
Blue Cross/Blue Shield	70.9	65.9
Self-insured	49.7	60.5
HMOs	36.5	45.2
Blue Cross/Blue Shield	1.6	6.7
Insurance companies	5.4	6.5
Other	26.5	32.0

Source: Health Insurance Association Of America, Source Book of Health Insurance Data, 1995.

What can you learn from this table? For one thing, there's a movement away from traditional health insurance policies toward managed care. This is true at both the employer group level and at the individual policyowner level. Does this mean you should rush out and trade your health insurance policy for a managed care policy? No. This is a trend, not a stampede.

Do-It-Yourself Insurance

Some of the most significant growth has been in the area of *self-insurance*. This does not refer to the 40 million people in this country who are uninsured. There's a difference between self-insured and uninsured.

The growth in self-insurance from 50 to 60 billion, when group health insurance dropped from almost 89 million to 81 million, is a fair indicator where the new growth is coming from. Obviously, more and more employers are choosing to assume the liability of paying claims themselves. This is, in fact, what a self-insured group does. It provides an insurance plan and a policy. The terms of the plan may be identical to the coverage provided

Jargon Alert
Self-insurance is actually a program of insurance without an insurance company. It just happens to fund benefits through the policyholder, from the entity's own cash flow or cash reserves. It's usually found in large employer groups where the law of big numbers can operate to make claims predictable. It eliminates much of the cost of administration of the plan.

by a major insurance company. The policy contains less mandatory insurance company language, but it outlines the coverage and terms—just like a policy from a commercial carrier. The only difference is that an insurance company does insure the claims exposure, or at least most of the exposure. However, an employer may use an insurance company to protect against catastrophic claims, and it may use the insurer to administer the plan.

Having discussed the state of the industry briefly, you can get a feel for what is happening and why. This doesn't mean you can change it, but you need to do what's in your best interest and understand the critical issues in health care today. It's your health and your wallet that are at risk.

Bet You Didn't Know

Actually, the types of coverage enumerated in this chapter could be provided without an insurance company; you could provide them with self-insurance. In an earlier chapter you were introduced to self-insurance, a growing employer-sponsored alternative whereby companies pool their payments to share risks. In Chapter 23, you'll read about self-insured health plans.

Typically, the description of the covered expenses reads just like a traditional insurance contract. The only difference is that an employer or organization—rather than an insurance company—guarantees the payment of the benefits.

Hospital/Medical Expense Insurance

For decades, hospitalization insurance was the primary form of health insurance in this country. It reimburses the insured for expenses incurred during a hospital stay, which commonly includes room, board, and the expected services and supplies accompanying hospitalization.

For complete coverage, the basic hospital plan is augmented with physician/surgeon expense coverage, which is called medical expense insurance. The resulting combination is a plan that covers most of the charges incurred in or out of a hospital.

This combination of hospital and medical expense insurance was originally referred to as *first dollar coverage* because the insurance company actually paid from the first dollar of expenses. This approach has lost popularity with insurers in favor of *coinsurance* and *deductibles*. Both were introduced to limit overutilization of health insurance coverage by requiring the insured to share the expenses. It's frightening to imagine what costs could have been today without deductibles and coinsurance.

Jargon Alert

Coinsurance is the sharing of medical expenses between the insurance company and the insured. The contract specifies the percentage to be paid by each party, up to certain limits, beyond which the insurance company assumes the entire responsibility for payment. A *deductible* is the amount of a claim that the insured pays before the insurance company assumes part or all of the claim.

Hospital Expenses

The hospitalization portion of this traditional combination pays the daily room and board charges of the hospital. Under a hospital reimbursement form of contract, the policy specifies a maximum daily dollar benefit and a maximum number of days for each separate illness or accident.

The traditional hospital reimbursement policy will also have a provision for miscellaneous hospital expenses. Remember that the room and board charges are just part of your bill in a hospital. There will be charges for supplies, medications, diagnostic tests and exams, telephone and television, and so on.

Hospitalization may also be provided by service benefit plans, such as those found with Blue Cross plans. The "Blues" were early entrants into the health care industry and were responsible for much of the development of widespread coverage through employer and association group health plans.

Under the Blue Cross plan, the insured stays in member hospitals or facilities, and the prices for room, board, and other expenses are already agreed upon between Blue Cross and the hospital. This contractual arrangement was a precursor to current contractual plans.

Insider Tip
When buying hospitalization insurance, make sure the daily hospital room and board limit is at least high enough to pay for the average semiprivate room in your area. And make sure the total number of days allowed is liberal, such as 120 or 365 days.

Bet You Didn't Know

Blue Cross/Blue Shield plans are private health insurance plans that are administered by state or regional nonprofit organizations. The first such plan was in Baylor Hospital in Dallas, Texas, in 1929, where schoolteachers organized and negotiated with the hospital for a set price for room and board and related services for a fixed cost. The parent organization is the Blue Cross/Blue Shield Association.

The nonprofit structure of Blue Cross/Blue Shield is changing like everything else in the health care field. Private insurers are now buying "Blues."

Medical Expense Insurance

The medical expense portion of the policy covers your appointments with your doctor or your doctor's visit to see you. For those of you under the age of 40, I need to explain that once there was a custom in this country called a *house call*. As humorous as it sounds, the doctor actually *came to your home*. That was in the old days when doctors were not preoccupied with being efficient businesspeople. Today, a doctor may visit you in the hospital, and traditional medical expense insurance covers that visit up to a specified dollar limit.

Hospital Indemnity Insurance

This is less conventional coverage and of more limited value. The policy pays a flat dollar amount to the insured for each day hospitalized. The problem is that expenses will often exceed the flat dollar amount. Some policies will pay the claims only if the hospitalization is caused by an accident.

This is too restrictive to be effective hospitalization coverage and should be purchased only if you cannot afford traditional coverage.

Surgical Expense Insurance

Again, surgical expense insurance supplements the basic package of medical/hospital insurance. Typically, the surgical benefits are *scheduled benefits*.

The schedule will state the dollar amount it is willing to pay for each procedure. For example, a gall bladder removal benefit might be $1,100. The company will pay up to, but not more than, this amount for a normal removal.

Jargon Alert

Scheduled benefits are benefits under a health insurance plan that are paid according to a published schedule. The schedule should be a part of the contract and should be updated when necessary by the insurer. The purpose of the schedule is to limit the amount paid for a particular type of procedure to an amount the insurer considers reasonable.

Surgical expenses are paid under the Blue Shield portion of Blue Cross/Blue Shield plans. While these plans used scheduled benefits in older contracts, most Blue Shield plans now cover charges that are "usual, customary, and reasonable." Blue Shield is the final arbiter on what is considered to fit under this definition.

Insider Tip
Make sure the schedule is up to date and reasonable in your geographic area. You may find this information by calling the area hospitals for their fee schedules.

Major Medical Insurance

In response to escalating health care costs and the burden of claims paperwork, insurers introduced major medical insurance. It provides coverage under one roof for all manner of health expenses. Simplicity of design is the hallmark of these plans. High overall coverage limits is its second most distinguishing characteristic.

Unlike hospital/medical expense contracts, major medical plans cover all of the expenses of a sickness or accident, in or out of the hospital, under one policy.

A Picture Is Worth a Thousand...

If you were to show the policy graphically, it would resemble the graph in the following figure.

The major medical model, with a deductible, coinsurance, and high policy limits.

$ Maximum

100% INSURANCE COMPANY PAYS

COINSURANCE 20% YOU PAY	COINSURANCE 80% INSURANCE COMPANY PAYS

DEDUCTIBLE (YOU PAY)

$ 0

Now Deduct a Little Bit More

You'll notice that at the bottom of the above figure, which is the first dollar of medical expense, there is a deductible. Most major medical plans start with a deductible of $100, $250, or even higher, at your option. Remember, the deductible helps to keep the cost of the plan down because you're accepting responsibility for the most frequent charges—those under the deductible limit.

A larger deductible (lower premium) can make it possible to increase your overall limits of coverage. The top limits will be more important. Remember the big mistake/small mistake test. The difference between a $100 and $200 deductible is far less important than the difference between $50,000 and $1,000,000 of total coverage.

Now You Can Share

After the deductible is satisfied, you'll begin to share the expenses with the insurance company. This is the coinsurance portion previously defined. Most major medical plans coinsure on an 80/20 basis. This means that for each dollar above the deductible, the insurance company pays 80 cents and you pay 20 cents. Now this is beginning to look a little better.

But if you have a really large bill, this could still bury you. For example, assume you have a $10,000 hospital bill, covering surgery, room and board, and the television for a six-day stay. (If there is no television on your bill, you'll notice the hospital charges you for room and *bored* instead.)

174

If you had a major medical plan with a $100 deductible, the math would look like this:

Total Hospital Charges	10,000
Minus Your Deductible	– 100
Equals Charges After Deductible	9,900
Charges After Deductible	9,900
Times Your Share Of Coinsurance	× .20
Equals Your Co-Pay Expenses	1,980
Your Co-Pay Expenses	1,980
Plus Your Deductible	+ 100
Equals Your Total Out-of-Pocket Expense	2,080

You can see from this example that this type of coverage could leave you responsible for some serious money. That is what the term "out-of-pocket" is meant to convey—out of *your* pocket. And while $2,080 out of $10,000 may sound acceptable, how would you feel about a $50,000 bill? Now your out-of-pocket is $10,080, assuming the same $100 deductible. This is really serious money.

Stop the Loss!

Exactly. The insurance company will put a limit on your total exposure under the policy. To put it another way, they will limit your out-of-pocket expenses. The provision is called a *stop loss* clause.

A typical stop loss might be $1,000 per family member, with a maximum of $2,000 per family. What does this mean? It means that in any calendar year, you will pay no more than $1,000 for any family member, regardless of the size of the bill. Further, you will pay no more than $2,000 in expenses for your entire family's bills.

Jargon Alert
A *stop loss* provision puts a limit on the amount of money a policyowner will have to pay out for any one continuous claim. The loss is stated either on a per-claim or per-calendar-year basis. The latter is more common.

OOOH... **Insider Tip**

Stop loss is a very important provision in any major medical policy. You must know the stop loss terms before you buy the policy. If the stop loss is too high, you should create an emergency fund to meet just such an attack on your cash. Put the money in a quality interest-bearing account, such as a money market fund or short-term CDs.

Take It to the Limit

The next characteristic of major medical is the "major" part, the upper limits on the coverage. While most hospitalization and surgical policies cover the claim, up to the scheduled amount, including certain incidentals, the total dollar amount is not necessarily high. Major medical, on the other hand, meets the challenge of providing enough protection to cover the possibility of the huge claims. It is typical to have a major medical maximum of $1,000,000.

Do people actually have claims that run this high? Yes. But most insureds would be destitute long before the bill hit this plateau. Return to the idea expressed earlier, that with a large claim like $100,000, it's not the first $10,000 that ruins you, but the last $10,000.

Make sure your major medical policy has a large maximum—at least $250,000—but $1,000,000 is even more realistic today. Note that the maximum is usually a *lifetime maximum*.

Jargon Alert

The maximums can be *lifetime* or *per cause*. The former is more prevalent today and guarantees your coverage up to the maximum during the lifetime of the insured on a cumulative basis. If you have more than one illness, they're added together to arrive at the maximum. The *per cause* approach starts the calculation anew with each separate illness. The limits are higher overall with the lifetime maximum.

Is Your Major Medical Comprehensive?

Let's face it: You wouldn't admit that it wasn't, would you?

Jargon Alert
A *comprehensive* major medical plan is a stand-alone major medical and is most common with group insurance today.

Well, the term *comprehensive* has a special meaning in this arena. It refers to a health insurance policy that is designed to cover all of your medical expenses under a single policy. The major medical described earlier frequently is layered on top of a hospitalization policy, for example.

You'll usually be better off if you can buy a comprehensive major medical, an entire health insurance plan under one contract. This will have the advantage of being simpler to understand, making it easier to keep track of where you stand at all times. It will also mean that you have just one insurance company to deal with. Insurance is an area where the old KISS concept is valid (Keep It Simple, Stupid).

Dental Insurance

Dental insurance is an area you should become familiar with if you can obtain the coverage through an employer group or an association. Group dental insurance is especially valuable when you have children who are in and out of the dentist's and orthodontist's office every few months.

The range of plans is very broad, but a few generalities can be made. First, there is a great emphasis placed on preventive care. Even more so than most areas of general medicine, there is a great advantage to preventive maintenance with dental plans. Regular exams and cleanings will prevent larger problems later, and you'll be rewarded under most plans if you follow a schedule of regular visits. Second, the typical plan will pay most of the cost of routine dental visits and procedures, 80 to 100 percent, depending on the procedure and the reasonableness of the charges. Third, if you have children with the threat of braces just ahead of college tuition, then dental insurance could save you a bundle.

OOOH... **Insider Tip**

The availability of dental insurance outside the workplace is limited. Try to insure through your job first, then the outside marketplace. And if you're going to look outside the group plan, check and double-check the rates. Go back several years and see how much you actually spent on dental bills, noting what would have been covered if the insurance had been in effect and how much you would have paid in premiums.

The Least You Need to Know

Traditional health insurance is almost an evolving concept, because what was traditional yesterday is slowly being replaced with managed care (covered in the next chapter). However, many Americans still have basic hospitalization and medical expense coverage and/or major medical.

➤ You need to check the coverage under your policy or policies to make sure they're still reasonable. Health care costs are accelerating too quickly to rely on older policy limits.

➤ Choose comprehensive major medical over a combination of policies. It will be easier to understand and keep track of.

➤ Choose deductibles and coinsurance provisions that are consistent with your ability to absorb medical expenses on your own. If need be, run a worst-case hypothetical claim, using the approach outlined in this chapter.

➤ Consider dental insurance if available through a group plan, especially if you have school-age children.

Chapter 22

Managed Care

In This Chapter

➤ Understanding the concept of managed care

➤ The fundamentals of a Health Maintenance Organization (HMO) plan

➤ Differences between traditional insurance and an HMO

➤ Understanding the Preferred Provider Organizations (PPO) approach to health care

➤ Understanding Point-of-Source (POS) plans and how they function

According to many critics, *managed care* is a much-needed revolution sweeping American health care. To others, it represents a failure in health care cost containment. Whether it will be judged a success or a failure remains to be seen. But almost everyone agrees that something needed to be done to try to curb medical and insurance expenses.

Jargon Alert

Managed care is the term given to a range of health care alternatives that focus on services rendered to covered individuals under a contractual agreement with the providers. There are usually financial incentives for all parties to lower costs. The plans ideally have strict guidelines for physicians, facilities, and other health services providers. They also should have strict review procedures.

Of the more than 200 million Americans with health coverage, about half are covered by managed care plans. The trend is toward greater participation, so if you aren't already enrolled in one of these plans, chances are you'll have the opportunity to enroll in the future.

Health Maintenance Organizations (HMOs)

HMOs are not as new as you might think. They actually started in the 1930s as prepaid group practices. The plans then focused on a geographic area and a target population for enrollment. These characteristics have remained a part of the HMO.

Congress gave the concept a boost in 1973 when it passed the HMO Act aimed at helping to fund new HMOs. Federally qualified HMOs were established and became an important option for employers in geographic areas serviced by the local HMOs. As surprising as it may seem, the federal government actually wrote detailed guidelines for an HMO to qualify. The programs did in fact catch the attention of employers and the public, and their growth has been significant.

Some of the more enlightening statistics from the Health Insurance Association of America include:

➤ In the early 1970s, there were 25 HMOs nationwide. Today there are approximately 575.

➤ HMOs have enrolled approximately 20 percent of the U.S. population. Seventeen states have more than 20 percent of their populations in HMOs. California leads the states, with just under 40 percent of its population enrolled in HMOs.

➤ Only Alaska, West Virginia, and Wyoming were without at least one HMO in 1994.

➤ In 1994, there were 87 HMOs with more than 100,000 members each. This large enrollment group was one of the fastest-growing segments of HMOs and, in fact, accounted for 16 percent of all HMOs.

➤ The total number of HMO-insured individuals has grown from 19 million in 1985 to 56 million in 1995.

➤ Insurance companies realized the importance of HMOs and decided to join rather than fight the trend. Insurers now develop their own HMOs.

Types of HMOs

Since the first prepaid group practices, the HMO has evolved into several forms of business:

➤ *Group Practice*. This is exemplified by a physician group contracting with the organization doing the enrollment and administration. There's usually a per capita payment to the physician group. This per capita means that the group receives a flat payment for each enrollee.

➤ *Staff*. The HMO hires the physicians as employees of the HMO and pays them a salary to care for members.

➤ *Network*. The networking approach is similar to the group practice except that there are many groups providing services for a negotiated fee per participant.

➤ *Independent Practice*. This is a plan of individual physicians contracting to provide services at negotiated rates in the physicians' own offices.

➤ *Combinations*. As the growth of HMOs continues, newer and more innovative combinations of the types of arrangements emerge.

This distribution of HMOs among the various types listed above is shown in Table 22.1.

Table 22.1 Percentage of Types of HMOs in the Country in 1995

Type of HMO	Percentage of all HMOs
Group Practice	7.3 percent
Staff	4.6 percent
Network	8.4 percent
Independent Practice	52.9 percent
Combinations	22.0 percent
Other	4.8 percent

Source: Health Insurance Association of America, Source Book of Health Insurance Data, 1995

How an HMO Works

An HMO provides all or almost all of the medical care for the year to covered individuals for a flat fee each month. Usually, the benefits are provided at no additional cost to the participant, although there could be a small charge for a doctor visit (such as $1 to $10). You use the physicians that are affiliated with the HMO only. Visits to doctors not a part of the HMO group are not covered at all under most plans.

Table 22.2   The Most Common Types of Cost Control Used by HMOs in 1994

Type of Cost Control	Percentage of HMOs
Home health care	97.1 percent
Preventive health	90.2 percent
Preferred provider negotiations	83.6 percent

Source: Health Insurance Association of America, Source Book of Health Insurance Data, 1995

The HMO is able to offer such coverage because of its negotiated fee schedule with the providers. The small fee for some of the services, for example, a $10 prescription fee, can be viewed as a form of deductible.

As a rule, an HMO premium will be less than personal traditional insurance. Occasionally, however, the premium for an HMO plan will be a little higher than individual or family insurance coverage. The justification given is more inclusive coverage, which may or may not be the case, and the lower "out-of-pocket" expenditures. But costs to the insured are currently becoming lower and lower due to the large number of competitors in the health care arena. This should continue as the large number of competing HMOs and other providers bang heads in the war to woo your business. The competitive pricing will not last forever and may be different from region to region.

Another trend is consolidation of health organizations, whether it's HMOs merging with HMOs, HMOs being purchased by insurance companies, or insurance companies merging with insurance companies. There are analysts who believe that when the consolidation phase of this industry is complete, there will only be a handful of players and they'll be huge. This could bring an end to any really competitive pricing.

Seniors in HMOs

The number of Medicare and Medicaid enrollees who are joining HMOs is dramatic. In 1993, there were 2.1 million Medicaid enrollees. The number jumped to 2.7 million in 1994. The number of Medicare enrollees also jumped, from 2.7 to 2.9 million. This is a healthy trend, no pun intended, because it means the government programs will not be used as exclusive underwriters of health expenses.

Preferred Provider Organizations

A preferred provider organization (PPO) is another form of managed care. It's designed to allow the members more latitude in choosing the providers they want to treat them.

The focus of the PPO is similar to the HMO—negotiated fees are lower than the market in general. The PPO contracts with a broader range of providers, but the fees are still negotiated for the members.

Watch Out!

Most PPOs allow enrollees to receive services from providers who are not a part of their system. (In other words, they are not one of the network's "preferred providers.") However, there's usually a cost for doing so. They may impose a large deductible before outsider service fees are paid, or they may require a larger co-payment from the member. If you're in a PPO or are considering one, make sure you understand this provision before your first visit to an outside physician.

To put the PPOs in perspective as to utilization, according to the AMCRA Foundation, Inc., as reported in the Health Insurance Association of America *1995 Source Book*, there were 1,107 PPOs in operation in 1994. They covered more than 45 million employees.

Table 22.3   The Enrollment and Number of PPOs in Leading States in 1994

State	Number of PPOs	Millions Enrolled	Percent of Population
California	84	7.3	23.4
Texas	67	5.2	28.7
Florida	78	3.0	22.2
Illinois	50	2.9	24.4
Ohio	47	2.2	19.7
Colorado	33	1.8	50.9
Pennsylvania	56	1.7	13.8
Tennessee	37	1.6	31.8

Source: Health Insurance Association of America, Source Book of Health Insurance Data, 1995

Watch Out!

Another form of PPO is the exclusive provider organization (EPO). EPOs can be very costly because they're all-or-nothing plans, meaning the enrollee will only be reimbursed for approved and affiliated physicians and facilities. If you go outside the system, you pay 100 percent of the bills. Avoid this type of plan if at all possible.

Point of Service Plans (POS)

Point of Service (POS) plans look like HMOs and PPOs. The distinguishing characteristic of the plans, however, is the designation of a *primary care physician*. This designated physician is the referral source for all your other medical professionals.

Jargon Alert
A *primary care physician* is the contact person and physician who will be responsible for the enrollee. Matters beyond the expertise of the primary physician are referred to other specialists. If you don't go through the primary care physician for a referral, you'll pay a higher percentage or even the total amount of the cost of treatment.

The employee selects a primary care physician from the list of practitioners that are acceptable to the plan administrators. The problem with this approach is that if you're in a small geographic area, the choice of primary physicians may be very restricted or nonexistent. If you don't like that physician, you're stuck with a deductible and possibly a higher co-payment percentage as well.

There are approximately 120 POS plans in the country now. Their availability is narrower than either HMOs or PPOs. It is likely that they will continue to grow in popularity. Some of the larger insurance companies are offering these plans and are committed to their growth.

Choosing a Managed Care Plan

Are headaches that are caused by shopping for a managed care plan considered covered expenses? That may be the question of the hour if you've ever tried to gather information about and choose from the available plans in your area. Be advised that the process can be very difficult, time-consuming, and frustrating.

How to Gather Information

If you're going through your employer, ask for the marketing information from each of the plans made available through the company. Ask other employees about their experience. If you're shopping on your own, get out the telephone book and a legal pad. You may be inundated by the marketing departments of the various plans or insurers. But you need to go through it all if you truly want to study the options.

Before making comparisons, however, make a list of features or benefits that are important to you. Realize that you probably won't use the right terms and will not understand all the contractual options, but you know more than you think you do about what your needs are compared to someone else in the same position.

Some of the questions you should ask yourself are:

➤ How much can I afford out-of-pocket each year? Can I afford to self-insure certain coverage?

➤ How important is the cost, the monthly premium? Obviously everyone wants the best price, but if you're severely restricted in the amount you can pay, this is important.

➤ How important is the accessibility of the providers? This is a question of time and of distance. Some of the providers may not be close to your home. Will this matter to you?

➤ Does a possibility of a time delay in seeing the physician cause you concern? One of the most common complaints about managed care is the difficulty getting in to see providers in a timely manner.

➤ Is it important to you to have freedom of choice in selecting your physician and other service providers? Managed care can severely restrict your choice of practitioners, unless you foot the bill.

➤ Is preventive care encouraged by the plan: Does it pay for routine and regular exams? This should interest almost everyone.

➤ How important is coverage of lifestyle-related conditions, such as smoking, drinking, and so on? If it is important, how liberal is the coverage for help in dealing with these problems?

➤ How important is it to you to know about the physician's background? Are you willing to spend the time that will be necessary to ferret out the facts?

➤ Are dental benefits important?

➤ Is prescription drug coverage important?

These questions are just a starting point for you. Expand or shorten the list based on your situation and your experiences in the past. Educate yourself throughout the process. Go easy on yourself during the analysis because the process is tedious.

Obstacles to Overcome

There are several problem areas you may encounter in shopping for the right managed care plan. Some have no easy solution, but the assumption is that if you're aware of the problem, you have a better chance of resolving it than if you're blind to its existence.

The Wrong Information

When you call various managed care plans for information, you may find that there's a wealth of information, but that it isn't what you need to make a reasoned decision. To begin with, no two plans are likely to offer the same benefits and features. Therefore, a true cost comparison is impossible. None of the insurers or managed care plans will segregate the various provisions by cost, either. So you never really can compare apples and apples.

Also, you need to realize that the plan will send you the information it wants you to have. They're in the business of sales—selling the prospective enrollee on their plan. So you'll receive information designed to sell you on the plan. That in turn means that they'll highlight what they do well and obfuscate their weaknesses. You must learn to read between the sales hype and find what you believe to be most important, based on the list you made earlier.

Lack of Standards to Judge Quality of Physicians

Many Americans choose family physicians based on reputation and referral from friends and neighbors, often after painstaking research. But the old network doesn't always cover the physicians in managed care. And trying to get information about a managed care physician can be like trying to get Princess Di's phone number.

Some information is available if you ask, however. For example, because you may have a need for specialists, you'll want to know how many and who in the approved group are Board Certified. A physician becomes "Board Certified" through advanced training and the recommendation of experts in order to specialize in a field.

Lack of Reports from Participants

There's a serious lack of information from participants in the various plans as to their satisfaction. But in this area, at least, there is a trend toward more information. One organization in particular, the National Committee for Quality Assurance, has an accreditation process and guidelines for selecting a plan. Another organization, Health Pages Magazine, has created report cards for many managed care providers in major metropolitan markets.

Where to Write for Help

These resources will give you more information than you will want, but in the midst of all that data, there's probably a rationale for selecting one of the plans offered in your area over all the others. Just remember, this isn't an easy process.

The National Committee for Quality Assurance

2000 L Street, NW.
Suite 500
Washington, DC 20036
Phone: (202) 955-3515
World Wide Web: http://www.ncqa.org

This organization is the first place to go in seeking information about a managed care company. They survey plan participants, study the plan's operations, and follow up with the state insurance commissioners as part of a process of accreditation for the plan. If the plan does receive their accreditation, it may be used in the promotion efforts of the plan sponsor. The National Committee for Quality Assurance will answer inquiries about a particular institution's accreditation. However, they will not discuss reasons for a lack of accreditation. They also provide a booklet on how to select a plan.

Health Pages Magazine

135 Fifth Avenue
New York, NY 10010

This magazine has designed a report card for managed care providers and institutions on a regional basis. Not all plans are covered yet, but the major metropolitan areas are especially well-covered. The report cards are published in the regional issues. If you have difficulty obtaining the magazine at the library, write to the magazine and request the specific report on the plans in the area of your interest.

State Insurance Commissioner

See the Appendix for the state insurance commissioner's office for your state. If you're in a metropolitan area such as the tri-state area of New York, New Jersey, and Connecticut, contact all three. The commissioner's office may have generic information on the managed care business and will have statistics on the number of complaints filed by participants. Remember that this is a state agency empowered to help you, so take advantage of their resources.

The Center for the Study of Services

733 15th Street, NW.
Washington, DC 20005

The Center for the Study of Services has *The Consumer's Guide to Health Plans* for $12.00. It's a survey of thousands of federal employees taken in 1994. This survey should help you formulate the types of questions that will be helpful in making your list of priorities.

The Least You Need to Know

The trend in recent decades has been toward managed care, in a variety of forms ranging from HMOs to PPOs and POS plans. All aim and claim to benefit you and the industry by containing costs and monitoring performance. On the drawing board, they all look great. In reality, managed care has created a whole new set of problems.

➤ Strongly weigh the available managed care alternatives in your area against traditional insurance coverage. Compare the coverage as well as the premium.

➤ Make a list of concerns and priorities before making your decision. Each person's needs may differ. Choose the plan that most thoroughly gives you what you want and need.

➤ Call, write, or surf the Net for the information you need to make your analysis. There are no clear guidelines for choosing between options, but an informed decision should be better than a stab in the dark.

Chapter 23

Reading the Health Care Contract

In This Chapter

➤ Who the important parties to the contract are

➤ The most important provisions in any health policy

➤ Understanding the claims procedure

This chapter looks at the typical provisions in a health care policy. Several decades ago, this would have been a *section* of a chapter, and the subject matter would have covered a health insurance policy. Today, you have choices that include health insurance and managed care alternatives, Medigap, and long-term care insurance. (Medigap is covered in Chapter 24, long-term care in Chapter 25.)

Because of the many options, there may be some overlapping of provisions and some that are unique. Some are mentioned in the chapters on the policy types, such as long-term care. The important point is to understand these provisions and how they're used in your quest for adequate protection.

Key Provisions in Your Contract

The provisions in this section may have been introduced in an earlier chapter or will be in a later chapter. But they are important enough to mention again in this discussion of the important parts of your policy.

Pre-existing Conditions

Possibly no provision in a health insurance policy has ever created more confusion and ill will than the *pre-existing condition clause*. This clause was introduced by insurance companies to attempt to limit their exposure to *adverse selection* by insureds, which is what happens when too many people with health problems sign up for insurance.

Many health insurance policies that have this type of clause won't cover the pre-existing conditions. Most health insurance policies define a pre-existing condition as any condition that you saw a physician about within the six months before the effective date of the new coverage. This is different from the Medigap policies discussed in the chapter on Medicare. Medigap policies must cover pre-existing conditions after six months of being insured under the new policy. Some group plans state they will cover pre-existing conditions after one year without treatment. There are several variations possible.

Jargon Alert

Pre-existing conditions are health conditions, either physical or mental, that exist prior to the date that insurance coverage becomes effective. The insured may or may not be required to know of their existence at the time of application. Prospective insureds who know of a health problem will tend to seek insurance to protect themselves. This is known as *adverse selection*.

Always find out what the pre-existing condition provision is in any policy you apply for, whether individually or through a group. In some cases, if there is a time limit on the condition, you may want to continue your present policy until the pre-existing conditions are all covered. This is obviously a judgment decision on your part, which is greatly influenced by your knowledge of current health problems.

Insider Tip

Read the plan proposal or Outline of Coverage *before* you cancel your old insurance. Be wary of replacing an old policy without exclusions for pre-existing conditions for a new policy with the exclusion. Shop around for a plan that will cover pre-existing conditions under the most advantageous terms for you, based on your needs.

Coordination of Benefits

The *coordination of benefits* clause is designed to prevent the insured from profiting from an accident or illness. It states that if the insured has coverage under more than one policy, all policies will be considered in the payment of the claim. The typical clause also seeks to establish a priority among the policies. No, there is not a presumption of wrong-doing or sleight-of-hand at work here. Most insurers realize that people usually have multiple policies because of the increasing existence of two-earner families, each party with fringe benefits.

OOOH... Insider Tip

There's little you can do to negotiate around the coordination of benefits provision, assuming you would even want to. However, realizing that two policies covering the same insureds will not pay double benefits, you should review the policies with an eye toward reducing your premiums. Perhaps you could change the benefits under the secondary policy to cover the truly cata-strophic claim, and use the primary policy to take care of more predictable expenses.

Coinsurance, Copayments, Elimination Periods, and Deductibles

Each of the following devices is an attempt by the insurer to cut costs—theirs and yours. By agreeing not to cover first-dollar expenses, the insurer avoids many small claims that are both expensive to administer and troublesome to pay. Most medical expenses are not large. By assuming them yourself, you can save the insurer claims, and they in turn should save you premium.

OOOH... Insider Tip

Study your policy carefully for opportunities to reduce the premium cost to you. A few ways to do this are to accept higher deductibles, longer elimination periods, and higher co-insurance participation with your dollars. If you're in a position to have a cash reserve for emergencies at all times, then take advantage of these vehicles.

Maximum Benefits

The maximum benefits under your policy are of great importance because of the stagger-ing cost of some medical procedures and treatments today. It is not uncommon today to see bills exceeding $100,000 for ongoing treatments for a single injury or illness. This kind of medical expense will bankrupt most people. Again, employing the big mistake/small mistake test, it would be a big mistake not to have protection on the upper end of a large health claim. If you need to increase your deductible in order to afford a $250,000 or $1,000,000 maximum benefit, it is almost always advisable. Be sure to consider whether the maximum bought is *per cause* or *lifetime*. A lifetime benefit will have to be higher than a per cause, because it aggregates all of your clauses, from more than one injury or accident, to arrive at the maximum benefit.

> OOOH... **Insider Tip**
>
> With the potential for outrageous bills today, cover yourself for the catastrophic claim and the long run. Hospitals today are filled with machinery designed to keep you alive in conditions many would hardly consider living. This isn't to downplay the value of technology, or the tremendous abilities in modern medicine to prolong life. The advancements are truly incredible. Also, review your will planning, making sure you have addressed the issue of being kept alive with life support systems.

Assignment of Benefits

Most policies allow the assignment of benefits directly to a provider. You must sign a form authorizing the assignment. It is usually provided to you by your physician or at the office, and the company knows to pay the claim to the provider. The benefit to you may not be obvious, but the assignment takes you out of the loop for payment. If the provider is organized and the insurance company is timely in paying claims, it works to your advantage. However, if the process doesn't work like clockwork, you aren't relieved of the responsibility for the payment to the provider.

> OOOH... **Insider Tip**
>
> Research the claims-paying history of the insurer, whether it's an insurance company, your employer under a self-insured plan, or a managed care provider. You can do this by contacting the Insurance Commissioner's office in your state to see how many complaints are filed, compared to other insurers. There are plenty of horror stories of families relying on HMOs and insurers only to be dunned and harassed by credit agencies because the insurer paid slowly or not at all. Do your homework before you buy.

Reasonable and Customary Charges

Most policies promise to pay *reasonable and customary* charges. These are charges that satisfy both criteria: reasonableness and custom. A charge could be reasonable but higher than customary, or customary but not at all reasonable. One company defines the term as the lowest of three charges:

➤ The usual charge by the provider or other providers for the same service

➤ The usual charge of other providers in the same geographic area for the same services

➤ The actual charge

This is not the only definition you may encounter, but it is illustrative of how an insurance company approaches the fairness of charges under your policy.

Insider Tip
Read the clause that provides the basis for acceptability of claims. If the clause does not have a "reasonable and customary" definition, find out if it is more restrictive. If it is, shop around for a better policy. If you can't, make sure you are using physicians and facilities the insurer finds to be most often acceptable.

Renewability

You saw the issue of renewability in the section on Disability Income contracts in Chapter 18. But the issue can also arise in individual health insurance policies and long-term care contracts. Here are the options:

➤ *Noncancelable and guaranteed renewable.* The policy cannot be canceled by the insurance company *and* the premium cannot be raised. This is the most generous to you.

➤ *Guaranteed renewable.* The policy owner has a contractual right to renew the policy, but the insurer may increase the premiums on all like policies as a class.

➤ *Conditionally renewable.* The insurer has the option to cancel all policies of that type or to not renew in particular areas.

➤ *Optionally renewable.* This provides little protection to the insured. The insurance company decides whether to renew.

Insider Tip
Buy non-cancelable, guaranteed renewable policies if available. Avoid conditionally and optionally renewable policies.

This by no means exhausts the provisions in a typical health insurance policy. However, these are the provisions that can have the most impact on your satisfaction with the policy.

The Least You Need to Know

The range of organizations and the plans they offer have expanded significantly in the last decade. The trend is toward managed health care, at the expense of traditional health insurance. More choices means more homework.

➤ Shop for the coverage you need, and be firm in your resolve to find what's best for you. Avoid pressure sales practices. Don't be afraid to call your state Insurance Commissioner if you're being pressured and harassed.

➤ Replace existing coverage with great caution and high standards. Make absolutely certain the proposed insurance plan is better than your new coverage.

➤ Be careful not to buy duplicate coverage. It will not pay for you, because health insurance policies coordinate the benefits under multiple policies to protect against overpayment of claims.

Medicare, Medicaid, and Medigap

Any discussion of health insurance should include the federal, state, and local programs—as well as the new rules for insurance to supplement those programs. According to the Health Care Financing Administration (HCFA), government spent almost $400 billion in 1993 to fund health care services, research projects, and the construction of medical facilities. It was reported in the 1995 *Source Book of Health Insurance Data* of the Health Insurance Association of America that this $400 billion figure represents close to 44 percent of the total health expenditures in this country. The HCFA estimates that government expenditures will almost double by the end of the century—that is, will be $700 billion by the year 2000. That level of funding deserves some mention.

Medicare

Medicare is a federal health insurance program. It was created in 1965 and became effective in July 1966. Medicare provides hospitalization and medical insurance to several distinct groups of people:

➤ Persons age 65 and older

➤ Disabled persons under age 65 who receive benefits from the Social Security program or the Railroad Retirement program

➤ Persons with chronic kidney disease

➤ Aliens (no, not from outer space), for a monthly premium

➤ Some federal civil service employees, for a monthly premium

There are two parts to Medicare: Part A for hospitalization and confinement coverage, and Part B for physician and other services.

Part A: Compulsory Hospitalization Insurance (HI)

The Hospitalization Insurance (HI) portion of Medicare is funded by the private sector: employers, employees, and participants. The federal employer payroll tax is used to collect the funds from the contributors.

The benefits under Part A are hospitalization, skilled nursing home care, home health care services, and hospice care.

Inpatient Hospital Care Benefit

The hospitalization benefit includes semiprivate room and board, lab tests, x rays, and ordinary nursing expenses, equipment, and drugs. The plan pays the bills in full for 60 days after satisfaction of the deductible. In 1996, the deductible was $736. The deductible is subject to increase to keep track with rises in health care costs, as determined by the government. There is only one deductible per calendar year or per illness.

Again, the Medicare payment is 100 percent of the expenses after the deductible, for up to 60 days. On the 61st day, there is a coinsurance requirement of $184 per day through the 90th day. If you use all of your 90 days in a row, you may dip into a lifetime reserve bank of 60 days. There is a coinsurance payment of $368 per day for the reserve days. Remember, there are 60 reserve days in your lifetime, not each year or illness benefit period.

There are four conditions in order to qualify for the HI benefit:

➤ The physician must prescribe a hospital confinement as the appropriate care for your condition.

➤ The condition must be such that only hospital confinement will answer the problem.

➤ The hospital must be a part of the Medicare system.

➤ The appropriate review committee of the hospital must not consider the hospitalization as unnecessary.

Inpatient Skilled Nursing Facility Care

The skilled nursing home benefits provide coverage for up to 100 days in any calendar year. The important word here is "skilled." This coverage was not intended to be for custodial type care, where the treatment does not require skilled nursing care. The benefit was introduced to pay for skilled care. Most nursing benefits are not skilled benefits.

There are five requirements that must be met for someone to collect these benefits:

➤ The medical condition must require inpatient skilled nursing care.

➤ The insured must have been hospitalized for three consecutive days, not counting the discharge day.

➤ The insured must be admitted to the skilled nursing home within a short time after the hospitalization. This is usually interpreted to mean within 30 days.

➤ The condition that prompts the nursing home stay must be one that was treated during the hospitalization.

➤ The physician must certify the treatment to the facility.

Medicare will pay 100 percent of the covered expenses during the first 20 days. Then, from the 21st to the 100th day, the insured's co-payment is $92 a day. Expenses covered include a semiprivate room with board, nursing, supplies, and drugs.

Home Health Care Benefit

The third coverage is home health care. It can only come into play after a hospitalization of at least three days, and it must be prescribed by a physician. Medicare will pay for

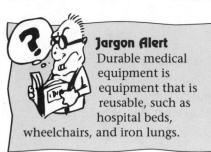

intermittent skilled nursing care, medical aide services, durable equipment, and supplies. The length of using the home health care benefit can be indefinite, but it is limited to four hours a day, seven days a week. The home health care coverage is the same under Parts A and B of Medicare.

There are four conditions to payment under Medicare:

➤ The care must include intermittent skilled nursing care, physical therapy, or speech therapy.

➤ The insured must be confined to home.

➤ The insured must be under the care of a physician who prescribes the home care.

➤ The provider agency must participate in the Medicare program.

All of the home health care costs are covered 100 percent of the approved amount, except for a 20 percent coinsur-ance requirement for durable medical equipment.

Hospice Care

Hospice care services are provided to the terminally ill. The services must be for pain relief, symptom management, or support. The services covered include intermittent skilled care, home health aide services, supplies, and durable equipment. The insurance pays all but limited amounts for outpatient drugs and for inpatient respite care. Respite care allows for the family caring for the terminally ill to get assistance from outside the home hospice workers on a temporary basis.

The three conditions for coverage are:

➤ The physician must diagnose the patient as terminally ill.

➤ The patient must opt for hospice care rather than the standard Medicare benefits.

➤ The care must be provided by a participating entity.

Part B: Medical Insurance

Part B is elective coverage. You're automatically covered when you come under the umbrella of Medicare, at 65 or whenever. The coverage can, however, be waived by the insured. If not waived, the enrollee must pay $42.50 per month. With the expenses that are covered, you pay a $100 deductible, then 20 percent of the approved amount. For most outpatient mental health services, the coinsurance increases to 50 percent.

The medical expenses covered include physician's services, inpatient and outpatient surgical services, physical and speech therapy, and durable equipment. Outpatient hospital services are also covered, as are home health care services.

Bet You Didn't Know

WOW!

The total enrollment in Medicare increased by approximately 700,000 people to a total of more than 36.9 million people from 1993 to 1994. Medicare spending that same year increased by 11.5 percent, with the federal government spending almost $160 billion on behalf of the participants. Approximately 30 percent of that figure was attributable to care for the elderly during their last year of life.

Claims and Appeals

The claims procedure under Medicare is designed to put the burden on the provider to process the paperwork. They are to submit claims directly to Medicare. The patient is not allowed to submit claims for hospitalization. The hospital is supposed to bill the patient for deductibles and coinsurance amounts.

Claims under the medical insurance part of Medicare are also the responsibility of the provider. Appeal procedures exist for claims denied by Medicare. There are offices called Peer Review Organizations (PRO) in each state.

Insider Tip

OOOH...

The provider is not allowed to require deposits before admitting a patient for inpatient care that is or may be covered under HI. A provider may ask you for one, however. Pay a deposit only if you are able and willing. Do not allow any provider to push you financially.

Insider Tip

OOOH...

For an outstanding description of benefits and administrative guidelines, order *All About Medicare '96 Edition*. This guide book is published by The National Underwriter Company, Department 2-EX, 505 Gest Street, Cincinnati, OH 45203-1716. The phone number is (800) 543-0874.

Medicaid

Medicaid is a national program of medical assistance for low income families. It is a joint program between the federal government and your state government. Federal law and accompanying regulations require basic services that must be a part of each state's program. These services are:

WOW! **Bet You Didn't Know** Of the 40 million people eligible for Medicaid in 1994, 95 percent, or 38.1 million, received some benefit. The total amount paid out was $107.9 billion. This represented a 6.1 percent increase in outlays over 1993. (Health Insurance Association of America.)

➤ Inpatient hospital services

➤ Outpatient hospital services

➤ Physician's services

➤ X rays and lab services

➤ Skilled nursing care

➤ Home health care services

➤ Family planning services for children under 21

➤ Mid-wife services

➤ Prenatal care and pediatric and family nurse practitioners

The federal law does not require states to participate, but all 50 do. One of the reasons that participation is at 100 percent is that each state sets its own rules for eligibility. The differences from state to state can be quite wide.

The Entitlement Debate

Unless you go out of your way to avoid the news, you're aware that the expenditures for Medicare and Medicaid are growing rapidly and that with much gnashing of teeth and spewing of rhetoric, Congress is trying to muster up the courage to address these emotionally charged issues. It is not my intention to join the debate, at least not in this book. But you should get facts from *someone*, because the facts appear to have escaped Congress.

In the fall of 1992, the Health Care Financing Agency of the U.S. Department of Health and Human Services made their projections of the total expenditures projected on Medicare and Medicaid for the year 2000. While this information, shown in Table 24.1, does not provide a solution, it certainly screams out the problem.

Table 24.1 Comparison of Actual Expenditures in 1991 and Projected in 2000 in Billions of Dollars

Expenditures	Medicare		Medicaid	
	1991	2000	1991	2000
Services/supplies	122.9	327.6	98.2	359.8
Hospital care	74.3	191.0	40.6	162.1
Physician services	33.9	104.1	6.7	24.9
Other professional services	3.5	9.0	2.8	12.5
Home health care	3.6	9.0	2.6	15.8
Drugs/medicine nondurable	N/A		6.1	19.5
Vision/medicine durable	2.4	5.8	N/A	
Nursing home care	2.6	4.4	28.7	72.1
Other personal	N/A		5.7	39.2
Administration	2.6	4.3	4.2	11.2

Source: Health Insurance Association of America, Source Book of Health Insurance Data, 1995

The bottom line from the study shown in Table 24.1 is that unless there are some changes made in the ways Medicare and Medicaid are designed and funded, expenditures are expected to jump from less than $250 billion in 1991 to $675 billion in the year 2000. This represents an increase of 270 percent in less than a decade.

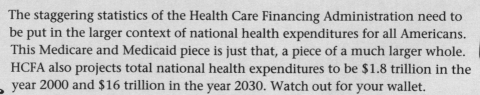

Watch Out!

The staggering statistics of the Health Care Financing Administration need to be put in the larger context of national health expenditures for all Americans. This Medicare and Medicaid piece is just that, a piece of a much larger whole. HCFA also projects total national health expenditures to be $1.8 trillion in the year 2000 and $16 trillion in the year 2030. Watch out for your wallet.

Medigap Insurance

Medigap insurance is private health insurance sold by private insurance companies as a *supplement* to Medicare. It is not a substitute. It dovetails with Medicare to cover the deductibles and coinsurance portions of the federal plan, as well as certain other non-covered expenses.

While the policies are private, Congress dictated the terms of the policies that could be offered. The states have followed up by prescribing the number of policies that can be offered. Most states now limit the offerings of private insurers to 10 policies.

Required Benefits

All Medigap policies must contain the following minimum benefits:

➤ Hospital Insurance (HI) coinsurance from the 61st to the 90th day under Part A of Medicare.

➤ HI coinsurance for the 91st through the 150th day in the hospital.

➤ Hospital insurance protection for an additional 365 days.

➤ The deductible for the cost of the first three pints of blood under both Parts A and B.

➤ Part B coinsurance, the 20 percent payable by the participant.

Variable Medigap Benefits

Additional benefits can be offered in addition to the required benefits itemized in the previous section. The inclusion or exclusion of some or all of these benefits is what makes the difference in the ten plans sanctioned by most states:

Insider Tip
While the policy forms are standard in each insurance company, don't assume that the premiums are the same. They aren't. Shop around with the major insurance companies that offer the coverage. Buy what you need—not what the salesperson wants you to buy.

➤ The deductible for the HI benefit of currently $736

➤ The coinsurance amount under the skilled nursing facility benefit, currently $92 a day

➤ The Part B deductible of $100

➤ 80 percent of the billing covered by the Medical Insurance benefit that is not paid because the physician does not accept assignments from Medicare

➤ 100 percent of the same billing as above

➤ 50 percent of the outpatient drug costs, with a $250 deductible and a maximum of $1,250 annually

➤ 50 percent of the outpatient drug costs, with a $250 deductible and a $3,000 annual limit

➤ Emergency care covering 80 percent of costs while traveling outside the U.S.

➤ Preventive measures and screening expenses up to $120

➤ Short term, assisted living benefits up to $1,600 each year

The combination of these core benefits required by law and the 10 additional benefits allowed by law make up the 10 policies creatively named A through J.

Open Enrollment

There's an open enrollment period for Medigap insurance. This means that for six months following your eligibility for Medicare Medical Insurance, Part B, you cannot be refused Medigap coverage or charged a higher rate because of your health history or problems.

OOOH... **Insider Tip**

When you're approaching age 65, or when you qualify for Part B coverage under Medicare, shop for a Medigap policy. Do not wait until it's too late. Your insurability is protected for only that first six months.

Medicare SELECT

Congress enacted a special policy to supplement Medicare in 1994 called Medicare SELECT. The plan was experimental in 15 states and now has been expanded to all 50 states. The program is still subject to a "clean bill of health" from the Department of Health and Human Services and will remain experimental (a demonstration program) until June 30, 1998, subject to the Department's approval.

The policy is designed to coordinate with a Medicare HMO. The policy limits Medigap benefits to the services of specified health care providers. It is designed to complement HMOs and other managed care providers. The attraction should be a lower premium.

If you can afford the more expanded version of Medigap policies, this will probably make better sense until the experimental Medicare SELECT plan is certified workable in 1998.

Duplicate Benefits

The primary reason the federal government got involved in the design of the core and supplemental policy forms was the insurance industry's inability to police itself in the area of duplicate benefits. Overzealous agents selling Medicare supplement policies (Medigap) were adding two, three, or more policies together when insurance companies would never pay more than the basic policy. It was the older insureds who were being taken advantage of—when they're most vulnerable.

Watch Out!

In response to the sale of duplicate policies, Congress passed the 10 policy scenario. But they also made serious penalties for overselling duplicate benefits. If you find you have been sold or are being encouraged to buy duplicate benefits, call 1-800-638-6833. This will put you in touch with the right governmental agency to discuss the possible illegal sales practices.

The Least You Need to Know

The Medicare and Medicaid programs are available to all Americans to help meet the rising costs of hospitalization and medical expenses. The programs are a great start, and, if you're in a position to afford the expanded coverage of Medigap plans, you should do so.

➤ Learn the essentials of Medicare before you become eligible.

➤ Study the 10 policy alternatives to see which best meets your needs. Then, shop for the best premium with a reputable insurance company.

➤ Be wary of duplicating benefits. There are steep penalties for offering such overlapping coverage, but sales are sales, and insurance companies are rarely intimidated into doing the right thing for the customer.

Chapter 25

Long-Term Care Insurance

In This Chapter

➤ What the risk of long-term care is today

➤ Understanding the place for long-term care insurance in your insurance program

➤ What the different coverage options are

➤ Understanding important policy provisions

➤ When to buy long-term care and for what amount

The popularity of long-term care insurance is a recent phenomenon; it arose just in the last decade. The range of possible coverage from the 188 insurance companies offering the product in 1994 were broad and widely priced. The Health Insurance Association of America estimates that there were 3.4 million long-term care (LTC) policies in existence by the close of 1993. Their records also indicate that almost 1,000 employers were offering the coverage to their employees in 1993.

Long-term care refers to custodial and maintenance services for the chronically ill and the disabled. It includes inpatient and outpatient services, typically in a nursing home, hospitals, or at home. Long-term care insurance is designed to pay these medical/health-related expenses. In this chapter, you'll learn more about the product and its appropriate use.

Who Needs Long-Term Care Insurance?

There are several factors that are prompting the growing awareness of LTC insurance: escalating health care costs, the high cost of nursing home facilities, the ballooning baby boomer generation's invasion of middle age, and the severe limitations on Medicare and Medigap insurance to pay for unskilled nursing home bills.

The people who can benefit most from long-term care insurance are those who, when they retire (or stop earning), will have assets between $100,000 and $1 million. Why? People with assets below $100,000 will probably not be able to afford the premiums, and people with assets over $1 million should be able to pay for nursing home care with their own money.

Obviously, these are generalizations and you need to analyze your particular situation before you make any decision. The important point here is that not everyone needs this coverage. However, if you're vulnerable, it could be the most important health insurance premium you pay.

Arguments for LTC Insurance

There are several very compelling arguments in favor of LTC insurance:

➤ The HCFA (Health Care Financing Administration) estimates that $69.6 billion was spent in 1993 on nursing home care. Only 63 percent was paid for by government programs or insurance. This left $26 billion to be paid for by the patients and their families. LTC insurance only covered $1.7 billion. This isn't because of exclusions but lack of widespread coverage.

➤ Despite the growing number of nursing and home health care organizations qualifying for Medicare and Medicaid, there's evidence that the largest area of need, for baby boomers particularly, will be unskilled custodial care facilities to meet medical needs not covered by federal and state health plans.

➤ According to Dana Shilling, author of *Financial Planning for the Older Client*, the federal government estimated that there were 6.5 million persons 65 or older with physical limitations. By the year 2040, that number is expected to triple. Medicare and Medicaid are not likely to expand to help pay for these costs. Congress is trying to figure out how to cut those benefits.

➤ According to Shilling, 55 percent of the over-65 population is confined to nursing homes at any point in time. The percentage increases with the age of the population. Almost 25 percent of 85-year-olds are confined in nursing homes. Forty percent of the elderly will spend some time in a nursing home, with up to 25 percent spending more than one year.

➤ The fastest growing segment of the population is the over-75 segment. This is the group most likely to experience the greatest difficulty in day-to-day living, including walking, lifting, shopping, bathing, and eating. These are the kinds of services performed by the unskilled custodial nursing homes or assisted living communities.

➤ Medicare and Medicaid. The coverage under Medicare is for *skilled* nursing facilities only; most nursing home needs are for unskilled. The coverage under Medicaid is for low-income individuals. If you qualify for Medicaid, you cannot afford LTC, and you won't have the assets that most purchasers of LTC are trying to protect. Medicare and Medicaid are not substitutes for LTC insurance.

Arguments Against LTC Insurance

There are several reasons why you might not be interested in LTC insurance. But as stated earlier, you must consider your own needs before you decide.

➤ The "you can't take it with you" attitude. Everyone is entitled to their own philosophy of life and death and inheritance. There's no right viewpoint—it's your money. You could be like the old presumed millionaire with the one-line will and testament that read, "Being of sound mind I spent it." But, if that isn't your objective, you should consider LTC insurance.

➤ Those with adequate assets to pay nursing home expenses out of their own pocket will probably prefer to do so. You will want to weigh the burden of the premium while you are healthy against the potential loss of your estate if you need nursing home care.

The Insurance Company's Pitch

Insurance companies make money when there are healthy sales (pun intended). They're not likely to turn down applications because they believe you'll have the assets to pay for nursing home expenses yourself. Nor do they reject applications from those who've been scared into buying the protection even when they couldn't afford it. It's up to you to decide whether your assets and income level are right for this kind of insurance purchase.

The essence of the issue of whether to buy LTC is that you jeopardize all of your assets by hoping either that you won't need nursing home care or that you'll be able to pay for the care with your

Insider Tip
It isn't too late to find a professional insurance agent or a financial planner who will give you an honest and accurate appraisal of your need for LTC insurance.

income and assets. There are many horror stories of life savings being dissipated for expenses not covered by government programs.

Whose Money Are We Talking About?

The two great variables in life—time and perspective—come into play in looking at LTC insurance.

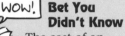

Bet You Didn't Know

The cost of an unskilled nursing home stay has been estimated to be between $36,000 and $40,000 on average across the country. Expenses of $50,000 per year are not unusual. Call a few nursing home facilities in your city (look in the yellow pages) and see what the cost is in your area.

Insider Tip

The premiums for LTC insurance are essentially low until the age of 60, at which point the cost increases dramatically each year you wait. As with many types of insurance where the rate is age-dependent, you can fix the premium rate at the time you purchase the policy. In other words, once you buy the coverage, the premium remains level in the future.

If you're looking at the coverage from the standpoint of a married 65-year-old with a retirement nest egg in the $250,000-to-$500,000 range, your concern is immediate. You're probably afraid that there won't be enough money to protect both you and your spouse for the 25 or more years that you or your spouse will live. Assets of $500,000 invested at 6 percent provide $30,000 a year of income. Coupled with Social Security, your income is still under $50,000. A nursing home bill of $36,000 a year would make it very difficult for the spouse at home.

If you're a healthy 45-year-old with a good job and a working spouse, you're probably less concerned with the possibility of needing the coverage several decades into the future. And yet, at age 45, the premiums are quite affordable to protect yourself.

What if you're the same 45-year-old, but with parents who are now in their late 60s and who are entering into retirement with severe misgivings about being able to afford the future. In fact, assume they're the 65-year-old couple introduced in the beginning of this section. Would you, as their child, want to make sure they were adequately insured to protect their assets and lifestyle, but also ultimately your assets and income? If they lose it all, won't they have to turn to you? You may want to pay the premium to protect them with insurance.

Time and perspective are the backdrop against which to study the problem for yourself.

Insider Tip

If you're 45 years or older, or have parents who will possibly rely on you for support, take a cold, realistic look at the need for LTC protection in your situation. If 25 percent of older Americans are going to need nursing home confinement for more than one year, then this isn't a remote possibility. This is a real risk.

The Insurance Company Story

The story you'll most likely hear is that one out of every four Americans will need nursing home care and that the average stay will be 2 1/2 years. If the average stay is $40,000 per year, that's $100,000. If you suffer from Alzheimer's or a similarly debilitating, protracted illness, the nursing home stay could cost several hundred thousand dollars.

The problem is compounded if one spouse needs a nursing home facility while the other remains at home. Now there are two "households" to maintain income-wise.

The insurance company will unfortunately not tell you not to buy LTC insurance because you have adequate assets or not to buy LTC insurance because your assets are low enough that you'll qualify for Medicaid relief. You must make that judgment call.

Types of LTC Coverage Available Today

With almost 200 companies in the marketplace offering some type of LTC coverage, there's a broad spectrum of choices. However, some generalizations can be made.

There are basically two types of long-term custodial care that the policies may address. The first is confinement in a custodial care facility, such as a nursing home, hospital, or residential facility. The second is home health care. If the care you need is primarily custodial, you probably will not get help from Medicare or Medicaid.

Because this is a relatively new area of insurance, the insurance companies don't have the experience necessary to closely predict utilization or future costs—as they can with disability insurance or traditional health insurance. This has prompted the NAIC (National Association of Insurance Commissioners) to get involved with LTC regulations at the state level.

The NAIC concerns itself with policies that extend beyond one year and offer coverage for medically necessary treatment or custodial care.

The Most Important Policy Provisions

As with all insurance policies, the LTC insurance policy provisions are important to understand. This information is frequently found in the printed proposals prepared by the insurance company.

General

The first provision to look for is the *free look* period. This is the period of time you have to reconsider the purchase. If you decide to return the policy for some reason during this period, you're entitled to your premium back in full. The free look period can run from 10 to 30 days. The longer the free look period, the better for you.

Inflation protection is another important provision, especially if you're purchasing the coverage in your 40s and 50s. Inflation is currently about 3 percent. That means that the hypothetical cost of living will double every 24 years. To a 45-year-old, that is a strong likelihood. If inflation averages 4 percent, the cost of living will double in 18 years. Compare the premiums with and without the inflation rider. If you're in your 70s, the protection may not be worth the expense.

There are two types of inflation protection provisions most commonly used. The first guarantees a flat percentage increase in daily benefits each year, such as 3 percent. If your daily benefit is $100 on the day you bought the policy, the benefit would increase to $103 in year 2, $106 in year 3, and so on. The other type of inflation protection is compounded increases. Using the same 3 percent, in year 2 the daily benefit would be $103, but in year 3 the company increases the benefit by 3 percent of your $103 benefit. This latter approach results in a higher daily benefit.

A *waiver of premium* is another valuable provision. You may remember from the life and disability income insurance discussions that this clause waives your future premiums after a disability of some specified duration. For LTC, a common waiver time period is 90 days of continuous confinement. A waiver of premium provision should be included.

Benefits and Features

The type of expense covered can be either nursing home care and/or home and community care. Both are important for a complete policy. Unless the policy is only affordable when covering nursing home confinement, select a policy that covers both areas.

The *benefit approach* is also variable. Some policies cover nursing home care on a *reimbursement* basis and others on an *indemnity* basis. Under the reimbursement approach, the insurance company will pay the amount of the claim as billed to you or to the provider, up to a daily maximum. This is the most efficient as long as the maximum benefit is high enough. The insurer reimburses you only for actual charges. The indemnification approach works in a different way. It pays you a set benefit if you're under the defined and covered care. You will have selected the benefit level at the time of application for the policy. You will also have been paying the premium for that benefit. The reimbursement approach is better for you and for the insurance company.

The *benefit period* is important. Some insurers define the period in time, such as one, two, three, or five years. Some provide a lifetime benefit period. Still another option might be a benefit period that depends on the total dollars of protection selected. In other words, the benefit period is the amount of time that it takes to exhaust the purchased dollar coverage. A lifetime benefit is obviously the most liberal, but it may be too expensive. Apply the big mistake/small mistake test to help you decide whether to pay for the lifetime benefit.

The *renewability* feature will be important in long-term care insurance, just as it was in disability income insurance (discussed in Chapter 18). You want a policy that renews at your option. It must not be cancelable by the insurance company for any reason other than your failure to pay the premium. And the premiums should not be subject to increase for any reason. This latter point is important because the claims experience under LTC insurance is relatively new. Time may reveal that premiums in general are too low, and insurers may have to charge more. Let them charge new policyholders the higher premium.

Daily maximums address the total benefit for the nursing home or home care, and can vary from $10 to $300 or more per day. Obviously, you're charged a premium based on the total amount you purchase.

> **Jargon Alert**
> *Respite care* is care provided to relieve the person or persons who normally care for the insured. It recognizes the need to care for the family and friends that care for the patient. There are an increasing variety of facilities to meet the needs of the custodial care patient. *Assisted care facilities* are facilities devoted to continuous care and support to patients who are unable to perform a prescribed number of activities of daily living.

This can be viewed as a limitation as well as a benefit, because the insurer will not pay more than the maximum you purchase. Buy a reasonable amount based on your current living expenses.

Home and community care benefits are intended to cover the expenses generated in your own home, alternative care facilities, adult day care centers, and *respite care*. They should cover all levels of care: skilled, intermediate, and custodial.

Assisted care facility benefits are advantageous in your policy. Frequently, there's a maximum benefit expressed as a percentage of your daily maximum benefit.

Benefit Triggers

Benefits under LTC policies are usually triggered by limitations in *activities of daily living* (ADLs). The most common listed in LTC policies are:

➤ Eating

➤ Walking

➤ Bathing

➤ Using toilet facilities

➤ Dressing

➤ Moving from a bed to a wheelchair or a chair

One major insurer in this area requires two out of five ADLs or an injury, sickness, or some cognitive impairment before allowing nursing home reimbursement. The same policy requires two ADLs for assisted care or home and community care. Again, the objective is to find the right policy for you.

Limitations and Exclusions

Some of the limitations are a matter of choice while others are built into the contract. One over which you usually have a choice is the *elimination period*. This is a form of deductible that defers the benefits until the completion of a number of days. It usually applies to the nursing home benefit and assisted care, but it can apply to custodial care as well. The elimination period can range from 0 to 100 days. The greater the period, the lower the premium. Read the terms of the elimination period before buying. A better provision will not require continuous days to meet the period.

Pre-existing conditions are the most important of the limitations. Not all policies exclude pre-existing conditions. Those that do exclude them usually define them as a medical condition that was treated by a physician or that had symptoms such that it should have been treated by a physician. The aim of the exclusion is to prevent insureds from waiting until they have a problem to seek insurance coverage. A typical pre-existing condition clause will require a waiting period of six months before all conditions are covered. This is the longest allowable waiting period for insureds age 65 and over in most states. For under 65, the waiting period can be as long as 24 months.

OOOH... **Insider Tip**

Buy a policy without a pre-existing condition clause if possible. If not, try to find a period no longer than 90 days. Don't wait until the last minute to buy the LTC policy. If you buy the policy when you're healthy, the pre-existing clause will not likely be a factor.

Other typical limitations and exclusions include the following:

➤ Care provided by family members, even if they're professionals in the field of health care.

➤ Care and services provided in veteran's hospitals or other federal government facilities for which you are not charged.

➤ Care occasioned by war or an act of war.

➤ Services required because of attempted suicide or self-inflicted injury.

➤ Care when no charges would have been made except for the existence of insurance. This prevents care providers from manufacturing prescribed care in order to use insurance benefits.

➤ Care for alcoholism or drug addiction except on the advice or instructions of a physician.

➤ Care covered by Medicare or any other insurance program, except to the extent that expenses are shared under the policies by *coordination of benefits*. This provision allows the insured to receive benefits under more than one form of coverage, but never for more than the cost of the charges. This prevents overutilization of insurance, even if you own more than you need.

➤ Care related to mental illness and personality disorders.

The Cost and When to Assume It

What should you expect to pay for LTC? The author Dana Shilling, cited previously, referred to a survey in *Life Association News* magazine in 1989 that emphasized the wide range of premiums for LTC. The article reported that a $60-a-day benefit was priced at premiums between $79.80 and $976.50 per year. That's a scary difference. The pricing isn't in line with reality. Unfortunately, there is not enough claims experience in LTC insurance to say who is closest to a fair premium.

Watch It!
Consider purchasing LTC when you don't need it, before the problems that are covered appear. Buy based on need, not greed. Remember that premiums will fluctuate based on the coverage and your age.

Obviously, age is part of the equation. According to that same issue of *Life Association News*, the average premium for a 50-year-old was $483. The average was $1,135 for a 65-year-old. The best wisdom seems to be to buy the coverage earlier, when premiums are lower. Again, the premiums begin to escalate significantly at age 60.

The Least You Need to Know

LTC is one of the fastest growing need-based sales areas in the country. The coverage can be widely priced. The benefits can be quite varied. But the need for the protection is justified in most personal situations.

➤ Analyze your personal financial situation to determine whether you have sufficient income-producing assets to pay for an extended nursing home confinement. Base your judgment on the expenses charged in your geographic area.

➤ Hone your shopping skills, because the variety in provisions and premiums can be dramatic.

➤ Look for benefits first, then cost comparisons. The quality of the coverage is most important, the rate secondary.

➤ Study alternatives for comparison purposes. Know what your options are before you make them a part of your insurance portfolio.

Part 5
Annuities

Along with the opportunity for a longer, more productive life is the threat of outliving your income. The retirement plans that were built around a retirement age of 65 and a life expectancy age of 72 could be under-funded and could result in severe shortfalls in income for the retiree. Learn how annuities can be used to generate an income you will not be able to outlive.

Annuities are also used as tax-deferral vehicles. You will read about the different annuity types and how the investment approach to the policy determines its viability in your portfolio. You will also read about the great tax doctrines of squeaking pigs and long-tailed dogs.

Annuity Basics

The annuity business has grown enormously in the last fifteen years. In 1994, according to the American Council of Life Insurance, the total annuity consideration in this country was $153.8 billion. These are premiums received by insurance companies during the calendar year. Of this figure, over $80 billion in premiums were from *individual* sales, as opposed to *group* sales (which would include pensions).

Jargon Alert

Individual sales are what the name implies—sales to individual purchasers who act as individuals and not as part of a group. The most typical *group* is an employer-based collection of people who are purchasing insurance or annuities together. The group can give the members some clout or leverage in terms of price or rates, although not always and not significantly.

It's not always easy to put all this in perspective. Table 26.1 shows the dramatic growth of individual annuity sales.

Table 26.1   Individual Annuity Considerations (Premiums in Billions for U.S. Life Insurance Companies)

Year	Premiums
1969	$0.885
1974	1.924
1979	4.976
1984	15.706
1989	49.407
1994	80.832

Source: American Council of Life Insurance, 1995 Life Insurance Fact Book Update.

Well, what in the world happened between 1979 and 1989? Annual premiums jumped from $4 billion to $49 billion in sales in a decade. That's what this part of the book is about—the emergence of annuities as popular savings and investment vehicles. But like any other financial product, they aren't for everyone. Read on to find out if they are for you.

What Is an Annuity?

An *annuity* is defined as a contract (in the form of a policy) between an insurer and the insured whereby the insurer promises to pay a stipulated income to the annuitant for a long period of time, often life. Naturally, there's more to it than that, or there would be millions of people lined up for some of that long-term income.

Income

If you remember from the discussion of insurance contracts in Chapter 14, one of the requirements for a valid contract is consideration. You have to pay a premium in order to guarantee the insurer's promise to pay an income.

Originally, the idea was to provide an income that the annuitant could not outlive.

Because of the experience of numerous insurance companies, which has been pooled together in the form of mortality tables, insurers are able to structure the annuity in a wide variety of ways to meet the needs of different people. And, in fact, it was this creative structuring of annuities that led to the boom in premiums illustrated in Table 26.1. The majority of the premiums shown in recent years has not been attracted to annuities because of the opportunity to receive an income for life, if at all. The dramatic increase in premiums is attributable to an annuity's tax benefits.

Jargon Alert
The *annuitant* is the person to whom the income is paid. Additionally, it is the person on whose life the terms of the annuity are measured.

Tax-Deferred Growth

The majority of today's annuities are sold with *tax deferral* as the primary objective, which will be covered in more detail in Chapter 29.

But annuities stand on their own as income and growth vehicles.

Jargon Alert

Tax deferral is the process of postponing the payment of taxes, especially income taxes, until a future date (hopefully when it is more advantageous to receive taxable income). An IRA is an example of a product that provides tax deferral of income earned from reinvestment. Don't confuse tax deferral with *tax deductibility*, which is the ability to reduce one's current taxes by subtracting the asset or transaction from one's taxable income.

Parties to the Contract

There are three parties to a typical annuity: annuitant, annuity owner, and beneficiary. The annuitant was previously defined as the person on whose life the terms of the annuity are measured. The *annuity owner* is the person who has all the *incidents of owner-ship*, the rights to the policy. The annuitant and annuity owner can be the same person, but not necessarily. For example, a wife can own a policy on her husband as the annuity.

Jargon Alert
The *incidents of ownership* in an annuity or life insurance com-pany are the rights in the contract, such as the right to the cash surrender value, the right to name a beneficiary, and the right to assign the policy. The *annuity owner* controls these rights in an annuity, as does the policyowner of a life insurance company.

The *beneficiary* is the person who will receive the death benefit of the annuity when and if it is paid out by reason of death of the annuitant. The death benefit of an annuity is different from the death benefit of a life insurance policy. It is usually the accumulated premiums plus any interest earned. There is no mortality element in most annuities. Having said that, be aware that there can be an additional death benefit, especially in variable annuities, as discussed in Chapter 28.

Because of the special rules for tax deferral, as well as how individual insurance companies draft their contracts, the ownership arrangements are critical to accomplishing your planning objectives.

Why Buy an Annuity?

There are two primary reasons to buy an annuity: income and tax-deferred growth. Your objectives will determine which type of annuity best suits your needs. There are several other factors that will also enter into the equation. "Equation" is not used loosely here—the configuration of the annuity depends on mathematical calculations based at least in part on the following:

➤ *The annuitant's age.* Remember, the annuitant's life is the one on whom the payouts are measured. Because you could be talking about an income for life, it will matter to the insurance company if the annuitant is 40 years old or 80. It probably matters to the annuitant too, especially if it is the 80-year-old.

➤ *The annuitant's sex.* Gender matters. There have been complaints and litigation in the past regarding the unifying of rates for males and females for insurance and annuities. It had been the norm to have separate rates because the life expectancy is different for the two groups (see Table 26.2). Females will pay more for an annuity income because they are expected to live longer. For the same reason, they pay less for life insurance.

Table 26.2   Life Expectancy in Years at Various Ages in 1994

Age	For Males	For Females
0	72.1	78.8
25	48.9	54.9
45	31.0	35.9
65	15.3	18.8
85	5.1	6.3

Source: American Council of Life Insurance, 1995 Life Insurance Fact Book Update.

➤ *Principal sum.* The amount of money invested in the annuity will obviously be a factor. The more invested, the more the income potential.

➤ *Credited interest.* The interest rate used by the insurance company will make a difference, just as the principal sum will. The higher the credited rate, the more to *annuitize* or accumulate.

➤ *Expenses.* The expense charges of the insurance company will impact the policy. The lower the company's expenses, the greater the opportunity to improve your payout under the annuity.

> **Jargon Alert**
> *Annuitization* is the process of turning a lump sum of money into income through the use of an annuity contract. It usually involves an insurance company that guarantees the values and income. However, an annuity can be issued by an individual.

The Basic Types of Annuities

There are several ways to classify annuities:

➤ By premium method

➤ By the annuity starting date

➤ By the investment characteristics

➤ By the options available

Annuities can be funded in two ways: a *single premium* or *periodic premiums*. A single premium policy does not usually allow for subsequent premiums to be deposited. A periodic premium policy does allow that freedom. Most periodic premium policies are *flexible premium* policies, although some contracts can require fixed and level premiums over time.

Bet You Didn't Know

WOW!

U.S. life insurance companies collected more than $80 billion in individual annuity premiums in 1994. Of that sum, $49 billion was single-premium business. Of the remaining $31 billion, $17 billion was first-year premiums and almost $13 billion was renewal premiums under periodic or flexible premium plans.

Annuities classified by the starting date of payments can be either *immediate* or *deferred*. The immediate annuity begins payments to the annuitant right away, usually a month after the premium is deposited. A deferred annuity accumulates principal and interest for payment at some future date. Remember the two reasons for buying an annuity—income or tax-deferred growth. Immediate and deferred annuities are the focus of the next two chapters.

The investment alternatives for annuities are *fixed* and *variable*. With the fixed annuity, you leave the investments up to the insurance company. With the variable annuity, you assume the responsibility for the investment returns. You saw the life insurance equivalent in Part 2, "Life Insurance," called variable life. These annuities are also focused on in the next two chapters.

WOW! **Bet You Didn't Know**
The majority of individual annuities issued today are deferred as opposed to immediate. This is because more people are buying them for tax-deferral purposes rather than income needs. According to the American Council of Life Insurance, there were 137,000 immediate annuities issued in 1994, compared to 4,051,000 deferred annuities issued that same year.

Annuities are also classified according to the payout option selected. These options were the reason the product was designed in the first place, when the overriding concern was a lifetime of income, not tax deferral. These options will be explored more deeply in the next chapter.

Putting It Together

If you examine the payout options separately, there are six factors to be considered: single premium or flexible premium, immediate or deferred benefits, and fixed or variable investments. Any combination of three of the factors is feasible. For example, you can have a single premium deferred fixed annuity or a single premium immediate variable annuity. The right combination will depend on your needs and objectives.

Where You Can Buy an Annuity

Annuities are insurance products. This means they're issued by life insurance companies and are usually sold by licensed life insurance salespeople. But, as you've already learned about the financial services industry today, you can find a licensed life insurance salesperson in almost any financial institution, including your stockbroker's office, your bank or savings and loan, or your insurance agent's office. Some annuities are even sold by associations on a direct-mail basis.

Does that mean there will be a competent person there to help you out? Unfortunately, no. Even though you will be doing business with a licensed life insurance sales representative, don't confuse *licensed* with *trained*—or even *experienced*. The amount of knowledge of annuities you need to pass an insurance exam these days is minimal. When you have a choice, buy your annuity from someone with experience with annuities.

How do you find this information? Ask the salesperson what experience they have. What if there is no salesperson? If you're buying from an association, for example, compare the policy offered with policies from other sources. If the credited rate or rates of return are comparable, you may be better off with a representative to turn to for planning and service assistance.

The Least You Need to Know

The annuity business has exploded in popularity in the last two decades due to the possibility of income tax deferral. But this emphasis on tax benefits overlooks the original reason for the annuity—an income you cannot outlive.

➤ Purchase annuities as you would any other financial product, because it is consistent with your financial objectives. If you have no objectives, start planning now.

➤ Make sure you understand the type of annuity you're buying. They can be very different from each other.

➤ Comparison shop for the best annuity, realizing the value of a professional underwriter in the process.

Chapter 27

Fixed Annuities—Immediate or Deferred

In This Chapter

➤ The classification of annuities by the timing of annuity payments

➤ The income options under an immediate annuity

➤ Understanding the important characteristics of a deferred annuity

➤ Understanding rates and rate guarantees in fixed annuities

➤ How to read a typical deferred annuity contract

In the previous chapter, you learned that there are several ways to categorize annuities, including the timing of the benefit payments and the investment features. A look at these two possibilities in the following figure may help.

You see that the immediate annuity comes in two basic forms: the fixed immediate and the variable immediate. By far, the fixed rate immediate is the most prevalent and will be the one discussed here at greater length. Of the deferred annuities, the emphasis over recent years is shifting toward the variable. Only time will tell if this trend continues.

*An Annuity Grid illus-
trates the possible combinations of annuity forms.*

	FIXED	VARIABLE
IMMEDIATE	I	II
DEFERRED	III	IV

The Immediate Annuity

To review, an *immediate annuity* begins to pay an income to the named annuitant approximately one month after receipt of the single lump-sum premium. If the premium is
not paid in one lump sum, but rather in installments over several years, then the income
begins after the last premium has been paid.

And, as a further review, remember that the amount of the payout is a function of several
factors: the annuitant's age, sex, total premium (consideration), and the insurer's credited
rates and expense factors.

When you're interested in purchasing an annuity, ask for a quote. However, unlike a
quote for insurance, for example, you will receive a rate of income for each dollar invested rather than a price. What you're looking for is the largest *income per thousand* based
on the same income option (as explained in the next section). This last qualification is
the most important variable in this process and leads to the next section.

Annuity Income Options

There are basically six options with insurance companies. The selection of one over the
other depends on the income recipient's needs.

Life Annuity Option

The *life annuity* was the original annuity designed to be an income that the annuitant could not outlive. The insurance company pays an income rate that is calculated taking into account the age and sex of the annuitant. The company knows the interest rate and expense assumptions it can make based on its own experience. If the insured is a 70-year-old woman, for example, the insurance company knows what the actuarial tables say will be the average longevity for all 70-year-old women. It can then price a stream of income for this woman in particular.

One insurance company will pay a 70-year-old man $8.42 per thousand dollars for life. Therefore, for a $100,000 single premium, they will pay him an income of $842 per month for his lifetime.

What happens if he dies at the end of two years? His income stops. He made a bad choice to buy this type of annuity. He will have received $20,208 total ($842/mo. × 24 months). He paid in $100,000. He clearly lost money on the transaction.

On the other hand, what if he lived to be 95 years old? This has been a good deal for him and not so good for the insurance company who has paid out $252,600 in total income, assuming he died on the policy anniversary.

Because of the high degree of risk in losing much of the principal or premium you invest, the life annuity pays the highest income of all of the income options.

Insider Tip
Buy a straight life annuity only if you're convinced that you'll live long enough to beat the life expectancy tables. And only if you can afford to take that risk with the money. If you have survivors who likewise depend on that money for their continued support, don't choose this option.

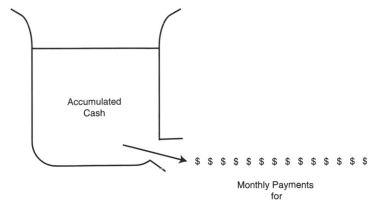

Accumulated Cash

$ $ $ $ $ $ $ $ $ $ $ $ $

Monthly Payments
for
Annuitant's Lifetime

Life Annuity, illustrating an income you cannot outlive.

Cash Refund Annuity

The *cash refund annuity* is one answer to the risk inherent in the life annuity. If you're the type of person who chooses not to take the life annuity gamble, the cash refund annuity gives a measure of protection of at least your premium.

The policy pays an income for the annuitant's life, no matter how long. However, if the annuitant dies prior to the return of all of the premium, then the insurer agrees to refund the difference in one lump sum.

Cash Refund Annuity, illustrating a guaranteed return of premium.

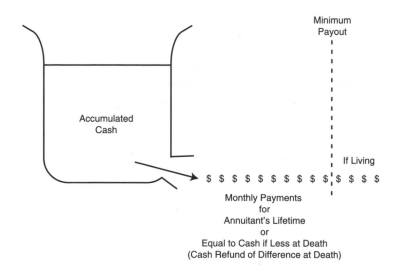

Accumulated Cash

Minimum Payout

If Living

$ $ $ $ $ $ $ $ $ $ $ $ $ $ $ $

Monthly Payments
for
Annuitant's Lifetime
or
Equal to Cash if Less at Death
(Cash Refund of Difference at Death)

Insider Tip

OOOH...

The cash refund annuity is a good choice if you need income for your life, but don't want to risk losing any of your principal for your heirs. This option frequently appeals to those who have worked hard for their retirement monies and the annuity represents a large percentage of their assets.

Installment Refund Annuity Option

The complement to the cash refund is the *installment refund,* which, as you might imagine, continues the income to the annuitant's beneficiary until the principal sum is returned. This difference from the cash refund annuity is shown in the following figure.

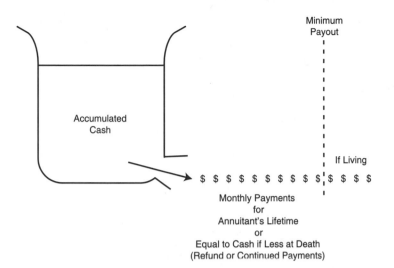

Installment refund annuity, illustrating a return of premium in continuing installments.

The major difference between the two refund options, then, is the nature of the refund itself—all at death or spread out over the original payment schedule.

> OOOH... **Insider Tip**
>
> The installment refund is ideal to guarantee the continuation of the same stream of income to the annuitant's beneficiary, usually the surviving spouse. Use this option if there is concern with how the survivor would manage a refund in cash.

Life Annuity with Term Certain Option

The *life annuity with term certain* is another approach to guaranteeing a minimum amount of income even if the annuitant dies early. It mitigates against the risk in the straight life annuity. The relationship between the level of income and the length of the period certain is important. The longer the guarantee period, the smaller the life income monthly payment. You can see this guarantee in the following figure.

Life annuity with period certain, illustrating the minimum term of the annuity.

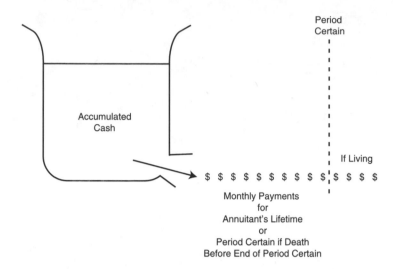

A comparison of income levels can be illustrated with the following income quoted by a major insurance company. For an annuitant 70-year-old male with a $100,000 lump sum premium, the straight life annuity would be $842 per month. Remember, this option has no refund or guarantee feature. If this same annuitant opted for a life annuity with a 10-year term certain guarantee, the monthly income from the same company would be $762 per month. And, if you increase the guarantee period to 20 years, the monthly income drops to $643.

OOOH...

Insider Tip

Choose this option if you have a definite income need for a specified period of time, and you have someone else who relies on the income. An example might be an income need for 10 years before a company pension kicks in.

Joint and Survivor Annuity Option

The *joint and survivor annuity* is designed to pay an income for two lives. When one of the two annuitants dies, the income simply continues.

The joint and survivor annuity can be structured to meet the needs of different situations. Some people are concerned with a higher level of income only while both parties are living. The assumption is that some of the income is consumed by each annuitant. Therefore, the income level could decrease at the first death. If the joint annuitants are willing to accept these terms, the income potential at the inception of the annuity can be higher.

Typical alternatives to the joint and full survivor annuity is the joint and two-thirds annuity or the joint and one-half annuity. Again, the annuity payments begin on the two lives and continue after the death of the first joint annuitant, only at a reduced level, such as 2/3 or 1/2 of the initial income figure.

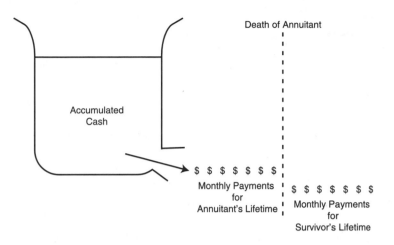

Joint and survivor annuity, illustrating an income for two lives.

Insider Tip

OOOH...

The joint and survivor annuity is ideal for a husband and wife with limited retirement assets, and who are concerned with adequate income for both spouses. Be wary of the reduced survivor benefits, because they fail to take into account the erosive power of inflation. What seems like a reasonable reduction at the first death may be unreasonable when it occurs because inflation has decreased the purchasing power of the original income.

Income Comparisons

Let's look at a hypothetical situation now where a retiring husband and wife have $100,000 to use to produce income. Assume each is 70 years old, they're in reasonably good health, and that this represents their major income-producing asset. In Table 27.1, you'll see how one large insurance company would quote various alternative options on a fixed-rate basis.

Table 27.1   Annuity Income Options

Annuity Income Option	Monthly Income
Life Annuity Husband Only	$842
Life With 10 Year Certain	$762

continues

Table 27.1 Continued

Annuity Income Option	Monthly Income
Life With 20 Year Certain	$643
Joint With 10 Year Certain	$645
Joint With 20 Year Certain	$643

Interest Only

There is one further choice for individuals who have significant sums on balance with insurance companies, but who may not need much income or who prefer to use as little of the principal as possible. That is the option to leave the principal with the insurer and receive interest only on the principal. You are in effect turning your annuity into a certificate of deposit. The company will credit you with an interest rate that fluctuates from time to time as interest rates, in general, fluctuate.

Annuities and Settlement Options

Finally, a word about the difference between annuities and settlement options under life insurance policies. For those of you who were so excited about the earlier chapters on life insurance contracts that you went to your files to read your life insurance policies, you will have noticed that the terms used to describe the annuity income options are the same as those choices in your policy called *settlement options*. That's because the settlement options are in fact annuities purchased with the accumulated cash surrender values in your policies.

The Basics of Fixed Deferred Annuities

The preceding discussion centered on income options. But most annuity buyers aren't interested in immediate income. They're accumulating dollars for retirement or at least until some future date when they may opt for an income stream. These buyers want *deferred annuities*.

Deferred annuities may be purchased with a single premium, and are commonly called an *SPDA*, or Single Premium Deferred Annuity. Or they may be purchased with periodic premiums, either fixed or flexible. The flexible premium is the most common form of the periodic annuity today.

Remember also that single premium deferred annuities can be fixed or variable. The variable is the one where the premium is invested at your direction into a choice of separate accounts, separate from the general assets of the insurer. Variable annuities are the focus of Chapter 28. Here the current focus is on SPDAs.

Characteristics of SPDAs

SPDAs are still the most popular form of annuity because of the perceived safety of the vehicle, as well as the inherent tax advantages. They are not for everyone, but you'll have a better idea if they can work for you after you learn their characteristics.

Single Premium

You probably guessed this one. It's significant because it highlights the investment aspects of the contract. The policy requires no ongoing contributions and no thresholds of premium other than the minimums acceptable to the issuing insurer.

Rate Guarantee

The most important aspect of the SPDA is the rate guarantee. The insurance company guarantees an interest rate to be credited to the policy for a stated number of years. The most common rate guarantee period is one year.

If you bought an SPDA with a $10,000 premium, the company might offer several rate plans to choose from. For example, they might offer one-, three-, and five-year rate guarantees. In a typical rate environment, the longer the rate period selected, the higher the guaranteed rate. Why is that?

Typically, the rates on *government debt instruments* are lower at the shorter maturities and increase as the term of the debt instrument grows longer.

In this typical environment, a treasury bill might yield 4.5 percent while a 30-year treasury bond would yield 7.0 percent. This is a normal yield relationship. Occasionally, short-term yields are higher than long-term, in which case the curve is said to be *inverted*. How does this relate to the rate guarantees by insurers? The largest percentage of insurance company assets is in bonds, governments and corporate, as shown in Table 27.2.

Jargon Alert
Government debt instruments are the evidences of debt when the U.S. government borrows money from you and me to continue to fund its deficit-based economy. These instruments include treasury bills with a maturity of one year or less, treasury notes with maturities from one to ten years, and treasury bonds with maturities from ten to thirty years.

Table 27.2   1994 Distribution of Assets of All U.S. Life Insurance Companies

Asset	Percent
Government Securities	20.4
Corporate Bonds	40.7
Corporate Stocks	14.5
Mortgages	11.1
Real Estate	2.8
Policy Loans	4.4
Miscellaneous	6.2
Total	100.1

The insurance company invests your premium in a portfolio of assets that gives them a greater rate of return than they will credit your annuity. For example, if the company knows that it must credit 6 percent on a one-year annuity to be competitive, and that it must earn 1.75 percent to pay expenses (including commissions and overhead), then it must earn at least 7.75 percent on its assets to break even.

But most insurers are in business to make a profit, not to break even. So, an insurance company faced with this rate scenario would invest the total premiums received into a portfolio that yielded 8 percent overall. The company is managing its portfolio to make the *spread* between what it earns and what it pays out.

> **WOW!** **Bet You Didn't Know**
> Annuity insurance companies are not the only institutions in the spread business. No, not bedding companies, either. Banks, savings and loans, and credit unions also make a profit managing a portfolio to the spread. In the case of your bank, they're lending to you at a percentage below the yield on their portfolio.

To continue the example, if they credited 6 percent on the one-year plan, they might guarantee 6.25 percent for three years and 6.5 percent for five years. This means they would promise to pay that rate for each of the years in the rate guarantee period.

What about after that guarantee period? There is no guarantee after the initial guarantee period for most SPDAs. So what prevents the company from dropping the rate to 1 percent? Well, you could also ask: What prevents you from taking your annuity money somewhere else?

Most annuities have a reasonable minimum rate floor, such as 4 percent. This contractual provision establishes the lowest rate the company can credit. Frequently, this minimum is mandated by state regulations. But aren't the companies smart enough to find ways to keep your money with them? Read on.

Surrender Charges

Insurance companies build their expenses into the spread. But the spread is only 1.5 to 2.5 percent each year, while the expenses may be 6 to 7 percent the first year because of the commission. A typical commission is 5 to 6 percent. How does the insurance company ever make this up? By recapturing part of this initial expense over several years—for example, six years.

What happens if the annuity owner wants to move the policy to another company before the insurance company recoups its expenses? Without a safeguard, the insurance company would lose money. The safeguard is called a *surrender charge*.

Jargon Alert

A *surrender charge* is a penalty levied against the accumulated cash value of a policy that is clearly stated in the contract. It is usually graduated to approximate the outlay of expenses by the insurer up front. It will build in a little to cover the presumed cost to liquidate assets to pay out the cash.

A typical surrender charge might look like Table 27.3.

Table 27.3 Typical Surrender Charge Schedule

Year	Percent of Cash Value
1	6
2	5
3	4
4	3
5	2
6	1
7 and beyond	0

Source: American Council of Life Insurance, 1995 Life Insurance Fact Book Update

But what if a policy has a rate guarantee for only one year and a heavy surrender charge? It could pay an attractive yield to entice you to invest and then drop the *renewal rate* well below the going rate in the market. You would be trapped if there was an onerous surrender charge. The answer is a safeguard for you this time, called a *bailout provision*.

Jargon Alert

Insurance companies credit an initial rate for the stated number of years. After that rate expires, the company must credit a new rate, typically every year thereafter. That rate is called the *renewal rate*. It is based on the interest rate scenario at the time of renewal. If rates have come down at the bank, you can bet they will come down in the annuity and vice versa. The *bailout provision* is a contractual promise that if the company drops its renewal rate more than a specified percentage during the period of time that the surrender charges are effective, then you have a 30-day or similar time frame in which to move your money without a surrender penalty.

Bailouts were more prevalent in the 1980s, but they still exist and can be a great value to you, especially with a company that doesn't have a great track record in crediting renewal rates. But how do you find this history? Ask. Tell the agent you want to see the renewal rate history on the business the company has written in the past 10 to 15 years. If the agent balks, buy a different product or find a different agent.

Products without bailout protection are referred to as "trust me" contracts in the industry. Insurance companies found that bailouts put them at severe disadvantages when interest rates changed dramatically during the surrender charge period. This is especially the case if interest rates spike upward, because bond values move inversely to the move in interest rates.

Interest rate relationship, between rates and values of bonds.

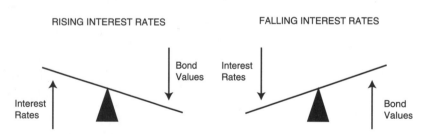

Notice the see-saw example, where one side must move up when the other moves down. So it is with interest rates and bond values. The reason is that if you bought a bond today for $10,000 with a stated yield of 6 percent, you would expect $600 each year in income. If you went to sell the bond several years later, but now interest rates were 8 percent, no one would be willing to pay $10,000 for a bond yielding 6 percent. However, they would be willing to pay less. Enough less, in fact, that the yield on their purchase would be exactly 8 percent.

This is why insurers can lose money when the interest rate swings upward. They obviously gain when interest rates fall.

So, how do you protect yourself in "trust me" products? You don't.

Some companies offer an outrageously high rate just to get you in the door, but you will have a difficult time getting out of the contract whole. It's a little like a financial house of mirrors. If you see a policy with a first-year rate of 10 percent when the current interest rate environment is 5 percent, watch out. Make very certain you understand what the entire policy is made out of.

> **OOOH...**
>
> **Insider Tip**
> Don't buy a policy on rate alone! The quality of the insurer, its reputation and history of fair rate renewals, and the contractual provisions are more important. Be wary of very high credited rates for the first year only. These are "come-on rates" and are frequently not based on anything other than hype.

Partial Withdrawals

At some time in the future, you will want to get money out of the contract. It could be because of an emergency during the surrender charge period, and that could be costly. To overcome this particular flaw in the annuity, most contracts allow for *partial withdrawals*.

A common provision is to allow 10 percent of the accumulated cash value in any given year, or the contract may allow withdrawal of all earnings in the contract without surrender charges. Because you buy an SPDA to accumulate monies rather than for immediate income, most partial withdrawal provisions will be adequate.

> **Jargon Alert**
> A *partial withdrawal* is a withdrawal of less than the full value of the contract. The provision allows for such withdrawals up to a certain percentage or dollar amount without the imposition of a surrender charge. The provision is only necessary during the period in which a surrender charge is levied.

> **OOOH...** **Insider Tip**
>
> Make sure any SPDA you buy has some provision for early withdrawal. Also, if the surrender charge period is 10 years or longer, you should look for a different SPDA. A typical surrender period is six or seven years.

The SPDA is a tax-favored product. (Chapter 29 covers tax treatments.) However, in the previous discussion of withdrawal provisions, be aware that the discussion dealt only with the policy penalties and relief from policy penalties. It did not discuss tax penalties, and there can be tax penalties. Make sure you understand both before you purchase an SPDA (and if you already own one, before you make a withdrawal).

The Least You Need to Know

Annuities can be immediate or deferred. Either of those can be fixed or variable. Immediate annuities are income vehicles based on actuarial calculations given the age, gender, premium, and income needs of the applicant. SPDAs are deferred accumulation vehicles usually purchased for tax-deferred savings for retirement.

➤ Look at immediate annuities for income alternatives as you approach retirement age. They offer yields you cannot outlive without the burden of investing your nest egg for yourself.

➤ Realistically assess your income needs, including a factor for inflation. This is a time when a professional agent or broker can be of great help. Choose income plans that suit your specific needs.

➤ Buy SPDAs to save for retirement on a tax advantaged basis. Know what you're buying, however. All SPDAs are not created equal.

➤ Buy SPDAs and immediate annuities only from companies that meet the test of solvency and safety discussed in Part 2, "Life Insurance." This is critical.

➤ Remember that buying an SPDA is like buying anything else. If it sounds too good to be true, it probably is. This is especially true of credited interest rates at the beginning of the contract.

Variable Annuities

Variable annuities can be immediate or deferred. Sound familiar? It should, because it's the mirror image of the fixed annuity choices.

The number of people who opt for a variable immediate annuity are hardly enough to fill a stadium each year. So, most of the attention in this chapter will be devoted to the variable deferred annuity. Just be aware that with a variable immediate annuity, the monthly income payment you receive will fluctuate with the value of the underlying fund. On to the variable deferred.

Who's Going To Take the Risk?

If you're saving and investing in an annuity for retirement, the first question you need to ask yourself is "Who's going to manage the money?" This is an enormous question for most people because they're not sophisticated investors. In fact, most people are intimidated by the investment markets.

If you're one of the people without investment experience, the fixed annuity, with the rate guaranteed by the insurance company, may be the best alternative for you. That's because the variable annuity shifts the responsibility for the investment of the premiums from the insurance company to you. (A review of the variable life explanation in Chapter 13 would be helpful.)

How? When you buy a fixed annuity, the expenses of the contract are subtracted from the premium, and the balance is deposited in the *general account* discussed under variable life insurance. These are the assets of the company behind all of their promises to pay death and living benefits.

But with the variable annuity, expenses are subtracted from the premium and the remainder is invested in accounts that are separate from the insurer's general accounts. In fact, they're called *separate accounts*. These are mutual fund–like accounts, where your premium buys a number of units based on their value that day. You choose which funds to invest in, just as with a mutual fund. You decide when to change funds from one account to another. In short, the risk is yours.

Passing the Buck

What happens if you turn the investment job over to someone else? You can pass the buck (or at least the responsibility for investing the buck) to whomever you want. However, the responsibility is still yours as far as the insurance company is concerned. The owner has the onus. (Okay, so it's not Robert Frost, but you get the point I'm sure.)

This warning should not be construed to mean that there are no good programs to help individuals decide where to invest the variable annuity monies. There are, and they're introduced later in this chapter under the title "Asset Allocation Funds and Services."

Variable Annuity Investment Choices

The variable annuity typically offers you a variety of investment alternatives. The theory is that by investing in *equities* and other investment options, you can get better performance results than in the general account.

Jargon Alert

Equities are investments that represent an ownership interest in a company. Owning stock in IBM is an example. By contrast, when you own a bond, you have a debtor relationship with the company—you have loaned the company money, and the company promises to pay it back with interest later.

The most common fund alternatives are stock, bonds, international, global, growth and income, and guaranteed funds. These are investment accounts that are governed by securities law as well as insurance regulations. Some products will offer a dozen or more choices, which can be quite confusing unless you have experience as a mutual fund investor. But with the explosive growth of money invested in mutual funds in the last decade, more and more investors are making these long-term decisions, and for them, the variable annuity is an excellent vehicle for tax-deferred growth.

Common Stock Funds

The real appeal of the variable annuity in the last decade has been the opportunity to share in the exceptional growth of common stocks. There's quite a range of options within the field of common stocks. They should be viewed in terms of riskiness.

Aggressive Growth Funds

The riskiest are the stock funds that are classified as "aggressive growth." These are usually smaller capitalization stocks or stocks in a particular segment of the market. They will be more volatile, and while they have the greatest likelihood of bigger returns, they also have the best chance of larger dips in down markets. They may be likened to rocket ships: up and down in a hurry.

OOOH... **Insider Tip**

The investments inside your variable annuity should be made as part of your entire investment plan, not in a vacuum. If you're heavily invested in aggressive growth stocks and funds elsewhere, don't ignore that fact when you choose your funds inside the annuity. Just because the annuity is tax deferred does not isolate it from your overall objectives. If you don't have a plan, get some help and adopt one.

Growth Funds

The objective of a growth fund is long-term growth, primarily through capital appreciation. They're not as volatile as their aggressive cousin. They invest in more stable, more mature firms and include dividend-paying stocks.

> **OOOH...** **Insider Tip**
>
> Just as with mutual funds, read the prospectus to make sure you know what each fund's stated objective is and what its holdings are. If you know a little about stocks, you can tell a great deal by looking at the fund's top holdings. The prospectus also details the expenses and track record of the fund.

Growth and Income Funds

These funds aim to combine growth stocks in well-established companies with income-producing securities such as bonds and dividend-paying stocks. They're frequently called equity-income or total return funds and are less risky still than the first two offerings. These are an outstanding long-term choice in most fund families.

Bond Funds

These funds provide growth through fixed income investments. They can vary from conservative government bond funds to riskier high-yield bond funds. The name of the bond fund will usually tell you how the monies are being invested.

> **OOOH...** **Insider Tip**
>
> Again, read the marketing materials and prospectus to determine whether the funds meet your objectives. One of the great advantages of the variable annuity is the ability to invest in several funds under the tax sheltered umbrella of one product. Choose the funds as part of an integrated plan.

Foreign Funds

One of the areas receiving great attention over the last five years is the overseas investing arena. Touted especially by the major Wall Street firms, *international* and *global* funds are often options within variable annuities. They offer the two choices for stock and/or bond funds. Within those two classes, they can have aggressive, growth, income, or the other objectives.

Jargon Alert

Overseas funds can have one of two configurations. An *international fund* invests overseas, but not in the U.S. The fund will usually diversify among numerous countries. A *global* fund, on the other hand, can invest world-wide, including the U.S. Some variable annuities will also offer single country funds, such as a Japan fund. These are *sector* funds.

Index Funds

The *index funds* are increasing in popularity as investors realize how difficult it is to beat the averages year-in and year-out. One way to ensure you never do worse than the S & P average, for example, is to buy the S & P stocks. Not literally, but to mimic the S & P through an index fund that will buy the same 500 stocks in the same percentage as the S & P.

Jargon Alert

The *S & P index* refers to the Standard & Poor's 500 stocks. This is a broad range of stocks—broader than the Dow Industrials, which is 30 stocks—and considered to be a good gauge of the overall stock market's behavior.

Asset Allocation Funds and Services

Fund companies realized that to attract many investors who lacked experience, they needed to offer to help the annuity owner to invest for the long term. The answer was an asset allocation fund. The fund diversifies among stocks, bonds, international securities, and short-term cash vehicles, depending on the fund manager's reading of the overall investment climate.

Some variable annuities take a different approach. They offer an asset allocation service. The fund sponsor will pay a money manager to make monthly or irregular allocation recommendations between stock, bond, cash, and international funds inside the annuity. The insurance company will make the adjustments in the percentages of the funds owned as the calls change.

Neither approach is a panacea. But this is a good approach for the novice investor looking for balance and conservatism inside the product.

Guaranteed Fund

The guaranteed account is a fixed rate account. It is a parking place for the short term, or a fund from which to *dollar cost average* into equity funds. Most variable annuities have a dollar cost averaging program that uses the guaranteed rate account as the starting point for the systematic deposits. The insurer automatically makes the transfer each month or however often selected.

The fixed rate account is probably not the best place to put money long term because it does not take advantage of the bond and equity markets. If you want the fixed-rate approach for the long run, buy a fixed-rate deferred annuity instead.

Jargon Alert

Dollar cost averaging is an investment strategy for long-term investors—which you should be if you're buying a variable annuity. The strategy calls for regular, systematic investments over time into a fund or funds. By investing the same amount each period, you take out the perils of volatile markets by buying more shares when the market is down and fewer when the market goes up.

Transfers

One of the unique characteristics of a variable annuity is the ability to move from one fund to another. This can be an advantage or a hindrance, depending on whether the privilege is used or abused.

Most products now put a limit on the number of transfers per year. The rationale is to cut down on the administrative costs as well as to protect the fund shareholders from *market timers*. Both can be costly to the fund.

Jargon Alert

A *market timer* is an investor or investment advisor who tries to predict major moves in the stock market and react by selling just before downturns and buying just before upturns. Some timers have advisory services for mutual funds and variable annuities. The market timer's approach is the opposite of the strategy called *buy and hold*, in which an investor rides out all market fluctuations.

Moves from one fund to another involve paperwork and expenses. The expenses are levied against the fund. Market timers tend to generate expenses more frequently than other investors who generally *buy and hold* funds. Additionally, they can weaken a fund's results by forcing a liquidation of fund shares at potentially inopportune times, which can trigger gains or loses.

OOOH... **Insider Tip**

Unless you're a very experienced and sophisticated investor, avoid market timing. In the last 30 years, which had some 7,800 trading days, 95 percent of the gains in the Dow have occurred in 90 days. If you missed these 90 days, $1 invested in 1966 would have been worth $2 today. If you had just left the dollar alone and held on, your $1 would be worth $28 today.

The Importance of the Fund Manager

In the case of life insurance and fixed annuities, the solvency of the insurer is paramount. This is because your money is under their control. But with the variable annuity, the wisdom of the fund manager is more important. The success of the product will lie with the sagacity of the manager in the markets. The premium you invest will be separated from the insurance company's assets.

So how do you find out about the managers?

➤ The prospectus is the first place to look for the investment history of the fund.

➤ A more contemporaneous history of performance is found in *Barron's* weekly newspaper, with a section devoted to variable annuities and fund unit values.

➤ The third alternative is VARDS (Variable Annuity Research & Data Service), a rating service similar to A.M. Best (which was described in the life insurance discussions in Chapter 4). This is the premier rating service for variable annuities. You can contact VARDS in Atlanta at (404) 998-5186.

➤ The fourth source of information on performance is Morningstar, one of the top analysts of the mutual fund industry. You can call Morningstar at (800) 876-5005.

OOOH... **Insider Tip**

As with any investment, look at the long-term results. If there aren't any because the fund is too new, take this into consideration in your comparison shopping. Often, a fund may be new in a variable annuity, but the fund manager has a track record from other fund management positions. Ask.

The Least You Need to Know

Many of the considerations discussed in the preceding chapter on SPDAs are applicable here. However, variable annuities are very different in execution, if not in their ultimate purpose as a vehicle for tax-deferred retirement savings.

➤ Look for a reasonable surrender charge schedule. Eight to ten years is just too long.

➤ Compare the expense ratios of comparable policies.

➤ Choose quality. You will likely be more comfortable with high-quality, experienced life insurance companies and fund management companies. Avoid new companies. Let someone else be a pioneer with the Night Life Insurance Company of Your Region.

➤ If you're not an experienced investor, buy the annuity from someone who can help you make the right choices based on your long-range objectives.

Chapter 29

Tax Relief

In This Chapter

➤ Understanding the general rules for annuity taxation

➤ How to calculate the exclusion ratio for annuities

➤ Understanding the all-important tax law changes affecting annuities and grandfathering of certain older annuity contracts

➤ How the accounting rules of LIFO and FIFO come into play

➤ Understanding the rules for exchanges of contracts on a tax-favored basis

➤ How the annuity tables impact taxation

➤ How to use annuities in estate and gift situations

In this chapter, you'll learn about tax laws and annuities. The tax laws are complex and this brief generalization should not replace the tax advice of good accountants and lawyers. It will, however, make you aware of the general tax benefits of annuities.

Tax Deferred Accumulation

The tax simplification laws passed over the last decade have done more to ensure the continuation of the annuity as a viable investment opportunity than perhaps any other factor. Because most annuity buyers are at least partly motivated by tax deferral, it's important to know how an annuity will be taxed *before* you buy it!

The General Rule

Section 72 of the Internal Revenue Code governs most of the tax ramifications of owning an annuity. The most beneficial is the tax deferred accumulation of cash values inside the contract. The *general rule* of accumulation is that interest credited or gains realized inside the policy will not be taxed until distributed or surrendered. This rule is specific to annuities.

> ### Jargon Alert
>
> The term *general rule* is important because the Internal Revenue Code—the basics of tax law—is structured on the principle of a general rule, with exceptions, exceptions to exceptions, and so on. Those blessed with the capacity to think creatively and intuitively rather than logically and sequentially should refuse to read the Code, for fear of forever losing that gift.

Exception to the Rule

There is an exception to the general rule, however. Contributions made after February 28, 1986 to a deferred annuity owned by other than a "natural" person will not be considered annuity considerations. No, this does not mean you have to pass a test to determine if you are in any way an artificial person. "Unnatural" persons are corporations, trusts, partnerships, and the like. Except...

Exceptions to the Exceptions

...except that the preceding prohibition does not extend to annuity contracts that are held by the estate of the decedent because of death, held under a qualified retirement plan, or purchased by an employer pursuant to termination of a qualified plan.

Are you beginning to feel that throb in your temples that you get every year in mid-April? Is it difficult to visualize why the concept of a flat tax has caught so much attention? The only writings more obtuse and bewildering than the Internal Revenue Code are the regulations that the IRS writes to clarify the Code.

Having made the point of complexity, the remainder of the chapter will attempt to present the tax rules without undue complexity. Just remember that in the world of the law, nothing is as simple as it sounds.

Amounts not Received as an Annuity

The phrase serving as the heading of this section is actually the phrase used in the Code to describe all amounts taken from an annuity except by annuitizing the contract itself. It includes policy dividends, cash withdrawals, policy loans, policy assignments, and partial surrenders. Remember, annuitization is the process of converting a sum of money into a stream of income, choosing the option outlined in Chapter 27.

There is another critical date at play here. The tax law change in 1982 made the "amounts not received as an annuity" less favorable than before August 14, 1982. The new rule is that amounts received under the contract are treated as taxable income first, to the extent there is any gain in the contract.

An example may help. Assume you invested $10,000 into a deferred annuity in 1990 and it now has a cash surrender value of $14,000. The $14,000 increase in your cash value is the gain in the contract, as shown in the numerical example. The contract allows a 10 percent free withdrawal (no surrender charge). If you withdrew 10 percent ($1,400), the entire withdrawal would be taxable. Why? Because the rule is that withdrawals are taxable to the extent that you have a gain in the contract.

> **Bet You Didn't Know**
> Tax practitioners, like most busy people, tend to use abbreviations. One such instance is the shortening of the tax law names. The most sweeping law change for annuities was TEFRA, intended to be a tax reform act. Despite what your CPA may tell you, TEFRA does not stand for Tax Everything Feasible Right Away. It just seemed that way.

$14,000 cash value

$\underline{- 10,000 \text{ investment}}$

$ 4,000 gain in policy

Assume you had the same policy with the $14,000 cash value. If you withdrew $5,000 as an amount not received as an annuity, you would have taxable income of $4,000. The last $1,000 would be a return of your investment. Why? Because the rule is that withdrawals are taxable to the extent that you have a gain in the contract. The gain is $4,000.

Prior to the tax law changes in 1982, the $1,400 (as well as the $4,000 in the second case), would have been a nontaxable return of investment first, until the entire $10,000 premium was recovered. This is relevant because you may own an annuity taxed under the old rules.

LIFO and FIFO

No, these are not twin poodles. They're tax accounting terms that really should have no relevance to you except that the terms have been used in the annuity arena freely in the past. In the first example in the preceding section, when $1,400 is withdrawn from an annuity with a $4,000 interest gain, the treatment of the $1,400 of gain as taxable income is referred to as LIFO, or *last in first out*. The *last in* refers to interest credited. It will be considered *first out* when taken as a partial withdrawal, surrender, loan, and so on. The old law was FIFO—*first in first out*. In other words, the principal ($10,000) is withdrawn tax free first. Once the principal (first in) is exhausted, then the gain is withdrawn and taxed.

Jargon Alert
An *assignment* is a transfer of ownership for the purpose specified and to the extent specified, as described in the document used to create the assignment. It may be conditional on some future event such as the non-payment of a debt.

If you have an annuity started prior to August 14, 1982, it has valuable rights *grandfathered* by the tax law of the same year. Before you change the contract, consult your CPA or accountant.

Jargon Alert
When tax laws are changed by Congress, they are usually *prospective* in effect. This means the old law stays applicable until the new law takes effect. In the case of laws based on transactions, such as the purchase of an annuity, the new law will often state that the new law is effective for all transactions after the stated date. This continuation of prior law for prior transactions is called *grandfathering*, and it often preserves favorable tax treatment for you.

Policy Loans and Cash Value Assignments

Amounts received as policy loans from post-August 13, 1982 annuities are considered amounts not received as an annuity, just like the withdrawal previously described. Most annuity policies no longer allow loans; they prefer to let the policyowner rely on free withdrawals.

The same problem arises if the annuity is *assigned* for collateral. It's common, for example, for a bank to require collateral for loans beyond personal lines of credit. Life insurance or fixed annuity cash values are excellent sources of collateral. Unfortunately, the tax law in 1982 made assignments of annuity policies taxable events, to the extent of gain in the policy, as calculated in the prior section entitled "Amounts not Received as an Annuity."

Insider Tip
Never assign an annuity policy purchased after August 13, 1982 unless you have your tax adviser's approval. The policy will be subject to immediate taxation even though you have withdrawn no cash.

The 10 Percent Penalty Tax

Congress, in the 1982 tax act, wanted to make sure that annuities were being used as long-term retirement plans and not short-term tax vehicles. They imposed a penalty tax that is similar to the 10 percent penalty tax on premature withdrawals from IRAs. This penalty tax is levied against distributions that result in taxable income. This is the general rule.

And as you learned earlier, there are exceptions:

➤ Payments after the date the recipient reaches age 59 1/2.

➤ Payments made because the taxpayer is disabled.

➤ Payments made from qualified retirement plans.

➤ Payments made after the death of the holder of the annuity.

➤ Payments made from an immediate annuity that are substantially equal periodic payments. The aim here is to treat payments that are like a life annuity as a life annuity, and tax them as such. This tax treatment is discussed later in this chapter, in the section on Annuitization.

➤ Payments made from annuities purchased by an employer upon terminating a qualified retirement plan.

➤ Payments under negotiated structured settlements from an insurance company. Many legal judgments and settlements in liability cases today are secured by annuities purchased for the benefit of the defendant. These are called structured settlements.

➤ Payments that are part of a series of substantially equal periodic payments made for the life of the taxpayer. These are potentially complex rules that should be interpreted by your tax adviser. But again, as mentioned previously, the philosophy is to allow payments that emulate life annuities to be taxed as life annuities.

Bet You Didn't Know

This last exception illustrates the famous legal principle of the quacking duck. The principle states that if it looks like a duck, walks like a duck, and quacks like a duck, then it will be treated as a duck. It's advisable to leave the judgment of the duck's qualities to those trained in such matters, such as CPAs and tax attorneys.

Multiple Contracts

A corollary to the duck principle is the pig theory. It states that a pig in a tuxedo is still a pig. The application of the principle was most evident in an early tax law case where taxpayers created numerous trusts in order to slip around a tax rule aimed at one trust.

Well, some too-bright taxpayer (or tax practitioner) was going to do the same thing with SPDAs to minimize the application of the LIFO interest-first rules. If a taxpayer with $100,000 to invest in SPDAs wanted to pull out income without tax, he could buy ten contracts for $10,000 each. Then, by withdrawing from just one of the contracts, both interest and principal, he could draw a little income and more return of investment.

Single contract: $100,000 at 6 percent interest

$100,000 premium

$\times\ .06$
_____

$6,000 interest

If the owner wanted a $6,000 withdrawal, all would be taxed as income received and not as an annuity. (There might also be the 10 percent penalty.)

To circumvent this rule, the taxpayer could have bought ten $10,000 annuities. Each would have earned $600 in interest, and that would be the gain in each contract. But what if the shrewd taxpayer withdrew $6,000, all from one contract?

Multiple contracts: $10,000 at 6 percent interest × 10 contracts

$10,000 premium

× .06

$600 interest gain in each policy

$10,600 new cash value each policy

–6,000 total withdrawal from one policy

$4,600 remaining cash value

The withdrawal of $6,000 would be characterized as $600 of gain, hence income, and $5,400 as return of investment in the contract, not taxable.

Congress saw the handwriting on the wall of the sty and invoked the pig theory, stating that you could not use multiple contracts to avoid the interest-first rules. The IRS will aggregate all policies purchased in the same company during any calendar year.

Tax-Free Exchanges of Annuities

Section 1035 of the Internal Revenue Code permits the tax free exchange of one annuity contract for another. This is true even if one is a fixed deferred and another a variable deferred annuity. It is also applicable to exchanges into different companies.

There are procedures to follow when exchanging contracts, and it is advisable to enlist the assistance of a qualified life underwriter or broker. You want to avoid the IRS claiming that you surrendered the old contract and reinvested the proceeds. The best way to do this is to allow the monies to move from company to company directly.

When might an exchange be justified?

> ➤ A change of direction in your planning, moving from a fixed deferred annuity to a variable annuity to take advantage of the investment options.

> ➤ A valid concern with the soundness and solvency of the current SPDA insurance company.

Watch It!
The surrender charges on the old policy may be levied against the cash value before the transfer. This can reduce the amount available for reinvestment and can result in poorer performance in the new contract. If surrender charges will be levied on the exchange, get a written statement why the broker believes it is still a good idea to transfer.

Watch It!
Go slowly in exchanging one annuity for another. The replacing broker must submit the proper forms, and you need to know what you're signing. Replacements and exchanges can be justified. Make sure you're comfortable with the move, however.

➤ A commitment of higher rates on an SPDA for more than one year.

This change usually means starting surrender charges for the new contract. If you see a need for the cash before the end of that new surrender charge period, don't make the transfer.

➤ A clearly superior track record of managed funds over a long period of time. Some funds do better than others, but don't get carried away with last year's winners in a variable annuity. The new funds must be much better over a long period of time to justify the new surrender charges and free withdrawal schedules.

Annuitization

Annuitization, as you remember, is the process of converting a principal sum of money into income, usually through an insurance company. In Chapter 27, you learned that there were six traditional options for annuity income. Now, how will they be taxed? Again, this area can be quite complex. At the risk of oversimplification, this chapter will stick to the most basic rules.

The General Rule

The concept behind the taxation of annuity payments is to allocate part of each annuity payment to the return of the purchaser's investment and part to interest. The return of investment is not taxable. Interest is.

The Code creates an *exclusion ratio* for purposes of calculating the portion of each payment to be treated as tax-free.

Watch It!

While I've tried to make the next section as simple as possible, if you are painfully averse to fractions, you may want to bail out during the math exercises. Some people rely on the insurance company and their tax preparer to wade through the unclear waters of the Internal Revenue Code.

The ratio is as follows:

$$\frac{\text{investment in the contract}}{\text{expected return}}$$

That is straightforward enough. It is a somewhat typical general rule. The total amount you invested in the annuity is compared to the total amount expected to be returned.

For example, assume you have invested $25,000 into an annuity and, according to the insurance company, you can expect to receive $50,000 over your life expectancy.

$$\frac{\$25,000 \text{ investment}}{\$50,000 \text{ expected return}}$$

The ratio is 1/2. This is then applied to each payment you receive from the insurance company.

Forever, you ask? No. If the annuity starting date of your contract (when you start to receive the monthly payments) is after 1986, you receive the payments 1/2 tax-free only until you have recaptured all of your investment. The date is a minor worry if you're reading this book because you would know if you had been receiving payments already.

Finding the Expected Return

For a life annuity, you need to know the life expectancy of the annuitant. This figure can be obtained from any insurance company. After you have that number of years, you multiply it by the monthly annuity payments you will receive. That is the total you expect to receive, actuarially and for tax purposes. Naturally, you will live well beyond that time, but at least now you know how to figure out how much of each payment is tax-free and taxable.

For example, assume you purchased an immediate annuity with $80,000 on your 68th birthday, January 1. The insurance company promises to pay you $750 per month for the remainder of your life. That equates to $9,000 a year ($750 × 12 = $9,000). The prescribed annuity table states that your life expectancy at 68 is 17.6 years. What is your expected return?

The calculations would be as follows:

$9,000

× 17.6

$158,400

The expected return is $158,400. The next step is the exclusion ratio:

$$\frac{\$80,000 \text{ investment}}{\$158,400 \text{ expected return}}$$

or 51 percent.

This means that 51 percent of each $750 monthly payment is excludable from income for income tax purposes. That is $382.50. But the exclusion does not last forever under current tax laws. You only exclude income until you have recovered your cost—in this case $80,000. How do you know when that takes place?

$$\frac{\$80,000 \text{ investment}}{\$382.50 \text{ exclusion}}$$

or 209.15 months. This equates to 17 years and 5 months. You will be able to exclude 51 percent of each annuity payment for 17 years and 5 months, at which time you will be 85 years old. After the $80,000 is recaptured, the entire monthly payment is included in your taxable income.

Calculations for Other Annuities

Well, if you're fed up with numbers, fear not, the remainder of the discussion requires no pencil. The calculations for other life annuities, such as term certain, are similar, except there is a credit given for the guaranteed portion of the annuity calculation. The calculation is beyond the scope of this book. But the important point to remember is that if you take an annuity payout, make sure you get qualified tax opinions on the taxable portion of your annuity. Most insurance companies will give you this information via their computers.

Variable Annuitization

There is one other potential plan for immediate annuities, a variable immediate. It is used far less frequently than fixed immediates, primarily because of the risk involved. The annuitant purchases an immediate annuity that will fluctuate in value because the principal sum is invested in a variable portfolio, based on stocks and bonds. The rationale is that with time the payments will increase because they're equity based.

Mechanically, the purchaser buys into a fund (or several funds) at the current price per share. If the fund with $1,000,000 is valued at $10 a share and the purchaser puts in $10,000, he will buy 1,000 shares. This number of shares stays the same. They may increase or decrease in value as the $1,000,000 fund grows or decreases in value.

> OOOH... **Insider Tip**
>
> If in fact the equity markets continue to dramatically outperform the fixed rate markets, variable immediate annuities will presumably become a more popular retirement funding vehicle. If you can afford a fluctuating income, explore this alternative.

Estate and Gift Taxes

This is not the proper venue for a detailed discussion of estate and gift tax law, but be aware that annuities are assets that are subject to these complex laws. They can trigger a gift tax if gifted and an estate tax if included in the estate for tax purposes. So make your plans after seeking tax counsel.

The Least You Need to Know

The tax laws are complex and thorough. While deferred annuities can be tax favored, they aren't tax-free. Income from annuities can be structured to meet your needs.

➤ Don't be guilty of jumping over dollars to get to dimes. If your tax situation is complicated and you aren't devoted to the task of researching the law, hire a professional CPA or accountant with tax expertise to work with you.

➤ Buy deferred annuities for tax and income reasons—not just taxes. Along with the duck and pig principles, there is the dog principle. Don't let the "tax tail" wag the dog. The dog is paramount. The tail is secondary.

➤ Buy variable annuities only if you're committed to the long term, meaning over 10 years and preferably 20. It takes time to recapture your expenses.

➤ If you invest in a variable annuity, especially in equities, remember that the markets are two-way streets, with traffic going up and down. Don't let stock market euphoria color your long-term perspective.

Part 6
Property and Casualty Insurance

This final part examines your needs for insurance to protect your physical assets and to protect you against the increasing threat of lawsuits in America today.

How do you find the best protection for your home, your car, and other assets of like value? When should you self-insure against the threats of fire, theft, storms, and similar catastrophes?

What are the various alternatives for insuring yourself and your property? Find out what the policies are really saying. You will find Part 6 less expensive and less time-consuming than law school or hiring a lawyer to explain the legal mumbo-jumbo to you.

Chapter 30

Homeowners and Renters Insurance

In This Chapter

➤ Understanding the risks associated with owning a home

➤ The important provisions in any homeowners policy

➤ Picking your way through the policy

➤ Where the premium savings are in homeowners insurance

➤ The coverage recommended for renters

The lines between property, casualty, and health insurance are sometimes blurred. This book considers property insurance to include loss of your assets such as your home, auto, boat, and business assets. Casualty encompasses liability to someone else's property or person. It may also cover health coverage for accidental injuries, for example. Health insurance was covered in prior chapters, so here the focus is on property and liability losses and the areas of greatest concern to you—your home, auto, and other property.

The property and casualty side of the business (as opposed to the life and health insurance side) controlled over $700 billion in assets at the end of 1994, held by 3,300 out of

6,000 insurance companies. (The Insurance Information Institute (III), however, states that most of the property and casualty insurance in this country is written by 900 companies.) The premiums received by the property and casualty (P&C) insurers in that same year was $250 million. That is essentially the same amount of premium as the life insurers collected.

There's No Place Like Home

Homeowners insurance premiums have risen in the last decade from $14 billion in 1985 to $22.5 billion in 1994. Obviously, homeowners are concerned about the possibility of damage and loss to their property. So are mortgage lenders.

Jargon Alert

Homeowners insurance is insurance that protects the owner of a home used for personal living against the perils of fire, storm, theft, and related damage. There are standard provisions in the policies that are required by law.

Who's the Buyer?

Approximately 68 percent of Americans own their own homes. This number has been relatively consistent for the last decade or so. Likewise consistent is the percentage of homeowners who insure their homes—between 93 and 95 percent. One can only speculate on why someone would not insure their home, but the overwhelming majority recognize how critical that insurance is. You should be in the majority on this one.

You should also have insurance as a renter if you do not own. But according to the III, only 41 percent of renters have insurance to cover their contents and possessions. This represents a significant increase over the prior decade for renters, with 28 percent insured in 1984. Nevertheless, renters are assuming unnecessary risks.

You might have guessed that the increase in premiums from $14 billion to $22.5 billion over the last decade would reflect more people opting for the coverage. And yet, the statistics on the percentage of homeowners with insurance seems to indicate that some other force is at play. That force is probably inflation and its impact on the total value of the property to be insured. As the value of your home increases, as many did in the last decade, your premium will also increase, assuming you want the insurance to keep up with the value of the home. As you will learn later, this assumption is not automatic. You will need to be responsible for seeing to it that the insurance increases.

What's the Cost?

The III reported that the Bureau of Labor Standards estimated that Americans spent 6.8 percent of household spending on insurance in 1993. Of that figure, homeowners coverage was 0.6 percent. That is less than 1 percent of the entire household budget versus 2.2 percent for automobile insurance.

The III also reported that a study by the Alliance of American Insurers in 1991 revealed that on average, the American household spent $420 a year for homeowners insurance. The premium you pay will obviously depend on the value you're insuring. But the premium will also depend on the state you live in (the geographic location, not the confusion or turmoil). Property values as a rule may be higher in some states or around certain cities, and some states have a greater incidence of damage due to severe storms.

Table 30.1 The Average Homeowners Premium for Each Household for Selected States in 1991 (Based on Homes Worth $125,000 or More)

State	Average Premium	State Rank by Expense
Texas	$592	1
Massachusetts	$548	2
California	$539	3
Louisiana	$527	4
Mississippi	$526	5
South Carolina	$436	10
New York	$459	12
New Jersey	$452	13
Colorado	$448	15
Vermont	$412	20
Illinois	$363	30
North Dakota	$350	40
Wisconsin	$274	48

Source: Insurance Information Institute

Some of the premiums are surprising. Would you have guessed Louisiana's and Mississippi's? The influence of the hurricanes and flooding in the Gulf of Mexico may have driven the cost of insurance way up in this region.

Well, you know that the coverage isn't cheap. And you know that it will vary with the region or state. Now take a look at whether you need it.

What Are the Risks?

According to the III's *1996 Fact Book*, approximately 8 percent of all households filed a claim under their homeowners policy in the last 12 months. That's a good indication of the policy usage. But is there really that much lost? Read on.

Some Stats on Fires to Ponder

Homeowners stand to lose a great deal from fire. The statistics in Table 30.2 tell the story in human life terms. But that is only part of the story.

➤ A fire department responds to a call every 15 seconds in this country. Every 70 seconds there is a residential fire.

➤ One person dies from fire every 123 minutes. There is one fire injury every 19 seconds.

➤ Approximately 4,275 civilians died in 1994 as a result of fire. The greatest at-risk groups are children under 5 and adults over 65.

Table 30.2 The Number of Deaths by Fire per 100,000 Persons by Age Group

Year	0-4	5-14	15-24	25-44	45-64	64+
1985	4.1	1.3	1.0	1.3	2.2	5.2
1986	4.3	1.3	1.0	1.3	1.9	4.8
1987	4.5	1.2	0.9	1.2	1.8	4.9
1988	4.2	1.2	0.9	1.3	2.0	5.0
1989	3.9	1.3	0.8	1.3	1.8	4.6
1990	3.5	0.9	0.8	1.1	1.6	4.1
1991	3.8	1.1	0.7	1.1	1.4	3.9
1992	3.4	0.9	0.6	1.0	1.5	3.7
1993	3.5	0.8	0.5	0.8	1.4	4.3
1994	3.5	0.8	0.7	1.0	1.5	4.2

Source: National Safety Council and Insurance Information Institute.

➤ According to the U.S. Fire Administration and reported by III, cooking accounted for 20 percent of the reported residential fires in 1993. Heating problems accounted for 15 percent.

➤ Careless smoking was the number one cause of deaths in residential fires. Sometimes you don't have to wait to die from a protracted tobacco-related illness.

➤ Property losses in 1994 due to fire were estimated at $12.3 billion, according to Insurance Services Office. The III calculates that to be a loss of $47.37 per capita in the U.S. That's up from approximately $9.5 billion in 1990, or $38.26 per capita.

Catastrophes in 1994

The possibility of property damage from catastrophes is usually thought of well after the threat of loss from a fire or a burglary. But the statistics prepared by the Property Claim Service division of the American Insurance Services Group, Inc. and reported in III's *1996 Fact Book* are amazing:

➤ The total insured catastrophic losses in 1994 are estimated at $17 billion. The most costly was an earthquake and accompanying fires that caused losses estimated at $12.5 billion.

➤ A series of wind and hail storms and tornadoes caused flooding throughout the middle of the country from April 25-27, with a damage price tag of $750 million.

➤ Tropical storms Alberto and Beryl coupled with Hurricane Gordon for estimated insured loss payments of $235 million.

Table 30.3 shows the tremendous dollar cost of the most expensive catastrophes.

Table 30.3   The Ten Most Expensive Catastrophes for Insurers in History

Month/Year	Catastrophe	Estimate Dollar Loss
August/1992	Hurricane Andrew	15.5 billion
January/1994	Northridge, CA earthquake	12.5 billion
September/1989	Hurricane Hugo	4.2 billion
March/1993	Winter storm, 20 states	1.7 billion
October/1991	Oakland, CA fire	1.7 billion
September/1992	Hurricane Iniki	1.6 billion
October/1989	Loma Prieta, CA earthquake	.9 billion

continues

Table 30.3 Continued

Month/Year	Catastrophe	Estimate Dollar Loss
October/1993	California brush fires	.9 billion
May/1995	Texas and New Mexico storms	.9 billion
December/1983	Winter storm, 41 states	.8 billion

Source: Insurance Information Institute and Property Claim Services division of the American Insurance Services Group, Inc.

The picture is clear enough at this point that you don't need further statistical reasons for insuring your assets. If you don't believe it now, only a major loss of your own will change your mind.

The Important Provisions in Your Policy

The homeowners policy represents a packaged approach to property and casualty insurance. The most important byproduct of the packaging of several coverages under one policy has been the increase in previously ignored coverage, such as personal liability and contents protection.

The typical homeowners policy today includes fire insurance, personal liability insurance, theft insurance, and contents protection.

Policy Classifications

There are several standard policy types, designated as HO-1 up to HO-8. There are four standard coverage categories, A–D.

Table 30.4 Homeowners Coverage—Own Property Alternatives

	Standard Coverage Categories			
Policy Type	Dwelling(A)	Structures(B)	Contents(C)	Loss of Use(D)
HO-1 (Basic)	$15,000 min.	10% of A	50% of A	10% of A
HO-2 (Broad)	$15,000 min.	10% of A	50% of A	20% of A
HO-3 (Special)	$20,000 min.	10% of A	50% of A	20% of A
HO-4 (Tenant's)	None	None	$6,000 min.	20% of C
HO-6 (Condo)	$1,000	Included in A	$6,000 min.	40% 0f C
HO-8 (Modified)	$15,000	10% of A	50% of A	10% of A

Table 30.4 shows the relationships between the value of the dwelling in HOs 1–3 and 8. The tenant's policy is concerned with contents and loss of use. The condo policy limits the dwelling loss to $1,000. Does this mean if you have a condo you can't insure it for loss of the dwelling? No. The condominium association carries a policy in which you as an owner share the cost and benefits of the insurance coverage.

Perils Coverage

The perils covered vary from one policy form to another, as illustrated in Table 30.5. The perils listed in the various policies are straightforward, except for "open perils." This term is used to mean all perils are covered.

Table 30.5   Perils Covered by Policy Form

Policy Type	Perils Covered
HO-1 (Basic)	Fire, wind, lightning, hail, smoke, riot, aircraft, vehicles, vandalism, theft, glass breakage, and volcanic eruptions.
HO-2 (Broad)	Same as HO-1, plus coverage for falling objects; heating and air conditioning damage; snow, ice, and sleet damage; water damage; plumbing damage from freezing; and damage from artificially generated electricity.
HO-3 (Special)	Open perils on the structures; same perils as HO-2 unless endorsement for open perils.
HO-4 (Tenant's)	Same perils as HO-2.
HO-6 (Condo)	Same perils as HO-2.
HO-8 (Modified)	Same perils as HO-1, except theft only as to premises and limited to $1,000.

Source: Vaughn, Fundamentals of Risk and Insurance

Dwelling and Other Structures—Replacement Cost

The coverage under these two categories is for the home itself—the dwelling and separate buildings and structures. The term *structures* is important because it includes items that are not buildings, such as fences, pools, and detached studios or garages.

The standard homeowners policy provides for *replacement cost* coverage. This means that the insurer pays the amount that it costs to replace the dwelling—not the stated cash value. This is important because the house may cost more to replace than you would sell it for, and the cash value may not keep up with the rising replacement costs in times of inflation.

Insider Tip

OOOH...

Review your coverage now to make sure you're covered for replacement costs, not cash value. Even though the standard policy specifies replacement value, not all policies insure under that standard. Review your coverage on a regular basis, at least every few years, to make sure you have enough coverage on Coverage A to approximate the cost to rebuild your dwelling. Don't rely on anyone else to update your coverage.

Inflation Guard

One of the ways you can protect against rising costs of construction is to purchase an endorsement to your policy called the *Inflation Guard Endorsement.* You may select the rate of inflation you want to use for the increase in value of your home, such as 1, 3, or 5 percent. The percentage is usually applied on a quarterly basis.

Insider Tip

OOOH...

When you calculate the replacement value of your home, be sure to include other structures and additions, such as decks, pools, separate buildings, and the like. Insure for 100 percent of the replacement value, then add the Inflation Guard Endorsement.

The starting point for the value of your home should be its current replacement cost. That excludes the value of the land because the land will not have to be replaced unless you reside on a cliff somewhere. (If that is the case, check into Government Insurance Plans, which cover areas susceptible to catastrophes.) To get a good handle on replacement costs, check with your insurance agent and a reputable builder.

Guaranteed Replacement Cost Policy

The next option is what is called a *guaranteed replacement cost policy*. This solves the problem by just defining the insurance amount as the replacement cost.

Insider Tip

OOOH...

Ask for a quote based on a guaranteed replacement cost policy. Compare the premiums with the replacement cost and inflation guard approaches. Always get quotes from several carriers.

Contents Protection

The *contents coverage* is set as a percentage of the dwelling coverage. Check your policy to see what the percentage is—50 percent, 75 percent, or whatever. Let's say the contents coverage is set at 50 percent of the dwelling coverage. This does not mean that you will automatically receive 50 percent of the dwelling value for your contents. For example, the HO-3 (Special) policy form has a minimum dwelling coverage of $20,000. The minimum contents coverage then, is 50 percent of $20,000, or $10,000. If the value of your home is $100,000, your contents coverage will be $50,000. That's the good news. The bad news is that it is probably based on the cash value of the item, not its replacement cost.

For example, let's say you purchased a CD-ROM home computer with all the bells and whistles for $4,000. Fire destroys the computer along with other property two years later. If the insurance company argued that the depreciation on the computer was $2,500, they would pay $1,500, not the $4,000 original cost or the replacement cost.

Insider Tip

When preparing your list of special items, photograph each item of value. For items of exceptional value, such as artwork, have the piece appraised by an appraiser who specializes in the area. Keep the list and photographs in a safe place away from the building, such as a safe deposit box.

If you have valuable assets that cannot be replaced, such as antiques, art, or stamp collections, you should consider separate coverage. This is commonly called *scheduled coverage*. It means that the assets of value are listed separately and insured for replacement cost or appraised value. These special assets can be covered under a special policy, called a *floater policy*. Or the assets can be added to the homeowners policy and itemized. Check with the insurance company to determine the best way to handle these items under your insurance.

Loss of Use Coverage

This portion of the policy is designed to reimburse you for the cost of living elsewhere while your home is being repaired from damage caused by a covered peril. The same provision can cover your expenses and loss of rents if part of your property is a rental.

Where to Save Premium Dollars

There are a number of ideas that can help you save money on your homeowners coverage. Utilize as many as you can, but remember that the most important objective is to buy the right coverage, not to save money. If saving money was most important, you wouldn't buy the insurance at all.

➤ Select the highest deductible you can afford. The III estimates the savings on premium to be 12 percent, moving from the standard $250 to $500. A $1,000 deductible can save you up to 24 percent.

➤ If you're looking for a home, be aware that newer homes frequently have lower premiums than older homes because of the older homes' outdated building materials and codes.

➤ The type of construction will have a bearing on your premiums. The preferred materials may vary from region to region. Ask an insurance agent about the preferences in your area. This may be helpful before you purchase or repurchase a home.

➤ Try to combine your homeowners and automobile policies with the same insurance company. This can result in combined discounts of up to 15 percent. Check the costs first, before you change coverage.

➤ Improve your home security. Most insurers will discount premiums for fire and theft prevention devices, such as smoke detectors, burglar alarms, dead-bolt locks, and sprinkler systems.

➤ Stop smoking. Or at least stop smoking in the house. Some companies offer discounts for smoke-free homes.

➤ Check out group plans that you may qualify for because of membership or other affinity. Group plans are not automatically less expensive. Compare coverage terms and premiums.

➤ Comparison shop the coverage. It's surprising how many people will visit ten auto dealerships before buying a car, but will take the first insurance policy offered.

For More Information

There are a number of insurance groups that publish helpful brochures and guides or that provide telephone assistance or Internet information.

➤ The Insurance Information Institute is one of the best. Call or write to ask for their annual *Fact Book*. It lists dozens of such organizations in addition to the III.

> 110 William Street
> New York, NY 10038
> Phone: (212) 669-9200
> Fax: (212) 732-1916

➤ The National Insurance Consumer Hotline at (800) 942-4242 is a good resource for general questions about property and casualty coverage, including homeowners insurance. They also handle life insurance.

➤ A great starting point for Web surfers is the KPMG Website. This is an international accounting and consulting firm, with vast experience in insurance. The address is http://www.kpmg.ca/insurance_links.html.

The Least You Need to Know

The homeowners policy is divided into two broad sections: damage to your property and damage to the property of others. The former was covered in this chapter. If you own your home, you need homeowners insurance. You can choose from a variety of plans, but you need to know what to look for first. Take the time to educate yourself before you need to make the decision, not after the first claim.

➤ Shop for the broadest, most comprehensive coverage you can afford.

➤ Shop with enough insurers to satisfy yourself that you're getting a competitive premium.

➤ Check the A.M. Best's rating for the company. You should only do business with very large, very secure companies. Read the earlier chapter in the life insurance section that deals with rating insurance companies.

➤ If you have valuables, protect them specifically with scheduled coverage or with an endorsement that will recognize their fair market value.

➤ Review your homeowners insurance often or whenever your living situation changes.

Chapter 31

More on Property Insurance

In This Chapter

➤ Understanding the need for renters insurance

➤ How and when to purchase flood insurance

➤ The breakdown of floater policies under inland marine coverage

➤ Understanding title insurance

➤ How to protect your boat and other watercraft

While your home is the most obvious subject for property insurance, it isn't the only one. It doesn't take much imagination to look around yourself at home and realize just how much you really own. And yet there are policies you may need that cover some things you rarely see and hardly ever think about. Your title is one. No, Sir George, not that title. The title to your home. This chapter will explore property insurance beyond your home and take a closer look at contents insurance alternatives.

I'll Do the Cookin' Honey, You Pay the Rent

It never came to light whether Bill Bailey's arrangement included paying the premiums for renter's insurance, but it probably should have. According to the III, 41 percent of renters had insurance in 1993. That represented a significant increase from just four years earlier when the renting population that carried renter's insurance was only 26 percent.

Is there a risk significant enough to insure? And what is the risk if you don't own the building or any other structures? The answer to those questions depends on whether you own anything of value, have anything worth protecting from liability, and have adequate cash on hand to move to another place to live while your apartment is repaired. There is more to the coverage than first meets the eye. And don't get fooled into thinking that your landlord's insurance protects your assets.

Property Losses

In 1994, there were approximately 451,000 structural fires. Of these, 341,000 were in one- or two-family dwellings, 97,000 were in apartments, and 13,000 were in dormitories, boarding houses, hotels, and other rental units.

The property losses from these fires was $4,317,000,000. The amount lost in apartment fires was $678,000,000. Somebody obviously lost something of value. But how do you measure that value? Is it a figure that stands out on a credit application? Probably not. The loss for most renters is not necessarily a room full of antiques. More likely, it is everything they own and need to function on a day-to-day basis: clothes for work and play, appliances, medical supplies and prescriptions, and furniture to sit on or sleep on or keep a family entertained. Get the picture?

Renter's insurance will not only cover the cost of replacing your contents (assuming you bought enough protection), it will also provide loss of use protection that will help you pay for temporary housing while your apartment or rental house is being repaired. This can be significant when you're forced to move to a local motel or hotel while the construction crews arrive to clean up and rebuild. Most people don't think of that expense. You shouldn't be one of them.

Insider Tip

The ultimate test of whether to insure your assets is whether it would create a financial hardship to replace them. That's how to look at renter's insurance, at least from a property stand-point. Do you have the cash on hand or the ready credit to go to the mall and replace everything tomorrow? If not, buy renter's insurance.

The liability part of the renter's policy will be discussed in the section on liability insurance, but a word first. It's easy to dismiss the idea of liability when you're renting. What could go wrong, and besides, who would want to sue you? Right? Wrong. If you have anything of value or if you're building your future with assets and aspirations, a lawsuit can change all that overnight. This society is litigation crazy. With as many lawyers as waiters in this country, it's becoming as easy to get served with a lawsuit as it is a cheeseburger. Without trying to debate the merits and demerits of today's legal system, suffice it to say that you need to buy protection from the legitimate and not-so-legitimate litigation that goes on today.

Floater Policies for Non-Swimmers and Swimmers Alike

You can forget the inflatable rafts and rubber ducks. These floaters refer to insurance policies that insure personal property. As mentioned previously, the modern homeowners policy is designed to meet most personal property insurance needs. However, there are assets that call for special treatment, such as expensive furs and jewelry, boats, and motor homes. This special coverage can be provided under your homeowners policy by endorsement or with a separate floater policy. Either will do the job.

The types of property that should be covered separately from the cash value coverage under your homeowners policy include:

➤ Personal jewelry

➤ Fine arts

➤ Silverware

➤ Stamp and coin collections

➤ Antiques and rare books

➤ Musical instruments

➤ Photographic and video cameras and players

Make a list of these assets to be covered under the floater, photograph them, and store the list and photos off the premises.

Insider Tip
Consider using a mini-cam or similar video camera for the pictures, especially one with sound. A walking tour of your home with a description of the assets and a running commentary can be very effective and thorough.

Noah's Ark with Flood Insurance

The typical homeowners policy excludes coverage for floods. If you live in areas close to rivers subject to rising waters or the ocean, this can be a major problem. Fortunately, Congress enacted the National Flood Insurance Program to help provide protection to the property owners in risk-prone areas. The federal government underwrites all of the insurance policies, although there are more than 80 private insurance companies that write flood insurance policies.

Bet You Didn't Know

WOW!

The federal program has issued or backed over 2.8 million policies. There are policies issued in every state, although there are some states with relatively few contracts. Montana, for example, has 496 policies as opposed to California with 41,597. (Source: Insurance Information Institute, *The Fact Book 1996*)

The coverage is not as expensive as you might imagine. The average premium in the U.S. was $293 for an average coverage of $96,841. Anyone who watched the rising waters of the Mississippi during the floods last year would consider the $300 well spent.

Bet You Didn't Know

WOW!

To give you an idea of the magnitude of the problem, there were 21,780 claims paid in 1994. There were 60,646 paid the year before when the flooding was so severe and widespread. The total claim payments in 1993 were $1,065,413,440 and $328,387,188 in 1994. That's an average claim of approximately $17,900 in either year. (Source: Insurance Information Institute, *The Fact Book 1996*)

The flood policy insures the dwelling, contents, and debris removal. The first two elements can be purchased separately. The definition of a flood is intended to be broad enough to provide coverage rather than exclude it. Flooding refers to the condition of either partial or complete inundation of normally dry land. The inundation can be temporary or permanent.

Insider Tip

OOOH..

When you purchase a home, the lender will usually ask for flood insurance if it believes you're in a flood-prone area. This area is sometimes called the *flood plain*. In any case, check with your insurer to see if the coverage is advisable. Don't wait until the water is rising.

The National Flood Insurance Program enlists the private insurance industry to help write the flood policies through a program called Write Your Own (WYO). According to III, 169 companies participated in the program last year, of which 86 actually wrote flood insurance. These companies issue the policies under their own name, but the federal government underwrites all of the coverage. The extent to which many states participate is shown in Table 31.1.

Table 31.1   Flood Insurance in the Largest Insured States for 1994

State	Number of Policies	Insurance
Florida	1,149,940	$122 billion
California	209,627	$23 billion
Texas	226,502	$22 billion
Louisiana	264,979	$22 billion
New Jersey	131,867	$15 billion
South Carolina	72,691	$9 billion
New York	77,016	$8 billion
North Carolina	53,838	$6 billion
Virginia	49,381	$5 billion
Georgia	38,624	$4 billion

Source: Federal Insurance Administration and Insurance Information Institute

Anchors Aweigh if You're Insured

The typical homeowners policy insures boats up to $500 or $1,000, and usually excludes theft away from your home. Because most of us don't drive our boats around our lawns, this is a bit too restrictive. If your boat, however, has a value of $1,000 or so and you live on a lake or river, this may be adequate.

On the other hand, if your boat (and trailer, if appropriate) is worth more than the homeowners coverage, or you like to keep the boat away from your premises, then shop around for a separate policy. There are basically two offerings. The outboard motorboat policy is the choice for small craft used on lakes, rivers, and inland waterways. The typical policy insures the cash value of the boat after a deductible. This is not designed to replace your five-year-old power boat with a brand new speed boat, or your ten-year-old john boat with a new bass boat and trailer.

The second coverage is yacht insurance. While the lines are not always clear between this and the outboard motorboat coverage, yacht insurance is thought of as protection for the oceangoing power

Insider Tip
Be certain to buy the broadest peril coverage possible. You want to be insured for loss, no matter how it happens. And most important, make sure you have liability coverage in the event of an accident or mishap at sea.

OOOH...

boat or sailboat. The coverage should be all peril or open peril coverage. If you're an oceangoing yachtsman, check with your insurer to make sure you are aware of any exclusions for "named tropical storms" in the Caribbean.

Title Insurance

Another form of property insurance protection is the title insurance policy. When you buy a home, you're buying what is called in the law a *fee simple interest*. This means that you're buying all the rights that normally attach to real estate. This bundle of rights is important, because it includes more than just the right of enjoyment—that is, the right to live in and use the property. And when you sell your home, the purchaser will want assurances that you're selling all of these rights, without liens, easements (granted rights of access over your property, such as a roadway), or other restrictions. That's where the title insurance comes into play. The title policy is an insurance policy that protects against losses from any problems associated with the title.

So, what can go wrong with the title? Here's a partial listing:

➤ Forgery by the prior seller

➤ Will contests and undiscovered wills and trusts

➤ Forgery in the public records affecting the property

➤ Easements

➤ Liens

➤ Encumbrances

Typically, when real property changes hands, there is an abstract of the title that is prepared by the attorneys. This is a public history of the title from owner to owner, with liens and other detractions from the title properly recorded. An attorney trained in real estate law will study the abstract to make sure you're buying the property without obstructions to a clear title. He can issue an opinion to that effect. If a problem arises in the future, you can sue the attorney and his liability insurance company.

Insider Tip

Always protect yourself and the property with title insurance. The one-time premium is a bargain compared to the possible loss. Use attorneys that specialize in real estate law.

A better approach is the purchase of title insurance. After the attorney completes his opinion of the state of the title, an insurance company can issue a title policy to protect you against subsequent difficulties with the ownership. The policy is delivered to you along with your documents at the time of the closing of the purchase.

It is interesting to note that the policy protects you from problems in the past, not the future. If a contractor renovates your home and you have a disagreement over the bill, he will file a lien against your property until the matter is resolved. But what if he doesn't subsequently remove the lien when it is satisfied? What if the dispute is not resolved when you try to sell the house? Your title insurance will be of no help. It covers defects at the time you bought the house.

The premium for the policy is a single premium, paid at the time of the closing. The benefits are dollars, not possession. If you're forced to vacate the premises after an issue is litigated, you'll receive money, not the house or a replacement house.

Below is a table of the leading writers of homeowners insurance ranked by the amount of premium they received in 1994. This does not mean they are the best or even that they write insurance in your state. But it does give you an idea as to their size.

Table 31.2   The 10 Leading Writers of Homeowners Insurance in the U.S. in 1994

Company/Group	Premiums	Percent Market Share
State Farm	$5.719 billion	23.6
Allstate	$2.883 billion	11.9
Farmers	$1.381 billion	5.7
USAA	$.784 billion	3.2
Nationwide	$.713 billion	2.9
Chubb	$.495 billion	2.0
Prudential	$.469 billion	1.9
Aetna	$.457 billion	1.9
Safeco	$.404 billion	1.7
ITT Hartford	$.379 billion	1.6

Source: A.M. Best Company and Insurance Information Institute

The Least You Need to Know

The other forms of property insurance are less significant than homeowners insurance in terms of premium, but not in importance. The loss of your contents is just as disastrous by flood as by theft or fire. Despite successful movement toward consolidating as much as possible under the homeowners form, there are assets and situations that call for separate policies. This does not necessarily mean separate companies.

➤ Inventory all of your valuable assets and then ask yourself if they're adequately covered for replacement or fair market value under your homeowners policy. If not, get a separate policy.

➤ Shop for the separate policy as you would any other coverage, but be sure to ask if there's a special discount for having the multiple policies in the same company.

➤ Be sure to check the flood possibility when you buy a home. Water damage from floods is excluded under almost all homeowners policies.

➤ Buy title insurance for any home that you buy, if available.

UH-OH...

Chapter 32

Auto Insurance

In This Chapter

➤ A brief history of auto insurance

➤ Understanding the basics of your automobile policy

➤ How and where to shop for the best coverage for the dollar

➤ How to read and interpret the limitations and exclusions under your policy

---

The automobile, America's obsession with a possession, has spawned hundreds of businesses to support its explosive growth. The promise of a chicken in every pot and a car in every garage seems a little empty to a generation of Americans who believe individual automobile ownership is an entitlement.

No business is more indicative of this obsession than the insurance industry. Look at some of the statistics that show how huge the "king auto" has become. Table 32.1 shows the premiums received by the companies that underwrite the most automobile insurance.

Table 32.1 The 10 Leading Writers of Automobile Insurance in the U.S. in 1994

Company/Group	Premiums	Percent Market Share
State Farm	$22.351 billion	19.2
Allstate	$12.131 billion	10.4
Farmers	$6.040 billion	5.2
Nationwide	$4.141 billion	3.6
USAA	$3.247 billion	2.8
Progressive	$2.535 billion	2.2
Geico	$2.308 billion	2.0
Liberty Mutual	$2.107 billion	1.8
ITT Hartford	$1.776 billion	1.5
American Family	$1.654 billion	1.4

Source: A. M. Best Company and Insurance Information Institute, The Fact Book 1996.

These are big numbers that really exist only to support the sale of automobiles. But the statistics show that the insurance is necessary. And not just because the law requires the coverage, but because we're still intent on playing bumper cars.

Tort Law, Tough to Swallow

Not only has an entire industry developed to meet the demands of automobile accidents and theft, but think of the number of lawyers who survive because of our driving habits. The obvious *tort* lawyers are complemented by their brothers at the bench, the criminal lawyers who defend and prosecute the drunk drivers, thieves, and criminally negligent.

Jargon Alert
Tort law deals with civil injury or wrongs, except for breach of contract wrongs. Injuring someone while driving in an automobile is an example.

Of course, there are lawyers who serve in the various state legislatures who write the laws governing our behavior behind the wheel. And then there must be judges to preside over disputes. The problem in this country is not too many lawyers. It's too many automobiles.

Before digging into the provisions in the typical policy, look at the important laws.

Bet You Didn't Know

WOW!

The cost of accidents is increasing. The average paid bodily injury claim in 1994 was $11,372. The average paid property damage claim was $1,900. This represents an increase of 66.9 percent and 56.1 percent respectively since 1985. This is faster than the cost of living increase in the same period, which was 37.7 percent. Update your coverage regularly.

Financial Responsibility and Compulsory Limits

Most states now require proof of financial responsibility (insurance) if you're involved in an accident, ticketed, or renewing your license. Most states also require owners of automobiles to carry a minimum amount of bodily injury and property damage liability insurance. These terms will be explained in more detail later in this chapter. For the moment, check out your state's requirements for insurance (see Table 32.2).

Table 32.2   The Requirements of Individual States as to Bodily Injury Liability per Person/per Accident/Property Liability, in Thousands

State	Liability Limits	State	Liability Limits
Alabama	20/40/10	Iowa	20/40/10
Alaska	50/100/25	Kansas	25/50/10
Arizona	15/30/10	Kentucky	25/50/10
Arkansas	20/50/15	Louisiana	10/20/10
California	15/30/5	Maine	20/40/10
Colorado	25/50/15	Maryland	20/40/10
Connecticut	20/40/10	Massachusetts	20/40/5
Delaware	15/30/10	Michigan	20/40/10
Florida	10/20/10	Minnesota	30/60/10
Georgia	15/30/10	Mississippi	10/20/5
Hawaii	25/25 per person/25	Missouri	25/50/10
Idaho	25/50/15	Montana	25/50/10
Illinois	20/40/15	Nebraska	25/50/25
Indiana	25/50/10	Nevada	15/30/10

continues

Table 32.2   Continued

State	Liability Limits	State	Liability Limits
New Hampshire	25/50/25	South Dakota	25/50/10
New Jersey	15/30/5	Tennessee	25/50/10
New Mexico	25/50/10	Texas	20/40/15
New York	25/50/10	Utah	25/50/15
North Carolina	25/50/15	Vermont	20/40/10
North Dakota	25/50/25	Virginia	25/50/20
Ohio	12.5/25/7.5	Washington, D.C.	25/50/10
Oklahoma	10/20/10	Washington	25/50/10
Oregon	25/50/10	West Virginia	20/40/10
Pennsylvania	15/30/5	Wisconsin	25/50/10
Rhode Island	25/50/25	Wyoming	25/50/20
South Carolina	15/30/5		

Source: Insurance Information Institute, The Fact Book 1996 *and the American Insurance Association*

For example, if your state is listed as requiring 25/50/20, you're required to carry bodily injury liability protection of $25,000 per person and $50,000 per accident. Additionally, you need $20,000 liability coverage for property damage.

Auto Policy Basics

The most common policy in force now is the personal auto policy. It breaks down the insurance protection into four areas: liability coverage, medical payments, uninsured motorist coverage, and physical damage to your auto. It's available to individuals (not businesses) who own automobiles.

OOOH...

Insider Tip
Business insurance for autos is beyond the scope of this book, but you should be aware that if you're a business owner with cars used in your business, you need to be especially sensitive to the liability issues with vehicles and the employees who drive them. Get a good property and casualty agent.

This basic policy is designed for private passenger automobiles only. If you drive a truck, check to make sure it's covered. With the overwhelming success of utility vehicles and trucks, the lines may blur. This doesn't mean that you won't be able to secure coverage for your truck—it just means you won't have access to this *particular* policy form. The fundamentals of the coverage will still be the same.

Liability

The liability portion of your contract covers damages which you become responsible for by virtue of an accident. Both *bodily injury* and *property damage* are covered under this section. The policy will cover you, your family, and any person using your covered auto. As Table 32.2 indicated, most states prescribe a minimum level of liability coverage. It is just a minimum.

> OOOH... **Insider Tip**
>
> If you have anything worth protecting in your name, buy as much liability protection as you can. The minimum in your state may be $20,000 per person and $40,000 for the entire accident. This is inadequate in today's world of "give it away" juries, who are generous because they know it's just an insurance company's money at risk. Buy as much as your insurance company will allow—coordinated with umbrella protection as outlined in Chapter 33. Apply the big mistake/small mistake test to help you decide on appropriate upper limits.

The insurance companies, by the way, agree in the policy to defend you in any litigation that results under the policy. But they also reserve the right to settle any litigation without your permission. So, if you happen to end up in court, don't be surprised if you discover that most of the lawsuits are not decided on the basis of who is right and who is wrong; they're negotiated on the basis of dollars and cents, not principles and sense. You can't take it personally if someone not at fault settles because the insurer thought it cheaper than fighting the lawsuit.

Liability Exclusions

There are several liability exclusions that should be reviewed:

➤ Intentionally inflicted bodily injury or property damage is excluded. It would be bad public policy to allow persons who deliberately cause damage to be protected.

➤ Property owned by the insured, rented by the insured, or in the care and custody of the insured is usually excluded, primarily because it ought to be covered elsewhere.

➤ Business usage of the automobile is also usually excluded, including renting the vehicle out for hire or in use by employees for business reasons.

➤ The policy form excludes coverage for persons who use the car without the belief that they were authorized to do so.

In summary, then, the liability portion of the policy is designed to protect you against any claims against you for damages either to another person or their property.

Bet You Didn't Know

Automobile insurance premiums in 1994 totaled $113.5 billion. Of that figure, $96.8 billion or 85 percent was attributable to private passenger autos. $16.7 billion (15 percent) was for commercial auto use. The liability portion of premiums in 1994 was $61,952,465,000, an increase of 4.5 percent over the prior year. In 1985, the premiums written were $28,243,882. (Source: A.M. Best Company, Inc. and III *1996 Fact Book*.)

Out-of-State Coverage

What happens if you purchase insurance that satisfies the financial responsibility laws in your state, but you're involved in an accident in another state with higher limits? There's a provision in the standard policy form that automatically adjusts your coverage for out-of-state limits. The clause also automatically adjusts to required compulsory statutes such as no-fault laws. Check your policy to make sure you have the clause entitled "Out-of-State Coverage."

Medical Payments

This section of your policy provides for the payment of reasonable medical expenses or funeral expenses caused by an accident and sustained by an insured. The policy's basic unit of coverage is $1,000, but you can expand the coverage to $10,000 for a reasonable premium increase.

The policy covers:

➤ The insured and family members of the insured

➤ Injuries while occupying the covered auto, including getting into and out of the car

➤ The insured and named family members while pedestrians

➤ Other persons while occupying your covered automobile

The exclusions are usually similar to the exclusions under the liability provisions, especially auto for hire and autos operated without a reasonable belief that the user had the authority.

Bet You Didn't Know

The III's *1996 Fact Book* lists statistics that highlight the importance of your insurance coverage. It estimated 33.9 million motor vehicle accidents in 1994, with an estimated number of injuries at 5,885,000 and 43,000 deaths. The total economic loss is estimated at more than $110 billion. Increase your medical payments to the maximum for your insurer.

Are some states more dangerous than others for automobiles? According to the National Safety Council as reported by III, Mississippi has the highest fatality rate—2.9 deaths per 100 million vehicle miles. Arkansas and Nevada were next highest with 2.5. Massachusetts and Rhode Island were the lowest in 1994 with 0.9 deaths in the same 100 million vehicle miles. California had the highest number of deaths, 4,212, but its population is so large that it boosts its vehicle miles. Its death rate was actually low at 1.5 deaths per 100 million vehicle miles.

Uninsured Motorists

It seems hard to believe there's anyone out there who is irresponsible when it comes to driving, but some people actually drive without insurance despite the laws to the contrary. The uninsured motorist provision covers your losses from their lack of responsibility.

The policy pays an amount that the insured could have collected had the uninsured driver carried the minimum required coverage in that state. Remember, this contractual promise is limited to the minimum. The protection extends to three situations:

Insider Tip
Increase your uninsured motorist coverage to the same limits applicable under the liability section of your policy. This is not an area in which you should try to save premiums.

➤ An uninsured or under-insured automobile under state laws

➤ Hit-and-run accidents

➤ Insured autos with insurance companies that become insolvent

Physical Damage Coverage

The physical damage section of the policy insures your covered automobile for damages due to collision or any other peril, such as theft or weather. Your policy can cover all physical damage to your car. This is usually provided under comprehensive coverage, which really is coverage for all risks of physical damage. *Collision* is a separate coverage item that includes damage to your auto from a collision with another car or any other object. The comprehensive coverage then would cover losses due to fire, theft, vandalism, storms, hitting animals, or explosions. The collision coverage will usually be scheduled separately. And it will relate to the value of your car. This is important, because not all cars are worth enough to insure against collision.

Insider Tip

Read the list of exclusions in your policy to make sure you can accept them. You may have significant money tied up in your stereo system, for example. You may be able to add a rider to cover these items or pick up the items through your other policies. Also make sure you understand the deductibles for both the comprehensive and collision portions of your policy.

Why wouldn't you want to cover collision for your auto? If your car's replacement value is exceptionally low, the insurance company is likely to consider any accident damage a total loss. The company will not want to pay to repair the old car. You may want to just start over with another car.

There are physical damage exclusions. Some of the more common include damage to tape players and other sound systems, antennas, and custom furnishings. The policy again typically excludes damage while the car is for hire.

No-Fault Insurance

The no-fault laws enable the insured to recover financial losses from their own insurance company regardless of blame or culpability. There are several no-fault states, but a wide variety in the accompanying laws as to right to sue and compulsory liability. It is beyond the scope of this book to differentiate the state's provisions. Just be aware that some states have different versions of no-fault coverage. Have your agent explain the law in your state and read that provision of the policy to make sure you understand it.

Driving And Drinking

The number of fatalities due to alcohol and automobiles is dropping. In 1994, the number of deaths from drunk-driving accidents decreased to 16,589 (40.8 percent). This is down from the 53.7 percent rate in 1985. There are a number of factors given credit for this decrease, but state laws making it tougher on drunk drivers are at the top. They include the following:

➤ Laws that limit alcohol consumption and purchase to persons 21 years of age

➤ Mandatory license revocations if caught driving with a blood-alcohol content above the state's limits

288

➤ Laws prohibiting open containers in a vehicle

➤ Sobriety checkpoints

➤ Canceling vehicle registrations in the event of a license suspension or revocation due to alcohol

You've heard it a thousand times before. Don't drink and drive. The cost in terms of human life, property damage, and career impediment—not to mention premium increases—is high.

Bet You Didn't Know

WOW!

A higher percentage of auto fatalities occurs in rural areas than urban areas—58.4 percent versus 41.0 percent (0.6 percent unaccounted for). This has been attributed to the potential for higher speeds in rural areas and the greater distance to hospitals.

How to Reduce Your Premiums

There are a number or ways to reduce your automobile insurance premiums. They include:

➤ Increase your deductibles, especially for property damage.

➤ Comparison shop your coverage. There can be significant differences in premium for the same coverage. After you receive your quotes, be sure to ask your homeowner insurer whether there's a discount for covering both home and auto with the same company.

➤ Ask for low-mileage discounts. The fewer miles you drive, the less likely you are to be involved in an accident.

➤ If you have an older car, consider dropping the very expensive collision coverage.

➤ When shopping for a car, check out the ratings on cars as to safety in collisions and from theft. "Low profile cars" can save you premium dollars.

Insider Tip
OOOH...
When you want to know about ratings, write or call the Insurance Institute for Highway Safety, 1005 North Glebe Road, Suite 800, Arlington, VA 22201. The phone number is (703) 247-1500. Ask for the Highway Loss Data Institute Chart.

➤ Ask about automatic seat belts and air bag discounts.

➤ Ask about anti-lock brake discounts.

➤ Ask about any other discounts, such as anti-theft devices, good drivers, student driver training, and students with good grades.

➤ Don't drive and drink.

➤ Keep your driving record free of moving violations and accidents.

The Least You Need to Know

The growth of the automobile industry has triggered an attendant rise in the insurance industry to support it. The cost of liability for accidents has become high enough to require insurance coverage. Most states acknowledge this fact with financial responsibility laws.

➤ Buy as much protection as you can afford, coordinating the coverage with umbrella protection (explained in Chapter 33). Increase deductibles and drop collision on old cars to help control costs, but carry all of the other protection you can reasonably afford.

➤ Your safe driving habits will impact your wallet. Just make sure your insurance company is aware of a good record.

➤ Think about insurance costs before you buy a car, not after you have driven it home.

Umbrella Liability and Other Insurance

In This Chapter

➤ The importance of liability insurance today

➤ The liability portion of your homeowners insurance policy

➤ The umbrella policy

The entire liability insurance area may be the most under-appreciated area in insurance today.

The need for liability protection for business owners, professionals, and the wealthy in this country has grown primarily because of the results of litigation in front of juries that are extremely generous with the insurance company's money. Million-dollar awards are commonplace and there's a strong bias by the insurers to settle lawsuits rather than litigate to the end. This makes anyone with assets and an insurance company in their corner wide open for aggressive *plaintiff's lawyers*—members of the Bar who file lawsuits against others for damages.

Jargon Alert

Liability insurance is insurance that protects you in the event that you carelessly cause bodily injury or property damage to other people. The liability can be because of negligence or a failure to live up to promises made under a contract.

This is not to say that there isn't a strong need for this area of the law. There is. Citizens need the protection of the law from unscrupulous businesses and negligent professionals. The law in this area of liability has developed responsibly to protect against abusive marketing, sales, and manufacturing, as well as negligence in medicine, law, and accounting. What has become unreasonable is the awards from juries.

The Personal Liability Umbrella

The insurance industry developed a broad-based liability policy to protect individuals from catastrophic liability awards. It's called an *umbrella policy* because it protects the individual like an umbrella that covers the entire space occupied by the individual. It covers automobile liability above and beyond your basic policy, and it covers general liability as well.

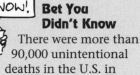

Bet You Didn't Know

There were more than 90,000 unintentional deaths in the U.S. in 1994. They were composed of 43,000 auto deaths, 26,700 deaths in the home, 5,000 deaths on the job, and 19,700 public deaths not related to autos. (Source: Insurance Information Institute, *The Fact Book 1996 1996* and the National Safety Council.)

The umbrella policy is designed to fit on top of other coverage, to dovetail with underlying policy limits. Different insurers have different requirements. One insurer may require, for example, an auto policy with limits of $100,000 of bodily injury per person and $300,000 per accident in total. It may also require $100,000 of property damage protection under your auto policy. Further, it may require $250,000 of coverage for liability under your homeowners policy. This is commonly known as *comprehensive personal liability* protection. Even if you opt not to carry an umbrella policy, you should increase your comprehensive personal liability coverage to the maximum allowed under the basic homeowners policy. The umbrella provides coverage from the point where the others end.

You've probably read about accidental deaths of children playing with guns or drowning in neighbors' pools. But what are the statistics?

III cites the National Safety Council's studies to report that of the 26,700 deaths in the home in 1994, most were children or those over 75 years old (see Table 33.1).

Table 33.1   The Distribution of Unintentional Death by Ages in 1994

Age	Number of Deaths
0-4	1,900
5-14	800
15-24	1,400
25-44	6,300
45-64	4,000
65-74	2,600
75+	9,700

Source: Insurance Information Institute, The Fact Book 1996 *and the National Safety Council*

Typical umbrella limits are $1,000,000 to $5,000,000. It is certainly foreseeable that the typical limits will rise with time. The limits you choose should be affordable and somewhat related to your worth and exposures. If you have swimming pools, watercraft, and similar potential sources of liability, then consider greater coverage. There's no scientific formula to calculate the exact right amount.

Tables 33.1 and 33.2 both illustrate the need for liability protection.

Table 33.2   The Distribution of Unintentional Injury Deaths in the Home in 1994, by Cause of Death

Cause of Death	Number of Deaths
Falls	8,500
Fires, burns	3,900
Suffocation	2,100
Poisoning by solids	6,400
Poisoning by gases	500
Firearms	900
Other	4,400

Source: Insurance Information Institute, The Fact Book 1996 *and the National Safety Council*

The function of the umbrella is to provide excess coverage above and beyond coverage under your basic auto and homeowners policies for liability. It also extends coverage to areas that may not have been covered previously by providing a broad insuring clause for all types of liability.

OOOH...   **Insider Tip**

Buy a personal umbrella policy with limits that exceed your worth if possible. Work with your existing insurer to make certain that the underlying auto and homeowners policies are up to the required limits in the new umbrella policy.

Snowmobiles, Jet Skis, and Other Toys

Most homeowners policies specifically exclude watercraft and snowmobiles except for limited liability. If you enjoy these sports vehicles, you need to check with your agent or read your policy to understand the coverage. Purchasing a separate policy often makes the most sense. This is especially true if you're going to purchase excess coverage through a personal umbrella policy. Remember that an umbrella policy regards as a deductible the base coverage you should have had to dovetail with the umbrella.

Offices at Home

There are an increasing number of people who work out of or in their homes. As you may remember from the homeowners chapter, most provisions exclude business pursuits. The same is true of your personal auto policy.

> **OOOH...** **Insider Tip**
>
> Read your homeowners policy. You'll likely see a provision that excludes coverage for business-related damages or limits the recovery to $1,000 or so. You need a separate policy to cover your business at home. Ask your current homeowner policy insurer. They may recommend a rider to your existing policy or a separate policy. The premium for this coverage is usually less than $200 a year and frequently less than $100. Also, check with business associations and trade groups you have joined for group coverage.

Travel Insurance

There are times when a cancellation of a vacation can be downright costly. In recent years, hurricanes and earthquakes have spoiled vacation plans for many travelers. But even worse, it can cost you money in nonrefundable deposits and tickets.

But you should not be thinking that natural disasters are the only threats to your vacation plans and funding. What about a death in the family or an illness during the trip? These can also result in a change of plans and a loss of big bucks.

Trip insurance is the answer.

There are several insurance companies that specialize in insurance to protect against trip cancellation or trip interruption. They can be contacted directly or through your travel agent. The travel agent is as valuable as your insurance agent in this area, especially if you've made your travel plans through the agent.

If you haven't and want to cover the trip on your own, here are several insurance resources:

➤ Access America at (800) 284-8300

➤ Travel Guard International at (800) 826-1300

➤ Travel Assistance International at (800) 821-2828

There are others, but this will get you started.

OOOH... **Insider Tip**

If you're scheduling a cruise, an extended travel excursion, or a vacation to an out-of-the-way place, look into trip insurance. For several percent of the cost of the trip, you can insure against natural disasters, illness, death in your immediate family, and other events that could interrupt or cancel your plans. Check for exclusions for pre-existing conditions and how the insurance company defines them.

The Least You Need to Know

There are great risks in society today with overzealous as well as well-founded litigation. You need to protect yourself against all manner of loss.

➤ Buy a personal umbrella policy to pick up where your homeowners and auto policies leave off. This will give you the coverage you need for the catastrophic award as well as the breadth of coverage under the underlying and blanket policy.

➤ Inventory your hobbies and avocations to ensure you're protected while recreating.

➤ If you work at home, buy coverage specifically for that purpose, either by rider, endorsement, or separate policy.

➤ When you plan your next big vacation, check into trip interruption and cancellation insurance.

Insurance Regulators' Names and Addresses

State	Regulator	Address	Phone
AK	Marianne K. Burke Director	Dept. of Commerce and Development Division of Insurance P.O. Box 110805 333 Willoughby Avenue 9th Floor Juneau, Alaska 99801	907-465-2515 fax: 907-465-3422
AK		3601 C Street Suite 1324 Anchorage, Alaska 99503-5948	907-269-7900 fax: 907-269-7910
AL	Michael DeBellis Commissioner	Department of Insurance 135 South Union Street Montgomery, Alabama 36130	334-269-3550 fax: 334-241-4292
AR	Lee Douglass Commissioner NAIC Immediate Past President	Department of Insurance 1200 West 3rd Street Little Rock, Arkansas 72201-1904	501-371-2600 fax: 501-371-2618
AZ	Chris Herstam Director	Department of Insurance 2910 North 44th Street, Suite 210 Phoenix, Arizona 85018-7256	602-912-8400 fax: 602-912-8452
CA	Chuck Quackenbush Commissioner	Department of Insurance 300 Capitol Mall Suite 1500 Sacramento, California 95814	916-445-5544 fax: 916-445-5280

State	Regulator	Address	Phone
CA		State of California 45 Fremont Street 23rd Floor San Francisco, California 94105	415-904-5410 fax: 415-904-5889
CA		425 Market Street, San Francisco, California 94105	415-904-6072 fax: 415-904-6085
CA		300 South Spring Street Los Angeles, California 90013	213-346-6400 fax: 213-897-6771
CO	Jack Ehnes Commissioner	Division of Insurance 1560 Broadway Suite 850 Denver, Colorado 80202	303-894-7499 fax: 303-894-7455
CT	George Reider, Jr. Commissioner	Department of Insurance P.O. Box 816 Hartford, Connecticut 06142-0816	203-297-3802 fax: 203-566-7410
DC	Patrick Kelly Acting Commissioner	Insurance Administration District of Columbia Government 441 Fourth Street NW 8th Floor North Washington, D.C. 20001	202-727-8000 ext. 3007 fax: 202-727-8055
DE	Donna Lee Williams Commissioner	Department of Insurance Rodney Building 841 Silver Lake Blvd. P.O. Box 7007 Dover, Delaware 19903	302-739-4251 fax: 302-739-5280
FL	Bill Nelson Commissioner	Department of Insurance State Capitol Plaza Level Eleven Tallahassee, Florida 32399-0300	904-922-3101 fax: 904-488-3334
GA	John Oxendine Commissioner	Department of Insurance 2 Martin L. King, Jr. Dr. Floyd Memorial Building 704 West Tower Atlanta, Georgia 30334	404-656-2056 fax: 404-657-7493

State	Regulator	Address	Phone
HI	Wayne C. Metcalf Commissioner	Insurance Division Dept. of Commerce and Consumer Affairs 250 S. King Street 5th Floor Honolulu, Hawaii 96813	808-586-2790 fax: 808-586-2806
IA	Terri Vaughan Commissioner	Division of Insurance Lucas State Office Building 6th Floor Des Moines, Iowa 50319	515-281-5705 fax: 515-281-3059
ID	James M. Alcorn Director	Department of Insurance 700 West State Street Third Floor Boise, Idaho 83720	208-334-4250 fax: 208-334-4398
IL	Mark Boozell Director	Department of Insurance 320 West Washington St. 4th Floor Springfield, Illinois 62767	217-785-0116 fax: 217-524-6500
		100 West Randolph Street Suite 15-100 Chicago, Illinois 60601	312-232-2385 fax: 312-814-5435
IN	Donna Bennett Commissioner	Department of Insurance 311 West Washington St. Suite 300 Indianapolis, Indiana 46204-2787	317-232-2385 fax: 317-232-5251
KS	Kathleen Sebelius Commissioner	Department of Insurance State of Kansas 420 S.W. 9th Street Topeka, Kansas 66612-1678	913-296-7801 fax: 913-296-2283
KY	George Nichols III Commissioner	Department of Insurance 215 West Main Street Frankfort, Kentucky 40602	502-564-6027 fax: 502-564-6090

continues

State	Regulator	Address	Phone
LA	James H. Brown Commissioner	Department of Insurance P.O. Box 94214 950 North 5th Street Attn: Patrick Frantz Baton Rouge, Louisiana 70801-9214	504-342-5423 fax: 504-342-8622
MA	Linda Ruthardt Commissioner	Division of Insurance Commonwealth of Massachusetts 470 Atlantic Avenue 6th Floor Boston, Massachusetts 02210-2223	617-521-7794 fax: 617-521-7770
MD	Dwight K. Bartlett, III Commissioner	Insurance Administration 501 St. Paul Place Stanbalt Building 7th Floor - South Baltimore, Maryland 21202-2272	410-333-2521 fax: 410-333-6650
ME	Brian Atchinson Superintendent NAIC President	Department of Professional and Financial Regulation Bureau of Insurance State Office Building State House Station 34 Augusta, Maine 04333	207-624-8475 fax: 207-624-8599
MI	D. Joseph Olson Commissioner	Insurance Bureau Department of Commerce 611 W. Ottawa Street 2nd Floor North Lansing, Michigan 48933	517-373-9273 fax: 517-335-4978
MN	David B. Gruenes Commissioner	Dept. of Commerce 133 East 7th Street St. Paul, Minnesota 55101	612-296-6848 fax: 612-296-4328
MO	Jay Angoff Director	Department of Insurance 301 West High Street 6 North Jefferson City, Missouri 65101	573-751-4126 fax: 573-751-1165

State	Regulator	Address	Phone
MS	George Dale Commissioner	Department of Insurance 1804 Walter Sillers Build. Jackson, Mississippi 39204	601-359-3569 fax: 601-359-2474
MT	Mark O'Keefe Commissioner	Department of Insurance 126 North Sanders Mitchell Building, Room 270 Helena, Montana 59601	406-444-2040 fax: 406-444-3497
NC	Jim Long Commissioner	Department of Insurance Dobbs Building 430 North Salisbury Street Suite 4140 Raleigh, North Carolina 27603	919-733-7349 fax: 919-733-6495
ND	Glenn Pomeroy Commissioner NAIC Secretary- Treasurer	Department of Insurance 600 E. Boulevard Bismarck, North Dakota 58505-0320	701-328-2440 fax: 701-328-4880
NE	Robert Lange Director	Department of Insurance Terminal Building 941 'O' Street Suite 400 Lincoln, Nebraska 68508	402-471-2201 fax: 402-471-4610
NH	Monica A. Ciolfi (acting) Commissioner	Department of Insurance 169 Manchester Street Concord, New Hampshire 03301	603-271-2261 fax: 603-271-1406
NJ	Elizabeth Randall Commissioner	Department of Insurance 20 West State Street CN325 Trenton, New Jersey 08625	609-292-5363 fax: 609-984-5273
NM	Chris P. Krahling Superintendent	Department of Insurance P.O. Drawer 1269 Santa Fe, New Mexico 87504-1269	505-827-4601 fax: 505-827-4734
NV	Alice Molansky Commissioner	Division of Insurance 1665 Hot Springs Road Suite 152 Carson City, Nevada 89710	702-687-4270 fax: 702-687-3937

continues

State	Regulator	Address	Phone
NY	Edward Muhl Superintendent	Department of Insurance State of New York 160 West Broadway New York, New York 10013	212-602-0429 fax: 212-602-0437
NY		Agency Building One Empire State Plaza Albany, New York 12257	518-474-6600 fax: 518-473-6814
OH	Harold T. Duryee Director	Department of Insurance 2100 Stella Court Columbus, Ohio 43215	614-644-2658 fax: 614-644-3743
OK	John Crawford Commissioner	Department of Insurance 1901 North Walnut Oklahoma City, Oklahoma 73105	405-521-2686 fax: 405-521-6635
OR	Kerry Barnett Director	Department of Consumer and Business Services Director's Office 350 Winter Street N.E. Room 200 Salem, Oregon 97310-0700	503-378-4271 fax: 503-378-4351
PA	Linda S. Kaiser Commissioner	Insurance Department 1326 Strawberry Square 13th Floor Harrisburg, Pennsylvania 17120	717-783-0442 fax: 717-772-1969
PR	Juan Antonio Garcia Commissioner	Office of the Commissioner of Insurance Cobian's Plaza Building 1607 Ponce de Leon Avenue Santurce, Puerto Rico 00909	787-722-8686 fax: 717-772-1969
RI	Alfonso E. Mastrostefano Commissioner	Insurance Division 233 Richmond Street Suite 233 Providence, Rhode Island 02903-4233	401-277-2223 fax: 401-751-4887
SC	Lee P. Jedziniak Director	Department of Insurance 1612 Marion Street P.O. Box 100105 Columbia, South Carolina 29202	803-737-6160 fax: 803-737-6229

State	Regulator	Address	Phone
SD	Darla L. Lyon Director	Division of Insurance Dept. of Commerce and Regulation State of South Dakota 500 E. Capitol Pierre, South Dakota 57501-3940	605-773-3563 fax: 605-733-5369
TN	Doug Sizemore Commissioner	Dept. of Commerce and Insurance Volunteer Plaza 500 James Robertson Pkwy Nashville, Tennessee 37243-0565	615-741-2241 fax: 615-532-6934
UT	Robert E. Wilcox Commissioner	Department of Insurance 3110 State Office Building Salt Lake City, Utah 84114-1201	801-538-3800 fax: 801-538-3829
VA	Alfred W. Gross Acting Commissioner	Bureau of Insurance State Corporation Commission 1300 East Main Street Richmond, Virginia 23219	804-371-9694 fax: 804-371-9873
VI	Gwen Hall Brady Acting Director	Division of Banking and Insurance 1131 King Street Christiansted St. Croix, Virgin Islands 00820	809-773-6449 fax: 809-773-4052
VT	Elizabeth Costle Commissioner	Division of Insurance Dept. of Banking, Insurance and Securities 89 Main Street Drawer 20 Montpelier, Vermont 05620-3101	802-828-3301 fax: 802-828-3306
WA	Deborah Senn Commissioner	Office of Insurance Commissioner Insurance Building- Capitol Campus 14th Avenue & Water Street P.O. Box 40255 Olympia, Washington 98504	360-753-7301 fax: 360-586-3535

continues

State	Regulator	Address	Phone
WI	Josephine Musser Commissioner NAIC President	Office of the Commissioner of Insurance State of Wisconsin 121 E. Wilson Madison, Wisconsin 53702	608-266-0102 fax: 608-266-9935
WV	Hanley C. Clark Commissioner	Department of Insurance 1124 Smith Street P.O. Box 50540 Charleston, West Virginia 25301	304-558-3354 fax: 304-558-0412
WY	John P. McBride Commissioner	Department of Insurance Herschler Building 122 West 25th Street 3rd East Cheyenne, Wyoming 82002-0440	307-777-7401 fax: 307-777-5895

Glossary

Activities of Daily Living (ADLs)   The activities associated with one's ability to care for oneself, such as eating, walking, bathing, and dressing.

Actuary   An individual trained in the mathematical sciences of insurance, risk, and related areas.

Agent   An individual or entity who solicits insurance business on behalf of the insurance company.

Annuitant   The person to whom the income under an annuity is paid, and the person on whose life the terms of the annuity are usually measured.

Annuitization   The conversion of a lump sum of money into income through the use of an annuity contract, usually with an insurance company.

Annuity   A contract between an insurer and the insured whereby the insurer promises to pay out a stipulated income to the annuitant for a long period of time, often life.

Assignment   A transfer of ownership of an insurance policy or a right under the policy for the purpose specified in the assignment document.

Beneficiary   The person or persons named by the owner of an insurance policy to receive the proceeds of the policy at the insured's death.

Bonds   Debt instruments issued by a borrower, which can be a corporation, municipality, or a government or one of its agencies.

Broker   A licensed insurance person who represents the insured rather than a particular company. Typically, the broker looks at several companies to obtain the best coverage in that situation.

Business overhead insurance   A form of disability income insurance that pays the bills of the business when the owner/insured is disabled due to accident or sickness.

Cafeteria plan   An employer-sponsored fringe benefit plan where the employer may select from a variety of fringe benefits.

Cash value   The savings or investment element in a permanent life insurance policy.

Casualty insurance   Insurance originally created to protect against loss or liability caused by accidents, but now covering all risks not included in property insurance.

Close   A salesperson's attempt to complete a sale, characterized by one or more attempts to get the prospective customer to agree to make the purchase. A *hard close* is uncomfortable pressure applied by the salesperson.

Coinsurance   The sharing of expenses between the insurance company and the insured.

Combination life insurance   Life insurance policies that combine term insurance and permanent insurance.

Competent parties   People capable of entering into a contract.

Compound interest   The crediting of an interest rate not only on the principal sum, but also on the prior accumulated interest. It is contrasted with simple interest—interest paid on the principal sum only.

Comprehensive major medical plan   A health plan that provides all the health coverage in one policy, as opposed to combinations of plans.

Consideration   Something of value given in exchange for the promise of another party, a requirement for a legal contract.

Consultant   An individual or organization that analyzes insurance needs or coverage for a fee rather than commission on a sale of product.

Contract   An agreement enforceable in a court of law, such as an insurance policy.

Counselor selling   A sales philosophy that focuses on building a relationship of trust between seller and buyer. The process puts the customer's needs first.

Current rate   The interest rate an insurance company actually credits to the cash value portion of a permanent policy.

Death benefit   The sum payable by the insurance company, either upon death of the insured, or later, if agreed upon in advance of the insured's death.

Deductible   The amount of an insurance claim that the insured pays before the insurance company assumes part or all of the claim.

Elimination period   A period of time before benefits under an insurance policy are paid.

Endowment   See **Maturity**.

Equities   Stocks or securities convertible to stocks, issued by companies as an evidence of ownership in the company.

Exclusion   A condition or result not covered by an insurance policy, and clearly spelled out in the contract.

Guaranteed issue   A policy that an insurance company agrees to issue to everyone who meets the criteria for inclusion, such as a member of an association. Issue is based on the membership, not medical underwriting.

Guaranteed rate   The interest rate an insurance company promises will be the lowest rate it will credit on the cash value portion of the contract.

Guaranteed renewable   A classification of insurance policy in which the policyowner has the guaranteed right to renew, but the insurance company retains the right to increase premiums.

Hazard   A condition that increases the likelihood that a loss will be more severe.

Health Maintenance Organization (HMO)   A form of managed care where an individual contracts with the plan sponsor for services through the organization in return for a monthly premium. The organization, in turn, contracts with certain providers to perform the health care services.

High yield bonds   Bonds that are of an inferior investment grade and therefore must pay a higher yield in order to attract investors to assume the risk of buying the bond. Also called junk bonds.

Human life value   The concept that a life has a value measured by the future earnings or services of that person. The future earnings are capitalized after making an allowance for maintenance of the earner.

Illustration   Life insurance proposals with numerical depictions of the performance of the policy over a period of time, typically 20 years or to age 65. It shows the premiums paid, death benefits payable, and the cash surrender values, at the very least.

Incidents of ownership   The valuable rights in an insurance contract that belong to the person or entity that owns the policy.

Inflation   The gradual increase in the price of goods and services that you purchase. It has the effect of decreasing the purchasing power of your income.

Insurability   An issue to be determined by the insurance company whether the applicant for an insurance policy is a risk that company is willing to assume.

Integration   A legal term for the process of considering a benefit plan's benefits along with other plans so that the total benefit does not exceed defined limits.

Junk bonds   See **High yield bonds**.

Law of large numbers   A fundamental mathematical principle of insurance, which states that the larger the number of individual risks combined in a single group, the greater the certainty of the predicted loss during a given time period.

Life underwriter   A life insurance salesperson.

Lifetime maximum benefit   The maximum health insurance benefit, in the aggregate, that an insurance company will assume for an insured over his or her lifetime, from all causes.

Long-term care   The custodial and maintenance services for the chronically ill and the disabled, including inpatient and outpatient services—in a nursing home, hospital, or at home.

Loss   A decrease or total elimination of economic value.

Lump sum   The payment of benefits or premiums in one payment, as contrasted with installments.

Managed care   Health care alternatives that focus on services rendered to covered individuals under a contractual arrangement with the providers of those services.

Marine insurance   Insurance coverage related to protection on or around the water.

Maturity   The time in the life of a whole life or other permanent life insurance policy when the accumulated cash value equals the death benefit. Also known as the endowment of a policy.

Medicaid   A joint state and federal program of medical assistance for low-income families and individuals.

Medicare   A federal health insurance program that provides hospitalization and medical insurance to persons 65 and older and certain other groups of persons.

Money market accounts   Cash vehicles usually invested in short-term debt instruments issued by banks or governmental agencies, which are very liquid and do not fluctuate in value as a rule.

Morbidity tables   Morbidity tables are statistical studies of the frequency and duration of disability.

Mortality charge or expense   The amount the insurance company charges for the actual death benefit in a policy.

Mortality tables   Mortality tables are statistical studies that show death rates at different ages.

Moral hazard   The mental attitudes of people that increase the likelihood of a loss increasing in severity.

Morale hazard   A form of moral hazard caused by the indifference or laziness of someone such that the likelihood of a loss is increased.

Mutual fund   An investment vehicle that combines the investment dollars of many investors with similar objectives into one fund that is under the professional expertise of a money manager or managers.

Mutual insurance company   An insurance company owned by its policyowners and managed by a Board of Directors elected by the policyowners. Profits are shared with the policyowners and not stockholders.

Needs selling   A sales philosophy that is based on the importance of the needs of the prospect. The focus is on selling product to satisfy the needs of the customer, not the salesperson.

No-fault insurance   Automobile insurance that enables the insured to recover financial losses from one's own insurance company regardless of blame or culpability.

Noncancelable policy   An insurance policy that cannot be cancelled by an insurance company, except for nonpayment of premiums. The premium is guaranteed not to increase.

Permanent insurance   Life insurance designed to meet long-term or permanent needs, and that has a cash surrender value. It is distinguished from term insurance.

Physical hazard   Specific tangible conditions that increase the likelihood that a loss will be greater in severity.

Point of Service (POS) plan   A form of managed care health insurance plan where the insured chooses a preferred provider from a list of physicians who have a contractual relationship with the sponsor to provide services to the members or refer them to other physicians who are a part of the plan.

Policy Specifications Page   The page in every life insurance policy that states the key information about the policy, such as the policy number, name of the insured, policy date, type of policy, premium for the policy, and any additional provisions or benefits.

Portfolio   The total investments of an insurance company. Analysis of the portfolio in relation to its obligations reveals the financial condition of the company.

Pre-existing conditions   Health conditions that exist prior to the date that insurance coverage becomes effective.

Preferred Provider Organization (PPO)   A form of managed care plan where the individual has a broad range of providers to choose from, but with negotiated rates for services.

Premium   The payment made to the insurance company to keep the insurance in force.

Principal   The sum of money on hand that is to be deposited in order to earn income.

Probate   The legal process of submitting the decedent's will to the court for verification of validity and to establish the administration of the estate. Most probate records are open to the public.

Property insurance   Insurance designed to protect the insured against the loss of an asset, such as fire insurance.

Pure risk   A risk that results in a loss or no loss.

Rate   A measure of cost of insurance, usually cited on a per-unit basis.

Reserves   Investments set aside by the insurance company for the settlement of future claims. State regulations dictate minimum acceptable reserves for companies licensed to do business in the state.

Risk   The uncertainty of loss, especially financial.

Scheduled benefits   Benefits in an insurance policy that are paid according to a published schedule in the policy.

Securities regulators   Governmental agencies responsible for the regulation of the investment industry and its salespeople.

Self-insurance   The practice of protecting one's self against loss, by personally assuming part or all of the risk.

Specimen contract   A policy that is a sample of the policy issued in that state by that company of that coverage.

Speculative risk   A risk that can result in either a gain or a loss.

Stock insurance company   An insurance company owned by stockholders who invest in the company's stock. Profits are shared with the stockholders.

Stop loss   A provision in an insurance policy, especially a major medical policy, that limits the amount of expenses an insured can be responsible for under the policy.

Surety bond   A promise by one party to be liable to a third party for the debt or obligation of a second party. Risk is not impacted; rather, it becomes someone else's responsibility.

Surrender charge   A penalty levied against the accumulated value of an insurance policy, annuity, or mutual fund, designed to reimburse the company for expenses they will be unable to recoup because the owner is withdrawing the cash value.

Tax deferral   The process of postponing the payment of taxes, especially income taxes, until a future date.

Term insurance   Life insurance coverage for a specified period of time, such as one, ten, or twenty years or to age 65. It is strictly indemnification in the event of the death of the insured.

Underwriter   The company that assumes responsibility for the risk, issues the insurance policy, and receives the premium. Also, the individual within the company who makes the decision whether to accept the risk.

Universal life   A form of permanent life insurance with flexible premium, death benefit, and cash values.

Variable life insurance   A form of permanent insurance that shifts the burden of investing the underlying assets supporting the product to the policyholder. It invests in separate accounts of the company rather than its general assets.

Whole life insurance   A form of permanent insurance, popular for most of this century, designed to last for life or to age 100.

Index

I

319

J-K

L

When You're Smart Enough to Know
That You Don't Know It All

For all the ups and downs you're sure to encounter in life, The Complete Idiot's Guides give you down-to-earth answers and practical solutions.

The Complete Idiot's Guide to Terrific Business Writing
ISBN: 0-02-861097-0 ▪ $16.95

The Complete Idiot's Guide to Winning Through Negotiation
ISBN: 0-02-861037-7 ▪ $16.95

The Complete Idiot's Guide to Managing People
ISBN: 0-02-861036-9 ▪ $18.95

The Complete Idiot's Guide to a Great Retirement
ISBN: 1-56761-601-1 ▪ $16.95

The Complete Idiot's Guide to Protecting Yourself From Everyday Legal Hassles
ISBN: 1-56761-602-X ▪ $16.99

The Complete Idiot's Guide to Surviving Divorce
ISBN: 0-02-861101-2 ▪ $16.95

The Complete Idiot's Guide to Getting the Job You Want
ISBN: 1-56761-608-9 ▪ $24.95

The Complete Idiot's Guide to Managing Your Time
ISBN: 0-02-861039-3 ▪ $14.95

The Complete Idiot's Guide to Starting Your Own Business
ISBN: 1-56761-529-5 ▪ $16.99

The Complete Idiot's Guide to Speaking in Public with Confidence
ISBN: 0-02-861038-5 ▪ $16.95

Y o u   c a n   h a n d l e   i t !

The Complete Idiot's Guide to Buying Insurance and Annuities
ISBN: 0-02-861113-6 ▪ $16.95

The Complete Idiot's Guide to Managing Your Money
ISBN: 1-56761-530-9 ▪ $16.95

Complete Idiot's Guide to Buying and Selling a Home
ISBN: 1-56761-510-4 ▪ $16.95

The Complete Idiot's Guide to Doing Your Extra Income Taxes 1996
ISBN: 1-56761-586-4 ▪ $14.99

The Complete Idiot's Guide to Making Money with Mutual Funds
ISBN: 1-56761-637-2 ▪ $16.95

The Complete Idiot's Guide to Getting Rich
ISBN: 1-56761-509-0 ▪ S16.95

Y o u   c a n   h a n d l e   i t !

Look for The Complete Idiot's Guides at your favorite bookstore, or call 1-800-428-5331 for more information.

The Complete Idiot's Guide to Learning French on Your Own
ISBN: 0-02-861043-1 ▪ $16.95

The Complete Idiot's Guide to Dating
ISBN: 0-02-861052-0 ▪ $14.95

The Complete Idiot's Guide to Hiking and Camping
ISBN: 0-02-861100-4 ▪ $16.95

The Complete Idiot's Guide to Cooking Basics
ISBN: 1-56761-523-6 ▪ $16.99

The Complete Idiot's Guide to Learning Spanish on Your Own
ISBN: 0-02-861040-7 ▪ $16.95

The Complete Idiot's Guide to Gambling Like a Pro
ISBN: 0-02-861102-0 ▪ $16.95

The Complete Idiot's Guide to Choosing, Training, and Raising a Dog
ISBN: 0-02-861098-9 ▪ $16.95

The Complete Idiot's Guide to Trouble-Free Car Care
ISBN: 0-02-861041-5 ▪ $16.95

The Complete Idiot's Guide to the Perfect Wedding
ISBN: 1-56761-532-5 ▪ $16.99

The Complete Idiot's Guide to Getting and Keeping Your Perfect Body
ISBN: 0-286105122 ▪ $16.99

The Complete Idiot's Guide to First Aid Basics
ISBN: 0-02-861099-7 ▪ $16.95

The Complete Idiot's Guide to the Perfect Vacation
ISBN: 1-56761-531-7 ▪ $14.99

The Complete Idiot's Guide to Trouble-Free Home Repair
ISBN: 0-02-861042-3 ▪ $16.95

The Complete Idiot's Guide to Getting into College
ISBN: 1-56761-508-2 ▪ $14.95

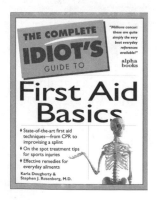

You can handle it!